INSTRUCTION AND IMAGERY
IN PROVERBS 1–9

Instruction and Imagery in Proverbs 1–9

STUART WEEKS

OXFORD
UNIVERSITY PRESS

OXFORD
UNIVERSITY PRESS

Great Clarendon Street, Oxford OX2 6DP

Oxford University Press is a department of the University of Oxford.
It furthers the University's objective of excellence in research, scholarship,
and education by publishing worldwide in

Oxford New York

Auckland Cape Town Dar es Salaam Hong Kong Karachi
Kuala Lumpur Madrid Melbourne Mexico City Nairobi
New Delhi Shanghai Taipei Toronto

With offices in

Argentina Austria Brazil Chile Czech Republic France Greece
Guatemala Hungary Italy Japan Poland Portugal Singapore
South Korea Switzerland Thailand Turkey Ukraine Vietnam

Oxford is a registered trade mark of Oxford University Press
in the UK and in certain other countries

Published in the United States
by Oxford University Press Inc., New York

British Library Cataloguing in Publication Data
Data available

Library of Congress Cataloging in Publication Data
Weeks, Stuart.
Instruction and imagery in Proverbs 1 9 / Stuart Weeks.
Includes bibliographical references and index.
ISBN-13: 978-0-19-929154-0 (alk. paper)
ISBN-10: 0-19-929154-3 (alk. paper)
1. Bible. O.T. Proverbs XIX—Criticism, interpretation, etc. I. Title.
BS1465.52.W44 2007
223'.706—dc22   2006039410

Typeset by SPI Publisher Services, Pondicherry, India
Printed in Great Britain
on acid-free paper by
Biddles Ltd., King's Lynn, Norfolk

ISBN 0-19-929154-3 978-0-19-929154-0

1 3 5 7 9 10 8 6 4 2

To Harry Weeks,
and to the memory of my father,
David Weeks

Acknowledgements

I began work on this book a dozen years ago. It was delayed first by personal circumstances, and later by other interests, projects and commitments, so it has seen the light of day only in the form of seminar papers delivered to various groups. While it languished on my hard disk, scholarly attitudes towards Proverbs 1–9 shifted from relative neglect to intense interest—at least judging by the number of recent studies that have appeared—and I have finally found the time to rewrite my material in the light of these. I am grateful to all who have offered valuable comments and criticisms over the years, especially my former supervisor, Professor John Day, and also to all my colleagues at Durham, who continue my education over coffee every morning. In particular, Loren Stuckenbruck has offered advice on the later materials, Walter Moberly made me think about theology, and Robert Hayward dragged my interests into the Second Temple period. My wife Frances has tolerated much with good humour, and my children, Harry, Charity, and David have provided distraction, sometimes welcome.

Contents

Abbreviations

AB	Anchor Bible
ABRL	Anchor Bible Reference Library
AEL	M. Lichtheim, *Ancient Egyptian Literature* (Berkeley: University of California Press, 1973, 1976, 1980)
AfO	*Archiv für Orientforschung*
BDB	F. Brown, S. R. Driver, and C. A. Briggs, *A Hebrew and English Lexicon of the Old Testament* (Oxford: Clarendon Press, 1906)
BKAT	Biblischer Kommentar: Altes Testament
BSOAS	*Bulletin of the School of Oriental and African Studies, University of London*
BZAW	Beihefte zur Zeitschrift für die alttestamentliche Wissenschaft
CB	Coniectanea Biblica
CBQ	*Catholic Biblical Quarterly*
CBQMS	Catholic Biblical Quarterly Monograph Series
DJD	Discoveries in the Judean Desert
DSD	*Dead Sea Discoveries*
EIW	S. Weeks, *Early Israelite Wisdom* (Oxford Theological Monographs; Oxford: Clarendon Press, 1994)
ET	English translation
FAT	Forschungen zum Alten Testament
GK	E. Kautzsch, *Gesenius' Hebrew Grammar*, second English edition revised by A. E. Cowley (Oxford: Clarendon Press, 1910)
HALOT	L. Koehler, W. Baumgartner, and J. J. Stamm, *The Hebrew and Aramaic Lexicon of the Old Testament*, translated and edited under the supervision of M. E. J. Richardson (Leiden: Brill, 1994–99).
HUCA	Hebrew Union College Annual

ICC	International Critical Commentary
IFAO	Institut Français D'Archéologie Orientale
ITC	International Theological Commentary
JAOS	*Journal of the American Oriental Society*
JBL	*Journal of Biblical Literature*
JEA	*Journal of Egyptian Archaeology*
JSJ	*Journal for the Study of Judaism*
JSOT	*Journal for the Study of the Old Testament*
JSOTS	Journal for the Study of the Old Testament Supplement Series
LA	*Liber Annuus* (Studii Biblici Franciscani)
LXX	Septuagint
MT	Masoretic Text
NICOT	The New International Commentary on the Old Testament
OA	*Oriens Antiquus*
OBO	Orbis Biblicus et Orientalis
OTL	Old Testament Library
OTS	*Oudtestamentische Studiën*
PEQ	*Palestine Exploration Quarterly*
RB	*Revue Biblique*
RdE	*Revue d'Égyptologie*
RES	*Revue des Études Sémitiques*
RevQ	*Revue de Qumran*
SBT	Studies in Biblical Theology
SJSJ	Supplements to the Journal for the Study of Judaism
SPAW	*Sitzungsberichte der Preussischen Akademie der Wissenschaften*
SSEA	Society for the Study of Egyptian Antiquities
SVT	Supplements to Vetus Testamentum
UF	*Ugarit-Forschungen*
VT	*Vetus Testamentum*

WA	H. Brunner, *Die Weisheitsbücher der Ägypter: Lehren für das Leben* (Zurich and Munich: Artemis, 1991)
WMANT	Wissenschaftliche Monographien zum Alten und Neuen Testament
WUNT	Wissenschaftliche Untersuchungen zum Neuen Testament
WZKM	*Wiener Zeitschrift für die Kunde des Morgenlandes*
ZÄS	*Zeitschrift für ägyptische Sprache und Altertumskunde*
ZAW	*Zeitschrift für die alttestamentliche Wissenschaft*

Introduction

It is generally accepted that the Book of Proverbs is not a single composition, but a collection or anthology of different works. Some of these have themselves, perhaps, been formed from the amalgamation of still earlier works, so that the compositional history of the book may be very complicated. At some stage, however, a system of subheadings was introduced, indicating the major divisions (most of which are marked, in any case, by abrupt changes of style). According to this system, the first part of the book lies in chapters 1–9, and those chapters do indeed seem to constitute a discrete unit, which may once have stood as an independent book.

There are important points of contact between chapters 1–9 and other parts of Proverbs, and some of its themes and images have certainly been picked up and elaborated in later literature. There is an essential distinctiveness to the work, however, which lends most of the material a certain continuity, and it is the contention of this short monograph that Proverbs 1–9 is basically, as this continuity would suggest, neither a collection, nor the result of extensive secondary accretion around some core, but a single composition, with a more-or-less coherent viewpoint. It is first and foremost, however, a series of poems, rather than a treatise. Using highly figurative language, and exploiting the familiarity to the original readership of its key motifs, it explores and commends the need to gain wisdom through instruction, and so to achieve the knowledge of God's will that is necessary for personal survival and prosperity. Moreover, although the content of the requisite instruction is not identified explicitly, the language used of it suggests that the readers were supposed to see a connection between that instruction and the

Law. Proverbs 1–9, in other words, is early Jewish religious poetry, close in its thought to similar works of a later period, but unusual in the way it presents and elaborates its ideas.

The distinctiveness of its presentation stems in part from the fact that Proverbs 1–9 is written as an 'instruction', and so belongs to an ancient and famous genre of poetic composition. That genre is relatively fluid in terms of form and content, but has a particular narrative setting, which Proverbs 1–9 adapts and builds upon. Another key factor, though, is the writer's decision to represent dangerous temptations using anonymous, typical villains, against whom a personified figure of Wisdom[1] is set in opposition. Over and above both these compositional decisions, the writer adopts, furthermore, a dense and difficult style, which lends itself more to poetic ingenuity than to clarity. The combination of these elements creates an extraordinary and intricate work, although not, perhaps, one that is entirely to the modern taste.

This description is, of course, radically different from the ways in which Proverbs 1–9 was usually discussed thirty or forty years ago, when scholarship on the work was dominated both by a curious literal-mindedness, and by a strong emphasis on now outmoded ideas about its genre. That sort of approach has not disappeared altogether, but it now jostles for space in a much more vibrant context of research. The mass of publications that have appeared more recently, and especially within the last decade or so, do not always do justice to the integrity of the work, but most show much greater interest in its poetry, in its links with other Jewish literature, and in its historical or social context. The price to be paid for so much scholarly interest is, of course, a resounding lack of consensus on almost all key points. Combined with the fact that trying to explain Proverbs 1–9 feels akin to explaining a joke or summarizing a song—the very process strips away all that is most important—this makes it difficult to write an account of the work that is neither ploddingly jejune nor constantly entangled in debate over specifics.

Rather than try to explicate its ideas directly or to engage in detail with all the other positions which have been adopted, I have chosen,

---

[1] As is now customary, I use the capitalized form for the personified figure (with the caveat that, in some places, the personification is partial or uncertain).

therefore, to approach Proverbs 1–9 on its own terms, through an exploration of its genre and its use of imagery. The first two chapters address what it means to say that Proverbs 1–9 is an 'instruction', firstly through a survey of the genre and its character, especially in Egypt, and then through a review of what this means for the interpretation of this work (and, with special reference to some older theories, what it does *not* mean). This is a rather fragmented undertaking, looking at important but varied aspects, but it is a necessary preliminary to what follows. The next three chapters focus on aspects of the imagery and underlying ideas, beginning with the key symbols and structural devices, and then focusing in more detail on particular elements and the way they interact. The last chapter looks forward, to the way in which elements from Proverbs 1–9 were taken up and interpreted in subsequent literature, and indicates the significance of the work more broadly for our understanding of wisdom literature.

The main discussion in these five chapters is followed by an 'annotated translation'. The annotations should not be taken to constitute a systematic commentary on the work, and do not engage in detail with the variety of opinions on each issue, but this part of the book provides a convenient translation for reference, and also a place for various philological or text-critical discussions that would otherwise clog the (already rather busy) footnotes.

1

The Instruction in the Ancient Near East

For all its unusual characteristics, Hebrew literature did not develop in a cultural or literary vacuum, and it is widely recognized that certain genres drew on forms and conventions borrowed from elsewhere. Among these are such important materials as the biblical law codes and psalms, but it is the wisdom literature, and especially the book of Proverbs, that has attracted most attention in this respect. Although it has sometimes given rise to assumptions that are highly questionable, that attention is warranted: much of Proverbs certainly does reflect compositional traditions that can be found elsewhere in the ancient world. The best known of these is the 'instruction'—a type of work that is widely attested, especially in Egypt—and the majority of modern commentators have associated Proverbs 1–9 with that genre.

1. THE CHARACTER OF EARLY INSTRUCTIONS

Egyptian instructions were poems that sought to win admiration for their carefully crafted language and style, as well as for their content, and so they are 'literary' creations in the sense that a modern critic might class them as *belles lettres*.[1] They are also 'literary', however, in

[1] For discussion of this elevated style in Egyptian instructions, see, for example, P. Kaplony, 'Die definition der schönen Literatur im alten Ägypten', in J. Assmann *et al.* (eds), *Fragen an die altägyptische Literatur: Studien zum Gedenken an Eberhard Otto* (Wiesbaden: Reichert, 1977), 289–314; W. K. Simpson, '*Belles Lettres* and Propaganda', in A. Loprieno (ed.), *Ancient Egyptian Literature: History and Forms*

the sense that they derive from written rather than oral prototypes. After the introduction of writing in Egypt, roughly around 3000 BCE, the hieroglyphic script attained its classic form by Old Kingdom times. During this period, it was used increasingly for funerary inscriptions, most notably prayers, incantations, and tomb autobiographies, and these texts exploited the ability of writing not only to fix and display a message, but to preserve it for an indefinite period. The words of the dead, or at least those attributed to them, could now live on, and serve the important function of keeping their memory alive. Future generations could thereby know and admire the achievements of the deceased, and even learn from them the proper behaviour that would ensure their own success and long life.

Instructional texts seem to have been a particular development of this idea,[2] and it is possible not only to discern connections between funerary inscriptions and early instructions, but to see a continuing relationship between the two.[3] This testamentary, memorial aspect

(Probleme der Ägyptologie 10; Leiden, New York, and Cologne: Brill, 1996), 435–43. S. N. Kramer, 'Sumerian Literature: A General Survey', in G. E. Wright (ed.), *The Bible and the Ancient Near East: Essays in Honour of William Foxwell Albright* (London: Routledge & Kegan Paul, 1961), 249–66, makes a similar point with respect to their Sumerian counterparts. Some of the key issues in such categorization of Egyptian texts are explored in S. Quirke, *Egyptian Literature 1800 BC: Questions and Readings* (London: Golden House, 2004), 24–8, and especially R. B. Parkinson, *Poetry and Culture in Middle Kingdom Egypt: A Dark Side to Perfection* (London and New York: Continuum, 2002), chapter 2.

[2] On the development of literature more generally from funerary inscriptions, see J. Assmann, 'Schrift, Tod und Identität: Das Grab als Vorschule der Literatur im alten Ägypten', in A. Assmann *et al.* (eds), *Schrift und Gedächtnis: Beitrage zur Archäologie der literarischen Kommunikation* (Munich: W. Fink, 1983), 64–93. This presentation is open to criticism on various fronts, and it is possible that other factors are involved; it seems unlikely, however, that instructions, in particular, drew more directly on oral prototypes; cf. Parkinson, *Poetry and Culture*, 58, following John Baines.

[3] See J. Bergman, 'Gedanken zum Thema "Lehre–Testament–Grab-Name"', in E. Hornung and O. Keel (eds), *Studien zu altägyptischen Lebenslehren* (OBO 28; Freiburg: Universitätsverlag Freiburg Schweiz, and Göttingen: Vandenhoeck & Ruprecht, 1979), 73–104. On the links between instructions and cults of the deified dead, see J. Baines, 'Society, Morality, and Religious Practice', in B. E. Schafer (ed.), *Religion in Ancient Egypt: Gods, Myths, and Personal Practice* (London: Routledge, 1991), 123–200, especially 147–61. A number of tomb inscriptions, with little or no discernible didactic content, describe themselves as *sbꜣyt*, 'instruction'. See especially A. H. Gardiner, 'The Tomb of Amenemhet, High-Priest of Amon', *ZÄS* 47 (1910), 87–99; also H. G. Fischer, 'A Didactic Text of the Late Middle Kingdom', *JEA* 68 (1982), 45–50, which implausibly takes the fragmentary inscription of Inpy to be

may explain, in part at least, why instructions are so rarely anonymous. It may also explain a certain emphasis on death in one of the earliest Egyptian works to describe itself as *sbꜣyt*, 'instruction'.[4] This text is attributed to a well-known prince of the Fourth Dynasty, Hardjedef (or Djedefhor), and is said to have been composed for his son.[5] Only the beginning of *Hardjedef* has been preserved, and this advises the son to marry and found a household to acquire an heir, but then goes on to stress the need for careful funerary preparations. The advice is presented in a series of poetic sayings, the length and structure of which are irregular, although they generally adhere to an admonitory style in which direct commands are followed by explanations.

Although it lacks such direct advice about funerary preparations, a second early instruction displays a similar concern with death and posterity, and is more explicitly a testament. Preserved for us in two separate editions, the *Instruction of Ptahhotep* tells the story of an elderly vizier in the Fifth Dynasty seeking royal permission to

didactic. W. Schenkel, 'Eine neue Weisheitslehre?', *JEA* 50 (1964), 6–12, challenges a similar claim by H. Goedicke in 'A Neglected Wisdom Text', *JEA* 48 (1962), 25–35. Since both attempted to describe behaviour in accordance with Egyptian ideals, there continued to be a close resemblance between the advice in instructions and the claims in tomb autobiographies; see J. Assmann, 'Schrift, Tod und Identität', and M. Lichtheim, *Ancient Egyptian Autobiographies Chiefly of the Middle Kingdom* (OBO 84; Freibourg: Universitätsverlag Freiburg Schweiz, and Göttingen: Vandenhoeck & Ruprecht, 1988). Finally, and correspondingly, it is interesting to note that the Middle Kingdom *Loyalist Instruction* (see below) was co-opted and adapted for use on the memorial stele of a later official, Sehotepibre.

[4] Bibliography and publication details for the texts discussed in this chapter are given in the appendix to my *Early Israelite Wisdom* (Oxford Theological Monographs; Oxford: Clarendon Press, 1994). For the sake of space, I shall simply give references here to that work (as *EIW*), along with any especially significant material or details not listed there. Translations in M. Lichtheim, *Ancient Egyptian Literature* (Berkeley: University of California Press, 1973, 1976, 1980) will be referenced by *AEL*, and *WA* used for those in H. Brunner, *Die Weisheitsbücher der Ägypter: Lehren für das Leben* (Zurich and Munich: Artemis, 1991); this is a revised version of H. Brunner, *Altägyptische Weisheit: Lehren für das Leben* (Darmstadt: Wissenschaftliche Buchgesellschaft, 1988).

[5] *EIW*, 163–4; *AEL* vol. 1, 58–9; *WA*, 101–3; Quirke, *Egyptian Literature*, 171–2. Egyptian script often places divine names out of order in phrases, a phenomenon known as 'honorific transposition', and this is the reason for uncertainty over the reading of the protagonist's name. Dating is a hazardous and controversial business for these texts, but the early Twelfth Dynasty (c. 1980–1801 BCE) seems likely.

instruct his son and make him a 'staff of old age'.[6] The king agrees
that the son should be taught the sayings of the past, handed down
from ancestors who had listened to the gods, so that he can become a
model for emulation by the children of the great. An introduction
to the advice describes it as 'The phrases of fine speech spoken
by... Ptahhotep, instructing the ignorant in knowledge and in the
standards of fine speech, as profit to any who will listen, as misery to
whomsoever will ignore it'.[7] What follows is a long series of sections
on a variety of topics, each usually, though not always, positing a
particular situation and giving appropriate advice, followed by an
explanation based on more general principles. The term 'fine speech'
in the introduction does indicate one general aspect of the work: it is
composed in an elevated poetic style.[8]

The prologue to *Ptahhotep* suggests that the advice is not
composed by the vizier himself, although he has lived by its dictates.
Rather, the son is receiving an ancient, more general body of
teaching. This certainly fits in with the broad range of situations
considered in the advice, which covers, for instance, the separate

---

[6] The most complete extant copy of *Ptahhotep* is found on Papyrus Prisse, but the
version in this copy differs substantially from that attested in others. *EIW*, 164–5;
AEL, vol. 1, 61–80; *WA*, 104–32. See also R. B. Parkinson, *The Tale of Sinuhe and
Other Ancient Egyptian Poems 1940–1640 BC* (Oxford: Clarendon Press, 1997), 246–72
(and his *Poetry and Culture*, 257–66) and Quirke, *Egyptian Literature*, 90–101. The
description of the textual situation is misleading in one well-known survey, J. D. Ray's
'Egyptian Wisdom Literature', in J. Day, R. P. Gordon, H. G. M. Williamson (eds),
Wisdom in Ancient Israel: Essays in Honour of J. A. Emerton (Cambridge: Cambridge
University Press, 1995), 17–29, especially 19: the version known from New Kingdom
MSS is also found in a Middle Kingdom text, so is not a substantially later edition.

[7] From Devaud's lines 42–50; see E. Devaud, *Les Maximes de Ptahhotep d'après le
Papyrus Prisse, les Papyrus 10371/10435 et 10509 du British museum, et la Tablette
Carnarvon* (Freibourg: s.n., 1916).

[8] 'Fine speech', *mdt nfrt*, reflects the concern to present truth in a fitting way, and
therefore refers to both style and content. This has primarily to do neither with
practised oratory or scribal polish, nor with skill in employing traditional sayings, as
Carole Fontaine suggests in her *Traditional Sayings in the Old Testament* (Bible and
Literature Series; Sheffield: Almond Press, 1982), 139–43; cf. G. Moers, 'Travel as
Narrative in Egyptian Literature', in G. Moers (ed.), *Definitely: Egyptian Literature.
Proceedings of the symposium Ancient Egyptian Literature: History and Forms*, Los
Angeles, 24–26 March 1995 (Lingua Aegyptiaca Studia Monographica 2; Göttingen:
Seminar für Ägyptologie und Koptologie, 1999), 43–61, especially 46–8. The first
maxim in lines 52–9 declares that such speech, although harder to find than emerald,
is yet to be found even among maids at the grindstone. On the broader implications
of the expression, see Parkinson, *Poetry and Culture*, 118–21.

possibilities that the hearer is rich or poor, a leader or a subordinate. This idea is also picked up in the lengthy epilogue that follows the direct teaching. Here the value of the sayings is affirmed not just for the particular hearer, but as something perpetual. To pass them on is to speak to posterity:

> If you heed my sayings,
> your every undertaking will go forward.
> Their value is in their *sp n mȝʿt.*[9]
> Their remembrance goes on[10] in the speech of humankind,
> Because of the fineness of what they say.
> While every word is carried on,
> They will never perish in this land.
> When advice[11] is given for the good,
> The nobles will speak in accordance with it.
> It is instructing a man in talking to posterity:
> Whoever hears it becomes an expert at hearing.
> It is good to speak to posterity—
> It will listen to it.

The epilogue also contains a section on the value of wisdom, and lengthy discussions on the importance of hearing and of considered speech. Picking up the issue of speaking to posterity, it includes a depiction of parental teaching as a potentially endless process, in which each son who has learned from his father passes that learning on to his own son. It would not be misleading to say that this epilogue constitutes, indeed, something close to a poetic essay on the timeless significance of such teaching.

It is almost a shock, then, when we are brought back at the very end to a more personal declaration by the vizier Ptahhotep, who claims to have enjoyed 110 years of life, and great honours, by doing justice for the king until his death. This assertion, with its echoes of funerary inscriptions, might even be read as posthumous, and sits

---

[9] The expression *sp n mȝʿt* is difficult, as *sp* has a number of different senses, including 'time', 'matter', and 'action'. The context here suggests that the expression may not be simply equivalent to *mȝʿt* by itself, as Lichtheim's translation assumes, but may refer to the sayings' perceived effectiveness as conveyors of *mȝʿt*.

[10] Devaud, apparently taking *rwi* to have its common meaning, 'depart', proposes the insertion of a negative *n*, but the verb may be understood to have the sense 'advance', 'go on', in this context; Devaud, *Ptahhotep*, ad loc.

[11] Reading *ir.t(w) sśsrt r nfr*, after Lichtheim.

uncomfortably beside the initial narrative.[12] That narrative itself, though, seems a little strange when the content of the verse is considered: why is this teaching being attributed specifically to Ptahhotep, and to a particular occasion, when it presents itself as something much older and more broadly targeted? The narrative and the advice seem unanimous in claiming that the vizier is only one link in a long chain of transmission, not the author or originator of the teaching.

It is possible that the narrative framework simply reflects historical reality: somebody has recorded Ptahhotep's conversation with the king and the teaching which he offered to his son, so preserving a snapshot of one phase in the teaching's much longer transmission. There are some important general considerations that tell against this, not least the suspicion of most modern scholars that the composition of the work occurred long after the time in which the narrative is set.[13] Even if we accept that Ptahhotep himself did give this instruction to his son, however, this does not itself explain why such trouble has been taken to recount the circumstances, or to attach such general teaching to such a specific setting. Here we return to the memorial, testamentary aspect of such works. It seems to be

---

[12] See Bergman, 'Gedanken,' 82–3, and especially 89: '...wir es hier mit Spuren einer postumen Rede des Ptahhotep zu tun haben. Oder sollen wir es ein wenig vorsichtiger so ausdrücken, dass der Schlussabschnitt bewusst so vag formuliert ist, um auch die Deutung der Anschiedsrede als postume Rede zu ermöglichen.' ('We are dealing here with indications of a posthumous speech by Ptahhotep. Or to put it a little more cautiously, the closing section is formulated to be so deliberately vague that it permits the possibility of interpreting the parting speech as posthumous speech.')

[13] Apart from general considerations about the development of Egyptian culture, the principal evidence for taking the 'Old Kingdom' instructions to be Middle Kingdom compositions is linguistic: all seem to be written in what is essentially Middle, rather than Old Egyptian. See, e.g. J. Assmann, 'Schrift, Tod und Identität', 86; J. Baines, 'Literacy and Ancient Egyptian Society', *Man* NS 18 (1983), 572–99, especially 578; and W. Helck, 'Zur Frage der Enstehung der ägyptischen Literatur', *WZKM* 63/64 (1972), 62–6. Miriam Lichtheim's attempt to place the early instructions later than they claim to be, but still within the Old Kingdom, is an unhappy compromise that has won little support; see *AEL*, vol. 1, 6–7. A rearguard action in favour of the early dates has been fought by Helmut Brunner in his various works on the instructions; see, for instance, his 'Zitate aus Lebenslehren', in Hornung and Keel, *Studien*, 105–71. In general now, however, the debate is not over whether, but precisely when the texts were composed in the Middle Kingdom. For a reasonably measured approach, see Parkinson, *Poetry and Culture*, 45–50, and his Appendix A.

crucial, even at this stage of development, to associate the advice offered in instruction with a particular individual, whose prosperity in life confirms its value. The extended narrative, much longer than *Hardjedef*, is able to incorporate royal approval of the advice as something to be emulated, while the end of the work is able to evoke conventional tomb inscriptions, in which the dead can boast of their deeds, and invite both imitation and remembrance.

The same idea of passing instruction to the next generation is picked up using extended narrative in a third work, although the beginning of this has been lost, and with it any attribution or explicit self-description as 'instruction'. This work again offers poetic advice, urging restraint in speech and self-advertisement. The advice, offered by another vizier, is followed by the tale of its reception: having come to an understanding of human ways, the vizier summons his children and urges them to heed 'all that is written in this book'. The children accept it gratefully, reciting and obeying it. The work then ends by describing events in the royal succession of the Third Dynasty, and the accession of a certain Kagemni to the offices of mayor and vizier. It seems apparent that Kagemni was one of the old vizier's children, and the work is usually known, therefore, as the *Instruction to Kagemni*.[14]

Because *Hardjedef*, *Ptahhotep* and *Kagemni* all offer advice, there are some very broad similarities of style and content. It is impossible, though, to pinpoint any particular form or mode of speech common to all three, beyond a general characterization of them as 'poetic teaching'.[15] Even that description, it should be noted, does little justice to

---

[14] *EIW*, 71–4; *AEL*, vol. 1, 59–61; *WA*, 133–6; Quirke, *Egyptian Literature*, 178.

[15] W. McKane, *Proverbs: A New Approach* (OTL; London: SCM, 1970), 51–208, examines a selection of the Egyptian and Mesopotamian texts in translation, and stresses the role of imperative constructions as a key characteristic of instructional address. Its persuasiveness is rather vitiated by McKane's willingness both to undertake such an analysis of the syntax with no knowledge of Egyptian, and to declare that much of the material cannot be defined as instruction, despite the fact that it explicitly claims to be. McKane, admittedly, is principally concerned to overturn an old form-critical supposition, that the long units in Proverbs must have developed out of the short sentences. Like Christa Kayatz, who takes a similar approach, he does succeed in showing that such sentences belong to a different type of literature; cf. C. Kayatz, *Studien zu Proverbien 1–9 : Eine form- und motivgeschichtliche Untersuchung unter Einbeziehung ägyptischen Vergleichsmaterials* (WMANT 22; Neukirchen-Vluyn: Neukirchener Verlag, 1966). In the process, however, both scholars put a

the narrative sections, or to *Ptahhotep's* reflections on the value of instruction. Arguably, the testamentary aspect is the only common formal factor that can be identified with any precision: all three works present their advice as speeches being passed on by one generation to the next, embodying ancient principles or personal experience.

It is interesting to note, in passing, that this presentation of material as a speech is itself a characteristic of tomb inscriptions. In these, a formulaic introduction names the individual, who is then said to speak the words that follow. Perhaps because of the link between such inscriptions and the emergence of 'literature', most early literary works from Egypt take a similar approach, presenting their content in the form of speeches, and the *Tale of Sinuhe* actually imitates the presentation of the tomb inscriptions. Instructions are far from atypical in this respect, then: the presentation of poems or narratives as speeches is a fundamental characteristic of classic Egyptian literature.

If there is some broad similarity between the styles and contents of the three instructions we have considered so far, when we turn to others, it rapidly becomes clear that no definition of the genre can be posited simply on such features. The *Instruction to Merikare*, for instance, is essentially a treatise on kingship, presented as a king's testament to his son.[16] The *Instruction of Amenemhet* is similarly given a royal setting, but seems principally concerned to show the assassinated king's approval for his son's accession to the throne,[17]

---

misleading emphasis on the form and syntax of instructions. The form-critical idea that instructional material has somehow 'developed' out of sentence-literature continues to lurk in some writing on the subject; cf. C. Westermann, *Roots of Wisdom: The Oldest Proverbs of Israel and Other Peoples* (Louisville, KY: Westminster/John Knox Press, 1995), 99.

[16] *EIW*, 165; *AEL*, vol. 1, 97–109; *WA*, 137–54. Also, J. F. Quack, *Studien zur Lehre für Merikare* (Göttinger Orientforschungen IV Reihe, Ägypten 23; Wiesbaden: Harrassowitz, 1992); Quirke, *Egyptian Literature*, 112–20. The work is known only from New Kingdom manuscripts; on the suggestion that it should be dated to that period, however, see Parkinson, *Poetry and Culture*, 316, and more generally 248–57.

[17] *EIW*, 165; *AEL*, vol. 1, 135–9; *WA*, 169–77; Quirke, *Egyptian Literature*, 127–9; Parkinson, *The Tale of Sinuhe*, 203–11. See also Parkinson, *Poetry and Culture*, 241–8. This work is attested in numerous copies, and recent textual discoveries have rather overtaken the editions listed in *EIW*; cf. Parkinson's bibliographies (*The Tale of Sinuhe*, 312–13; *Poetry and Culture*, 317). On the setting, see G. Burkard, '"Als Gott erschienen spricht er" Die Lehre des Amenemhet als postumes Vermächtnis', in J. Assmann and E. Blumenthal (eds), *Literatur und Politik im pharaonischen und ptolemäischen Ägypten: Vorträge der Tagung zum Gedenken an Georges Posener 5.–10.*

and royal eulogy or propaganda is a notable feature of certain other Middle Kingdom texts, most particularly the *Loyalist Instruction* and the so-called Oxford Wisdom Text.[18] Indeed, among the other early Egyptian instructions, only the *Instruction of Khety* includes any substantial amount of more general advice, reminiscent of *Ptahhotep* or *Kagemni*.[19] Texts up to the end of the Middle Kingdom, then, show no discernible uniformity of content. As for uniformity of style, we need only point out that part of *Merikare* is a lengthy hymn, or that *Khety* is most famous for its long, probably humorous denigration of the non-scribal professions.

Where they lack uniformity in terms of form or content, however, all of these texts share the same basic narrative setting, with advice passed down to the next generation by a protagonist who is usually quite eminent. That the teacher is apparently dead in at least one case serves only to emphasize that this advice is, in some sense, being bequeathed to his successor. For these early Egyptian texts, then, it seems to be the particular narrative setting that acts as a common bond, and as an indication of genre. This makes it possible to venture a very basic definition: in an 'instruction', one character delivers a speech addressed to his son, usually at the point when he is preparing to hand over to the next generation, or has already been compelled to do so.[20]

September 1996 in Leipzig (Bibliothèque d'Étude 127; Cairo: IFAO, 1999), 153–73. L. D. Morentz, 'Literature as a Construction of the Past in the Middle Kingdom', in J. Tait (ed.), *'Never Had the Like Occurred': Egypt's View of its Past* (Encounters with Ancient Egypt; London: UCL Press, and Portland, OR: Cavendish, 2003), 101–17, sees an element of parody in using the instructional format with a dead speaker (103–4), but I think this overlooks the mortuary associations of the genre itself.

[18] For the *Loyalist Instruction*, see *EIW*, 166. The Sehotepibre stela on which it was first found is translated in *AEL*, vol. 1, 125–9, and the instruction itself in *WA*, 178–84; see also Parkinson, *The Tale of Sinuhe*, 235–45, and *Poetry and Culture*, 266–72; Quirke, *Egyptian Literature*, 108–11; A. Loprieno, 'Loyalistic Instructions', in Loprieno, *Literature*, 403–14. For the Oxford Wisdom Text (Ashmol. 1964.489 a, b), see *EIW*, 168; *WA*, 193–5; Quirke, *Egyptian Literature*, 190.

[19] *EIW*, 166; *AEL*, vol. 1, 184–92; *WA*, 155–68; Parkinson, *The Tale of Sinuhe*, 273–83, *Poetry and Culture*, 273–7; Quirke, *Egyptian Literature*, 121–6. Additional fragments have been discovered since Helck's 1970 edition.

[20] M. V. Fox, 'Wisdom and the Self-Presentation of Wisdom Literature', in J. C. Exum and H. G. M. Williamson (eds), *Reading from Right to Left: Essays on the Hebrew Bible in Honour of David J. A. Clines* (JSOTS 373; T&T Clark International, 2003), 153–72, discusses the father–son setting as a characteristic of wisdom literature more generally, but it belongs properly (perhaps exclusively) to the instruction genre, at least in the Egyptian context.

This definition, of course, lays weight on the narrative setting, rather than on the content of the poetry. Consequently, the identity of the protagonists is potentially significant, and their situation may also be linked to the nature of the advice. *Merikare* and *Amenemhet* are obvious examples, where the situation is critical for an understanding of the advice, but the very eminence of such men as Ptahhotep or Kagemni is important as an affirmation of their teachings' value. Indeed, the setting may have been perceived as so important that some writers found it restrictive, and another Middle Kingdom work, the *Instruction by a Man for his Son* is explicitly anonymous, perhaps in an attempt to show that its message is universal.[21] All of this comes close to saying that early instructions should be viewed, like much other Egyptian literature, as stories dominated by the speech of a single character. In that case, we might well ask how far they are actually 'fictional' stories. Such a question is a modern one, though: it is doubtful that the ancient world would have recognized quite the same sort of distinctions that we make between fact and fiction, or between fiction and lies. In instructions, as in other literature from this period, the narrative forms a wrapping for the key material, often indicating its value by asserting a venerable antiquity or provenance, but sometimes, as in *Amenemhet* or *Merikare*, furnishing a precise context against which it is to be understood. Whether or not the narrative is historical in each—or any—case, 'fiction' is probably the wrong term to use.[22] These works have a very strong concern to put across what they

---

[21] *EIW*, 167. Also see H.-W. Fischer-Elfert, *Die Lehre eines Mannes für seinen Sohn: eine Etappe auf dem 'Gottesweg' des loyalen und solidarischen Beamten des Mittleren Reiches* (Ägyptologische Abhandlungen 60; Wiesbaden: Harrassowitz, 1999). Most of the known text is translated in K. A. Kitchen, 'Studies in Egyptian Wisdom Literature: I. The Instruction by a Man for his Son', *OA* 8 (1969), 189–208, and in *WA*, 185–92; cf. Quirke, *Egyptian Literature*, 102–7.

[22] On fictionalization of the texts in a technical sense, however, see Parkinson, *Poetry and Culture*, 87–9. Jan Assmann is happy to use the term, with qualification, in his 'Weisheit, Schrift und Literatur im alten Ägypten', in A. Assmann (ed.), *Weisheit* (Archäologie der literarischen Kommunikation 3; Munich: W. Fink, 1991), 475–500: 'Wir müssen jetzt nachtragen, daß es sich dabei um eine literarische Fiktion handelt. Natürlich hat diese Fiktion eine Entsprechung in der Wirklichkeit. Ohne die soziale Rolle des Vaters als Erzieher, die grundsätzliche Hochschätzung des Alters und der Autorität der Erfahrung... würde diese literarische Fiktion nicht über Jahrtausende funktionieren' ('We should add straight away that this is a matter of a literary fiction.

perceive to be 'truth', and they employ settings and attributions in pursuit of this greater truth, not as historical data.[23]

If it seems probable that the settings of Egyptian instructions may have symbolic rather than historical significance, there can be little doubt that this is the case for their early Mesopotamian counterparts. These texts are much rarer, and it is difficult to say much about their history and development. The oldest, extant in copies and separate editions from various periods, is entitled the *Instructions of Šuruppak*, and is presented as the teaching offered by Šuruppak to his son Ziusudra.[24] Dating is difficult, but this work may well be earlier than any of the extant Egyptian instructions, and it is certainly not just an imitation of the Egyptian texts: while it shares their narrative setting, the short sayings which make up the advice are strongly reminiscent of the common Mesopotamian 'sayings collections'.[25] There is not enough evidence to reach any firm conclusions, but it seems likely that *Šuruppak* is an independent development, which neither imitated nor influenced the development of Egyptian instructions.

This fiction has a counterpart in reality. Without the social role of the father as educator, the fundamental prestige of old age, and the authority of experience . . . this literary fiction would never have functioned over millennia.') (493).

[23] We should not presuppose, correspondingly, that the instructions reflect or idealize any conventional practice whereby Egyptian fathers commonly composed lengthy and sophisticated poems for their sons. To be sure, parents in Egypt, as elsewhere, must have offered advice to their children, but the literary genre shows no evidence of having emerged from this domestic context. The key evidence for 'real' paternal instruction comes from a New Kingdom letter, preserved in MS Ostracon Oriental Institute 12074, sometimes called the 'Instruction of Men(e)na' or 'Letter to a Wayward Son'. The very character of this letter, though, is significant: Menna and his son are apparently historical characters, but the letter itself is a poetic, literary piece, and may well have been written with a view to public consumption. See *EIW*, 171.

[24] See *EIW*, 179. Archaic versions are known from Abu Salabikh and Adab, and the Old Babylonian 'classical version' was translated into Akkadian. Two fragmentary copies of this translation are known: one of these, VAT 10151, is published in W. G. Lambert, *Babylonian Wisdom Literature* (Oxford: Clarendon Press, 1960), 92–4.

[25] See *EIW*, 180–2; there is an important new edition: B. Alster, *Proverbs of Ancient Sumer: The World's Earliest Proverb Collections* (Bethesda, MD: CDL Press, 1997); supplements to this are offered in N. Veldhuis, 'Sumerian Proverbs in their Curricular Context', *JAOS* 120 (2000), 383–99, part II. It is important to note that 'instruction' and 'sentence literature' are different types of composition, but are not mutually exclusive: the collections could be presented as instructions simply by putting them in the mouth of a protagonist teaching his son.

In the light of our conclusions about the Egyptian texts, though, it is interesting to observe that the setting in *Šuruppak* is most unlikely to be historical: Ziusudra, the son, is the hero of the Sumerian flood story. Lambert, interestingly, recalls a tradition preserved in Berossus, that the hero of the flood wrote 'beginnings, middles, and ends' on tablets, which were discovered after the waters had receded; if this tradition is old, it may be that the instruction is supposed to be associated with those tablets.[26] In any case, the setting is clearly intended to show that the advice is of great antiquity, and to associate it with the only man able to survive the flood. Another Sumerian work, the *Farmer's Instruction*, shows a similar mythological link, when it is revealed that the farmer teaching agricultural practices to his son is actually Ninurta.[27] If these two works were taken to represent a particular genre in Mesopotamia, then that genre was again understood in terms of setting rather than form or content.

To sum up briefly, by about the middle of the second millennium BCE instructions were well established as a type of composition in Egypt, where they had probably developed under the influence of funerary inscriptions. This influence is reflected in the testamentary character of early Egyptian instructions, which show little in common with each other beyond their poetic character and their depiction of advice as the words of an individual to his successor. Certainly at this stage, there is no specific 'instructional form', and it would be difficult to identify any theme that could be called conventional for the genre. In Egypt, and in the extant examples from Mesopotamia, however, there is a strong tendency to link the setting of the instructional speech with some famous individual from the past, who lends weight or a specific context to the advice, and

---

[26] Lambert, *Babylonian Wisdom Literature*, 93.

[27] *EIW*, 180. Given the limited potential readership, this work probably reflects an interest in agriculture that is more literary than practical. The extant instructional material in Sumerian is otherwise very limited. Apart from this text and the versions of *Šuruppak* mentioned above, we possess only a Sumerian preceptive work that gives general advice on a variety of topics, using units longer and more integrated than those in *Šuruppak*. No prologue is extant, but one of the sayings (rev. 5: 1) urges obedience to one's mother, and another (rev. 5: 4–7), commands respect for elder brothers and sisters; these might be taken to imply that a setting in familial instruction is assumed. For this text, see *EIW*, 179–80.

who is, therefore, identified by name. This is a narrative device, and should not be considered an authorial attribution in the modern sense.

2. SECONDARY DEVELOPMENTS IN THE GENRE

The development of Egyptian instructions in the New Kingdom has to be understood in the light of attitudes towards the earlier texts. Many of these were read and copied for centuries after their composition, despite the ever-growing gulf between their language and the spoken language of the readers. It is likely that the literary Egyptian used in some of these writings was archaic even at the time of their composition, and, centuries later, they may have posed a challenge even to experienced scribes familiar with the classical tongue. For the schoolboys who seem to have written many of our copies, they must have been very difficult indeed, especially after Middle Egyptian language and orthography finally ceased to be the official standard Egyptian under the Eighteenth Dynasty (1540–1295 BCE).[28]

Their pedagogical use is largely responsible for a widespread modern perception of instructions as 'textbooks' in Egypt, but such an understanding overlooks the fact that our evidence for that use of the Middle Kingdom texts dates from the New Kingdom:[29] although later used in formal education, there is no evidence that those texts were composed for that immediate purpose.[30] It also overlooks the

[28] John Baines, 'Classicism and Modernism in the Literature of the New Kingdom', in Loprieno, *Literature*, 157–74, notes (168) the existence of a translation into Late Egyptian of the beginning of the *Instruction of Any*, itself a New Kingdom work; cf. S. Schott, *Bücher und Bibliotheken im alten Ägypten: Verzeichnis der Buch- und Spruchtitel und der Termini technici* (Wiesbaden: Harrassowitz, 1990), 303, no. 1394.

[29] Parkinson, *Poetry and Culture*, 236: 'although there are some educational manuscripts from the Middle Kingdom, the educational use of literary genres...is unattested before the end of the Second Intermediate Period.'

[30] Jan Assmann has, in fact, argued in recent years that all Middle Kingdom literature was not just picked up, but specifically produced by the court for use in education, as a way of transmitting cultural identity to the next generation. This view is not universally held (cf. especially Parkinson, in *Poetry and Culture*, 69, and 'The Dream and the Knot: Contextualising Middle Kingdom Literature', in Moers,

similar educational use of narrative and other texts that were certainly not simple school manuals.[31] When we take into account the difficulty students would have had in comprehending the archaic instructions, it starts to become clear that an altogether different explanation is required for their pedagogical use, and this explanation is probably to be sought in the status that early instructional literature seems to have acquired.

The cultural ranking of texts and genres was a feature of Graeco-Roman culture, and seems also to have existed in the ancient Near East, although it is much harder to examine in that context. The paucity of direct evidence makes the few clues which we do have all the more significant, and a New Kingdom poem on the subject of great writers, preserved on Papyrus Chester Beatty IV, is probably the most important of these for Egypt.[32] After describing how the names of such writers live on when even their graves are forgotten and their bodies decayed, the poem asks:

> Is there any here like Hordedef?
> Is there another like Imhotep?
> There is none among our people like Neferti, or Khety, their chief.
> I shall make you know the name of Ptahemdjehuty and
> Khakheperreseneb.
> Is there another like Ptahhotep, or likewise Kaires?[33]

Later, the text goes on to praise Khety, attributing to him the composition of *Amenemhet*, but the list here is telling by itself: out of eight names, at least four belong to 'authors' of surviving instructions, and it is for their instructions that these men are

Definitely, 63–82) but it is, in any case, a long way from the 'school textbook' characterization. See J. Assmann, 'Cultural and Literary Texts', in Moers, *Definitely*, 1–15, especially 8–11, and his 'Kulturelle und literarische Texte', in Loprieno, *Ancient Egyptian Literature*, 59–82 (confusingly, the English version is based on a paper presented at a preparatory meeting for the Loprieno volume, but published after it).

[31] Judging from the number of extant copies, *Sinuhe* was probably the narrative most commonly read in schools.

[32] Published in A. H. Gardiner (ed.), *Hieratic Papyri in the British Museum. Third series: Chester Beatty Gift* (London: British Museum, 1935), vol. 1, 37–44, and vol. 2, pls. 18–22. Translation of this section in *AEL*, vol. 2, 175–8. See also Quirke, *Egyptian Literature*, 33–6. For other textual evidence, see Parkinson, *Poetry and Culture*, 29–32.

[33] Verso 3.5–7; Parkinson's translation, *Poetry and Culture*, 30. On the general significance, see Assmann, 'Weisheit, Schrift und Literatur'.

remembered, as the poem goes on to make clear. We do not know all of the others in the list, but Imhotep was famous as a sage,[34] and Kaires may have been considered the author of *Kagemni*.[35]

For this poet, at least, instructions seem to have dominated the list of 'classic' Egyptian writings (the other identifiable references are to the misleadingly named 'lament' genre, also often viewed as wisdom literature by Egyptologists). While Egypt had no equivalent to the later biblical canon, it seems reasonable to suppose that the texts he mentions had become more broadly 'canonical', in the way that Shakespeare, say, is commonly considered 'canonical' in English literature. It is probable, indeed, that this status was accorded to the genre as a whole. Here the concept of 'literature' is an important one; indeed, it may be crucial for an understanding of the ways in which the genre developed more generally. Modern literary theory often rejects the idea that some texts belong inherently to a category of 'literature', and can thereby be distinguished from others. In cultural terms, though, 'literature' is very much a reality, and many societies effectively create a canon of 'classic' or 'worthy' texts. Within such a process, genre and category play an important role: a sonnet, for instance, is inherently more likely to be considered 'literature' in modern Britain than is a limerick. Correspondingly, of course, a 'serious' novelist will enjoy greater prestige, though possibly a lower income, than a writer of pulp fiction or comic strips. For Egyptians in the New Kingdom, the instruction seems to have been an extremely prestigious genre, holding a position similar, perhaps, to that of epic poetry in the classical world, and probably read in schools for much the same reason.[36] Young scribes studied, copied, and memorized instructions not simply as a way of acquiring information, therefore,

---

[34] Opinions differ as to whether any instruction by Imhotep actually existed. Baines, for example, says bluntly that 'there probably never was one', Brunner that there was; cf. Baines, 'Society, Morality, and Religious Practice', 159; Brunner, 'Zitate aus Lebenslehren', 111–12.

[35] See, e.g. G. Posener, 'Quatre tablettes scolaires de Basse Epoque (Aménémopé et Hardjedef)', *RdE* 18 (1966), 45–65.

[36] The significance of literature in 'enculturation' more generally in the ancient world is discussed very fruitfully by David Carr, in his recent *Writing on the Tablet of the Heart: Origins of Scripture and Literature* (New York: Oxford University Press, 2005), which became available to me only shortly before completion of this book. On Egypt in particular, see 63–90.

but as a way of becoming 'educated', and drawn into the prevailing concept of Egyptian scribal and literary culture.

This attitude to the earlier instructions is probably the cause of some important developments in the genre. First, it provoked imitation by works that were more directly pedagogical in their aims. These are normally described as 'miscellanies' in English, although the Egyptian term seems to have been *sbꜣyt šꜤ(w)t*, 'instruction in letter-writing', and this is what most such texts call themselves.[37] Both terms are accurate descriptions: these texts collect examples of the sort of letters that scribes might be required to write, along with poems and other materials, to provide samples for copying and imitation.[38] Although the contents sometimes include admonitions and advice, or imitations of *Khety's* 'satire on the trades', these instructions in letter-writing rarely make any effort to pretend that their content is an instructional speech, or even that it is coherent. Rather, they borrow the customary attribution from the respected instruction genre, along with the setting, sometimes adapted to

[37] See especially A. H. Gardiner, *Late-Egyptian Miscellanies* (Bibliotheca Aegyptiaca VII; Brussels: Édition de la Fondation égyptologique reine Elizabeth, 1937) and R. A. Caminos, *Late-Egyptian Miscellanies* (Brown Egyptological Studies 1; London: Oxford University Press, 1954). Other works are described in *EIW*, 177–8. It is not always clear whether some texts are presenting themselves as miscellanies or as instructions proper. The text found in O. Gardiner 2, for instance, is described as a *sbꜣyt mtrt*, and attributed to a certain Hori; its content, however, is of the 'Be a scribe!' variety, apparently pioneered by *Khety*, but immensely popular in the miscellanies; see *EIW*, 178. For instances of the terms *sbꜣyt mtrt* and *sbꜣyt šꜤ(w)t*, see Schott, *Bücher*, nos. 1394–1400.

[38] The contents of the miscellanies defy any brief summary, but the headings in Gardiner's edition give a fairly good idea. The following are some of the titles he gives to material in MS Pap. Anastasi V: reproaches to an idle and incompetent scribe; the sorry plight of the soldier in summer-time; advice to the youthful scribe; prayer to Thoth for skill in writing; be a scribe, for the soldier's lot is a hard one; reprimand for failure to execute an order; congratulations to a military officer upon his promotion; letter about a bull, with a message to a lady; enquiries with regard to two runaway slaves; a letter to a quarryman enjoining obedience and industry; I have sent thee to school, be industrious there; a letter concerning the transport and erection of three stelae. Lang claims, extraordinarily: 'Eben ein solch unsystematisch kompiliertes Stück Schulliteratur ohne planvollen Aufbau, ohne gedanckliche Einheit und ohne inhaltlichen Fortschritt stellen Spr 1–9 dar!' ('Proverbs 1–9 represents just such an unsystematically compiled piece of school literature, with no methodical construction, no unity of thought, and no progression of content.'); B. Lang, *Die Weisheitliche Lehrrede: Eine Untersuchung von Sprüche 1–7* (Stuttgarter Bibelstudien 54; Stuttgart: KBW, 1972), 28.

a school context. Their different self-description probably reflects a consciousness that they are not 'proper' instructions, and they are best regarded as a separate type of composition, or, at most, a very particular sort of instruction.

Much later, the status of instructions also provoked parody.[39] In the New Kingdom, though, its most significant effect may have been to stifle the composition of new instructions. Unless the vagaries of archaeological discovery have just distorted the picture, it seems that the boom in composition came to an end with the Middle Kingdom. The miscellanies aside, indeed, we have only a handful of instructions composed between the middle of the second millennium and the very end of the first, a period of around fifteen hundred years.[40] At the end of this period, the genre then re-emerged energetically, but, as we shall see, in a rather different shape.

There is no demonstrable reason for the apparent decline in composition, if such it be, but we may speculate that attitudes towards the earlier instructions were a factor. Whatever the cause, we have only a small number of instructions from the New Kingdom, all fairly late, and one very broken text from the earlier part of the Late Period. We do not even have many fragments suggesting wider composition during this time.[41] In the New Kingdom and Late

[39] It is probable that the Demotic *Instruction of a Scribe of the House of Life*, in O.BM 50627, should be regarded as a parody of the genre, with its exaggerated style, lighthearted 'here's another one' introductions, and initial warnings about women addressed to the 'very, very young' recipient. See *EIW*, 176.

[40] Of these, Baines notes that 'they are almost more like continuations of the older central genre than a central part of the new Late Egyptian literature' ('Classicism', 168).

[41] In addition to the texts mentioned here, we have one tiny fragment of text on a wooden tablet, possibly from the Twenty-Fifth Dynasty (712–657 BCE), consisting of a single, partial line which reads ḥ3t m sb3yt, 'Beginning of the Instruction', in the first line, but little else. See R. Jasnow, *A Late Period Hieratic Wisdom Text (P. Brooklyn 47.218.135)* (Studies in Ancient Oriental Civilization 52; Chicago: Oriental Institute, University of Chicago, 1992), 39 n. 53; M. Bietak, *Theben-West (Luqsor): Vorbericht über die ersten vier Grabungskampagnen (1969–1971)* (Österreichische Akademie der Wissenschaften, Philosophisch-historische Klasse 278.4; Vienna: Böhlau, 1972), pl. 17. Two New Kingdom ostraca, IFAO (=ODeM) 1250 and Berlin P. 14371 also contain admonitory material appropriate to instructions, although the character of neither is certain; see *EIW*, 171. The first of these has now been edited by H.-W. Fischer-Elfert, *Lesefunde im literarischen Steinbruch von Deir el-Medineh* (Kleine ägyptische Texte 12; Wiesbaden: Harrassowitz, 1997), 24–5, who also suggests (8–9) an instructional character for the very difficult ODeM 1209.

Period, then, old instructions were read, copied and re-used a great deal, but new instructions seem to have been a rarity.

Of those that do exist, it is, perhaps, worth mentioning first a text that is unique in several respects, and might not be regarded as an instruction at all, but for its own self-description as *The Instruction According to Ancient Writings*.[42] This text can only be reconstituted from a number of separate fragments, the existence of which may point to a certain popularity. It is probable that the title belongs with the other fragments, but the matter is not beyond doubt; in any case, the contents are probably not ancient, and the language shows only the normal archaisms of Late Egyptian literature. What distinguishes the work above all is its abandonment of the instructional setting, and its use of a single, fixed form (the bipartite prohibition) for all of its sayings. In effect, the work presents itself as a digest or anthology of such sayings, and it may be more akin to miscellanies than to mainstream instructions.

From much later, probably the fourth or fifth century BCE, we have the very fragmentary Papyrus Brooklyn 4.218.135.[43] The composition of this piece may have been earlier than the papyrus, but cannot have been before the reign of Apries (589–570 BCE) in the Twenty-Sixth Dynasty: a narrative in the first two columns apparently sets the instruction at this time. Since, however, the Twenty-Sixth Dynasty was a favourite fictional setting for Late Period literature, the narrative may do no more than confirm that the work is back-dated. No attribution is preserved, but the story seems to involve a sanctuary in a foreign land, and the text is apparently punctuated elsewhere by mythological narrative material. The sayings themselves employ many different forms and cover a wide variety of topics, with some emphasis, perhaps, on the relationship between masters and servants. There seem to be more indicative sayings and fewer direct admonitions than in comparable Middle Kingdom texts, but the language is still poetic and highly figurative. The Brooklyn papyrus is too fragmentary for us to draw many

---

[42] See *EIW*, 169–70, where I have suggested a collation of the known fragments. The title is found in O. BM 5631, and it is likely, but not certain, that this is to be associated with the other texts. Some fragments are translated in *WA*, 215–17.

[43] *EIW*, 171–2; now published in R. Jasnow, *A Late Period Hieratic Wisdom Text*.

conclusions, although it is interesting to note that it does seem to have had a lengthy narrative setting, which was probably fictional or even mythological in character.

This is important when we return to the two, more fully preserved New Kingdom works, the *Instruction of Any* and the *Instruction of Amenemope.*[44] Both of these texts are attributed to relatively unimportant, middle-ranking scribes, and it is tempting to believe that they reflect a shift away from the more glamorous, but probably pseudonymous settings of the Middle Kingdom texts. Certainly, there is a possibility that the status of instructions led to some reversal in the role of attributions: when the old *Loyalist Instruction* was borrowed and re-attributed to Sehotepibre, for instance, we can see that individuals may sometimes have sought to gain lasting memorials through association with successful instructions. This is, indeed, very much in line with the ideas of the Chester Beatty eulogy, discussed above.

Before leaping to the conclusion, however, that Any and Amenemope were real individuals, and the authors of the instructions that bear their names, it is important to take account of certain other points. Perhaps most importantly, there is no evidence of any genuine authorial attribution in the Brooklyn papyrus or in the later Demotic instructions, and these New Kingdom instructions would have, therefore, to represent only a very temporary change. At the same time, the content of *Any*, as we shall see, reflects rather badly (by Egyptian standards) on Any's son, and it is hard to see that an Egyptian scribe, however lowly, would really subject his son to public humiliation in this way. It is quite possible, therefore, that the attributions in these New Kingdom works are intended to accomplish what the *Instruction by a Man for his Son* attempted in the Middle Kingdom, by making it clear that the advice is pertinent for ordinary members of the scribal class.

---

[44] For Any, see *EIW*, 168; now also J. F. Quack, *Die Lehren des Ani: Ein neuägyptischer Weisheitstext in seinem kulturellen Umfeld* (OBO 141; Freibourg: Universitätsverlag Freiburg Schweiz, and Göttingen: Vandenhoeck & Ruprecht, 1994). Translations in *AEL*, vol. 2, 135–46; *WA*, 196–214. For *Amenemope*: *EIW*, 168–9; *AEL*, vol. 2, 146–63; *WA*, 234–56. Dating is difficult: *Any* is generally placed in the Eighteenth Dynasty (although it is not attested that early), and *Amenemope* in the Twentieth or Twenty-First.

Any is not, in fact, a simple instruction. Although it begins in the time-honoured way, presenting a speech by Any in which he teaches his son, the work moves in a radically different direction when the son is given an opportunity to reply in his own speech. Unlike the enthusiastic children of Kagemni, Any's son Khonshotep is initially polite but lukewarm in his response, declaring the instruction to be beyond him. He suggests, furthermore, that advice must be both pleasing and limited in quantity if boys are to do more than just learn by rote the numerous admonitions in the books they are forced to recite. Any then responds by claiming that anyone, even animals, can be taught, and a short debate follows.[45]

Interestingly, much the same device is used in an Akkadian work, which may be of a comparable date. Nougayrol called this work *Counsels of Šube'awilum*, although his reading of the characters' names has been challenged.[46] Like *Any*, it gives the son his own speech, and the father's advice about proper behaviour is apparently followed by a bleak, pessimistic response, in which the vanity of life and of toiling for wealth are stressed. Two of its sayings may be expanded versions of sentences found in *Šuruppak*,[47] indicating a certain continuity in the Mesopotamian tradition, about which we can otherwise say as little for this period as for the earlier.[48]

---

[45] Discussed in M. V. Fox, 'Who Can Learn? A Dispute in Ancient Pedagogy', in M. L. Barré (ed.), *Wisdom, You Are My Sister: Studies in Honor of Roland E. Murphy, O. Carm., on the Occasion of his Eightieth Birthday* (CBQMS 29; Washington: Catholic Biblical Association of America, 1997), 62–77; cf. also J. L. Crenshaw, *Education in Ancient Israel: Across the Deadening Silence* (ABRL; New York: Doubleday, 1998), 199–201.

[46] *EIW*, 185. The fullest presentation of the text, including a German translation, is in M. Dietrich, 'Der Dialog zwischen Šupe-ameli und seinem "Vater": Die Tradition babylonischer Weisheitssprüche im Westen. Anhang von G. Keydana: Die hethitische Version', *UF* 23 (1991), 33–74. In his edition of the Ras Shamra text, Nougayrol read the names Šube'awilum for the son and Zurranku for the father; Arnaud, editing the copy from Emar, denied that proper names should be read here. See J. Nougayrol *et al.* (eds), *Ugaritica, 5: Nouveaux textes accadiens, hourrites et ugaritiques* (Mission de Ras Shamra 16; Bibliothèque archéologique et historique / Institut français d'archéologie de Beyrouth 80; Paris: P. Geuthner, 1968), 273–93, 779–84; D. Arnaud, *Recherches au Pays d'Aštata. Emar VI.4 Textes de la Bibliothèque: Transcriptions et traductions* (Synthèse 28; Paris: Éditions Recherche sur les Civilisations, 1987), 377–83.

[47] Compare col. 3, lines 5–14 in the Ras Shamra text with *Šuruppak* 17, 213, 217.

[48] The Mesopotamian material is usually more fragmentary than the Egyptian, and almost always much harder to date. We possess several other incomplete texts in Akkadian, of which the best known is one that Lambert entitled *Counsels of Wisdom*;

These works are most unlikely to be records of real conversations. Rather, they have taken the traditional monologue and transformed it into a dialogue between father and son. In *Any*, this dialogue becomes an examination of education, in which the father represents a very traditional position, and so is associated with a very classic genre. Its Akkadian counterpart opts to pursue a different issue, contrasting the optimism of advice literature with the realities of a world in which acting properly does not guarantee prosperity. Neither work is a simple instruction; indeed, both might be considered reactions against the claims of instructions.

The second Egyptian work, *Amenemope*, shows a different, less radical sort of development. Again, it is probably very conscious of its own character as an instruction and as a book. The prologue is lengthy, including both a formal statement of the work's purpose, and a detailed enumeration of Amenemope's posts and titles. An appeal to heed the advice being offered forms the first of the thirty distinct 'chapters' of advice, which vary in subject-matter, length, and form, but are all characterized by extraordinarily dense and figurative poetic language: *Amenemope* is, and probably always was, a very difficult book to read. Its poetic nature did not, of course, escape the notice of its copyists, and the principal copies lay the text out in metrical stichs. In stylistic terms, *Amenemope* is sophisticated to the point of obscurity.

Egyptian instructions were never secular compositions. Even setting aside the explicit religious concerns of *Merikare* and other texts, the writers were prescribing behaviour and existence in accordance with the proper order of the world, which it was the duty

he dates its composition to the Cassite period. Again, the advice is varied in form and topic, and, again, the prologue is apparently lost. A direct address to 'my son' in line 81, though, makes it apparent that the advice is presented as paternal instruction. Lambert suggests that one of two fragments, K 13770 and 80-7-19.283, may be a part of the missing prologue. The former apparently tells of a learned man exhorting his son to heed his advice, the latter, more obscurely, advises one to grasp the truth. See Lambert, *Babylonian Wisdom Literature*, 96–107. No setting can be established for the work on K 1453, which Lambert calls *Counsels of a Pessimist*. It gives brief advice on various topics, and apparently expresses a belief in the transitoriness of human achievement. See *Babylonian Wisdom Literature*, 107–9. *EIW*, 186–7. For a general survey, see S. Denning-Bolle, *Wisdom in Akkadian Literature: Expression, Instruction, Dialogue* (Mededelingen en Verhandelingen van het Vooraziatisch-Egyptisch Genootschap 'Ex Oriente Lux' 28; Leiden: Ex Oriente Lux, 1992), especially 124–33.

of gods and humans to maintain. *Amenemope*, though, introduces a new emphasis on personal piety and acceptance of the divine will, which may have been typical of the period in which it was written.[49] For all its self-conscious artistry and adherence to a traditional instructional setting, the book is not, therefore, simply an echo of the Middle Kingdom texts. Where *Any* employs the classic setting to examine the role of instructions, *Amenemope* uses it to convey ideas more in line with the needs and beliefs of its later context.

To sum up, then, instructions from the Middle Kingdom took on very high status in the New Kingdom, and would have been familiar to every scribe from their use as classic texts in schools. This status led to the emergence of 'instructions in letter writing', which were used for educational purposes, but few other instructions seem to have been composed. Those that were written tend to show considerable variety, and a consciousness of the genre's status, although the emphasis on narrative setting is retained, and there is no evidence that forms or themes became more fixed.

3. LATE INSTRUCTIONS

After this long period when instructions were essentially the literature of a past age, probably with few new examples being written, the genre suddenly saw an extraordinary revival in Egypt at the end of the first millennium BCE. The new texts are written in Demotic script and language, but differ from the older instructions in a much more fundamental way. Where Middle and New Kingdom texts always showed considerable variety in the forms they employed, the

---

[49] It is now widely accepted that *Amenemope* is reflecting changes within the context of Egyptian society rather than importing new or foreign ideas. See Baines, who, for example, cites a greetings formula found in Ramesside letters: 'I am alive; tomorrow is in the god's hands' ('Society, Morality, and Religious Practice', 194–8). The issue is explored at length, with numerous examples, in J. Assmann, 'Weisheit, Loyalismus und Frömmigkeit', in Hornung and Keel, *Studien*, 11–72; on Amenemope, see especially 12, n. 2. See also F.-J. Steiert, *Die Weisheit Israels—ein Fremd Körper im Alten Testament? Eine Untersuchung zum Buch der Sprüche auf dem Hintergrund der ägyptischen Weisheitslehren* (Freiburger theologische Studien; Freiburg im Breisgau: Herder, 1990), especially 25–6.

Demotic instructions typically consist almost entirely of aphoristic, one-line sayings. There are precedents for the use of such monostichs in Egyptian literature,[50] but these can hardly explain the sudden, wholesale shift to this style, or the more general resurgence of the genre.

It is probable that the strongest impulse came from a foreign work, the *Sayings of Ahiqar*, which most likely originated in Syria before the fifth century BCE, but which became something of an international best-seller.[51] It is difficult to account for the extraordinary success of this work, which should itself be considered an instruction, although the ease with which it was adapted to different environments was probably a key factor. *Ahiqar* tells the story of an official in the court of the Assyrian kings Sennacherib (704–681 BCE) and Esarhaddon (680–669 BCE), who is betrayed by his nephew and adopted heir, Nadin, but who escapes with the aid of an army officer, whom he had himself helped earlier. The story seems to be incomplete in our earliest version, from fifth-century BCE Elephantine,[52] but later versions include Ahiqar's restoration, and his revenge upon Nadin, who is instructed until he bursts. A long collection of sayings is inserted into this narrative, with the fuller versions of the story indicating that these are Ahiqar's words to Nadin. This collection

[50] The Brooklyn papyrus shows some tendencies in this direction (cf. Jasnow, *A Late Period Hieratic Wisdom Text*, 41), but see especially the text on the Middle Kingdom Papyrus Ramesseum II, which is a collection of short maxims, but not, apparently, an instruction. See *EIW*, 167. The bipartite prohibitions of the New Kingdom *Instruction According to Ancient Writings* also reflect, of course, a more specific use of short sayings, and such prohibitions are common in the Demotic instructions.

[51] On the influence, see especially M. Lichtheim, *Late Egyptian Wisdom Literature in the International Context: A Study of Demotic Instructions* (OBO 52; Freibourg: Universitätsverlag Freiburg Schweiz, and Göttingen: Vandenhoeck & Ruprecht, 1983).

[52] Published in E. Sachau, *Aramaische Papyrus und Ostraca aus einer jüdischen Militärkolonie zu Elephantine* (Hilfsbuecher zur Kunde des Alten Orients 4; Leipzig: J. C. Hinrichs, 1911), vol. 1, tables 44–50; vol. 2, 147–82. The text is in A. Cowley, *Aramaic Papyri of the Fifth Century BC* (Oxford: Clarendon Press, 1923), 204–48; B. Porten and A. Yardeni (eds), *Textbook of Aramaic Documents from Ancient Egypt*, vol. 3: *Literature, Accounts, Lists* (Hebrew University, Dept. of the History of the Jewish People, Texts and Studies for Students; Jerusalem: Hebrew University, 1993), 24–57. J. M. Lindenberger, *The Aramaic Proverbs of Ahiqar* (Johns Hopkins Near Eastern Studies; Baltimore: Johns Hopkins University Press, 1983), is an edition of the sayings section.

was widely adapted in the different versions, to embrace local sayings and other materials.[53]

Ahiqar is an instruction in much the same way as *Šuruppak* was: a collection of sayings presented as an instructional speech. Although probably not a Mesopotamian work originally, despite the fictional setting,[54] it shows a familiarity with the Mesopotamian tradition of creating such anthologies, or with some Syrian counterpart to that tradition.[55] We have no way, unfortunately, of knowing how far it also represents a Syrian or Levantine tradition of composing instructions. We cannot be certain of the date, either. The sayings in the Elephantine text have been dated to about the seventh century BCE, and they include apparent references to the story.[56] Although the narrative sections of that text are in a somewhat later Aramaic, it seems likely, therefore, that they have simply replaced an earlier version of the story. In any case, the story seems to have spread very widely over the next few hundred years, and was probably available in a Demotic version.[57]

[53] On these versions, see F. C. Conybeare, J. R. Harris, and A. S. Lewis, *The Story of Ahikar*, 2nd edn (Cambridge: Cambridge University Press, 1913).

[54] A late text from Uruk, which lists Ahiqar as a counsellor to Esarhaddon, is taken as evidence for Ahiqar's historical existence by, for instance, Lindenberger, *Aramaic Proverbs*, 22; J. C. Greenfield, 'The Background and Parallel to a Proverb of Ahiqar', in A. Caquot and M. Philonenko (eds), *Hommages à André Dupont-Sommer* (Paris: Librairie d'Amérique et d'Orient Adrien-Maisonneuve, 1971), 49–59. The text itself, however, is from the Seleucid Period, and probably reflects no more than an attempt to place the now famous character into the context with which he was associated; cf. J. C. Greenfield, 'The Wisdom of Ahiqar', in Day *et al.* (eds), *Wisdom in Ancient Israel*, 43–52, especially 44. There are many ancient stories set abroad—we need think only of the biblical tales of Joseph, Esther, and Daniel—and the Assyrian court, during an age of Assyrian power and glory, is not a surprising setting for a Syrian story.

[55] Contrary to many earlier opinions, it is now clear that the Aramaic text shows no sign of being a translation from Akkadian, and some sayings even include Aramaic puns; the Aramaic dialect of the sayings, moreover, is not that of Mesopotamia. cf. Lindenberger, *Aramaic Proverbs*, 16–17.

[56] The language is examined in Lindenberger, *The Aramaic Proverbs of Ahiqar*, and in I. Kottsieper, *Die Sprache der Ahiqarsprüche* (BZAW 194; Berlin: de Gruyter, 1990). The divine names used in the text are also used as a criterion for dating: see J. M. Lindenberger, 'The Gods of Ahiqar', *UF* 14 (1982), 105–17.

[57] The name Ahiqar is found in some fragments of Demotic texts, although so far as we can tell these do not appear to be versions of this actual work. See K. T. Zauzich, 'Neue literarische Texte in demotischer Schrift', *Enchoria* 8/2 (1978), 33–8. Translations by Zauzich of the relevant texts are conveniently reproduced in M. Küchler,

There is a strong general resemblance between *Ahiqar* and the best known of the Demotic instructions, the *Instruction of ᶜOnkhshe-shonqy*.[58] This text, probably dating from the Ptolemaic period, also includes a long narrative, which is set back in the royal court of the Twenty-Sixth Dynasty. Briefly, the hero is imprisoned for failing to inform the king of an attempted coup, after he had been overheard trying to dissuade his old friend from involvement. When he is not released during a general amnesty, ᶜOnkhsheshonqy asks permission to write an instruction for his son at Heliopolis, and, along with an initial hymn about social justice, this instruction is then presented as a long series of sayings.[59]

Despite its probable imitation of *Ahiqar*, ᶜOnkhsheshonqy shows a certain consciousness of earlier Egyptian literature. The brevity of the individual sayings, uncharacteristic of earlier instructions, is carefully explained in the narrative, where ᶜOnkhsheshonqy is allowed a pen but no papyrus, and so has to write his instruction, a little at a time, on pieces of the jars used to bring him wine. These fragments are, without his knowledge, read daily to the king (perhaps echoing a motif in the classic *Tale of the Eloquent Peasant*). ᶜOnkhsheshonqy, in fact, shows considerable sophistication in its resurrection of the instruction,[60] although in a different way from the other long

Frühjüdische Weisheitstraditionen: Zum Fortgang weisheitlichen Denkens im Bereich des frühjüdischen Jahweglaubens (OBO 26; Freibourg: Universitätsverlag Freiburg Schweiz, 1979), 333–7, and English versions of these are given in Lindenberger, *Aramaic Proverbs*, 310–12, under the misleading title 'Demotic Fragments of Ahiqar'.

    [58] *EIW*, 172–3; *AEL*, 159–84; *WA*, 257–91.

    [59] W. J. Tait, 'Demotic Literature: Forms and Genres', in Loprieno, *Literature*, 175–87, notes that a fragment has been found at Copenhagen with a version of the same story.

    [60] It is all the more unfortunate, therefore, that biblical scholars have been influenced by the absurd idea that this work is popular, farmers' literature. B. Gemser, 'The Instructions of ᶜOnchsheshonqy and Biblical Wisdom Literature', SVT 7 (1960), 102–28 bears much of the responsibility for this misapprehension, on which see Lichtheim, *Late Egyptian Wisdom Literature*, 4, and H. J. Thissen, *Die Lehre des Anchscheshonqi (p. BM 10508)* (Papyrologische Texte und Abhandlungen 32; Bonn: Habelt, 1984), 1. The work refers to agricultural matters more than do most Egyptian instructions, but within the context of many sayings on a wide variety of subjects. Also, few if any Egyptian farmers would have been able to read such a work, let alone write it; on Egyptian literacy, see especially Baines, 'Literacy'; Carr, *Writing*, 70–1.

Demotic work that has survived in Papyrus Insinger.[61] This latter text is too late for a detailed discussion of it to be appropriate here, but it is worth noting its most distinctive characteristic: in each section, sayings on a theme are typically followed by further sayings that contradict them, so as to promote a general message that the divine will, and not human activity, determines the outcome of events.

A great deal more could be said about Demotic instructions more generally, and about the ways in which the instruction genre of the Near East went on to influence Hellenistic and other literature. We are already, however, reaching a date some way beyond the period during which Proverbs 1–9 must have been composed. To summarize in a few words, then, this latest period is marked towards its end by the re-emergence of the instruction as a popular genre in Egypt, probably under the influence of the Syrian work *Ahiqar*. Despite a greater rigidity of form in the later works, this influence clearly did nothing to undercut the importance of the narrative setting, with *cOnkhsheshonqy*, like *Ahiqar*, placing its sayings in a much more sophisticated narrative framework than any instruction had attempted earlier.

4. THE CHARACTER OF THE GENRE

This survey of the literature has been brief, but has, I hope, shown that instructions were very far from the plain-speaking school text-books that many works on biblical literature take them to have been. In Egypt they emerged under the influence of tomb inscriptions, and retained a testamentary character during the Middle Kingdom period in which most of them were written. Thereafter, only a few instructions were composed until much later, but the genre retained very high cultural status, and was read as classic literature in schools. This may have inhibited the composition of new works, and it most likely left an impression on those that were written. Only in the last few centuries BCE was there a clear revival, and this was probably

---

[61] *EIW*, 173; *AEL*, 184–217; *WA*, 295–349. Various titles have been proposed for this composition, which is found in copies other than Papyrus Insinger.

provoked by the success of a foreign work, the *Sayings of Ahiqar*. This was probably Syrian, but it has many links with the literature of Mesopotamia, where instructions had similarly been written from a very early date. We possess very few of these works, however, and it is unlikely that they were as common as in Middle Kingdom or Ptolemaic Egypt. Indeed, the development of instructions in Mesopotamia may have been a quite independent phenomenon, and there is no evidence even for indirect contact with the Egyptian texts, at least until *Ahiqar* formed a bridge between the traditions.

In neither Egypt nor Mesopotamia do we find any strong convention of form or content: what made an instruction was principally its depiction of material as advice passed from one generation to the next, usually father to son. To be sure, certain themes recur in the Egyptian texts, perhaps most notably an emphasis on kingship in some of the Middle Kingdom texts. There is no evidence for a body of traditional motifs, however, just as there is no standard form for the expression of the advice—except, of course, the tendency to aphoristic brevity in the Demotic instructions and in *Ahiqar*. It follows that Egyptian and Mesopotamian instructions provide no basis for any attempt to describe a 'standard' instruction, in terms of either theme or form.

Although they were used in Egyptian education from the time of the New Kingdom, instructions should not be regarded as textbooks, and their origin is probably outside the educational sphere. They are essentially works of literature, closely related to other ancient literary compositions, whether the tales and laments of Middle Kingdom Egypt or the sayings collections of Mesopotamia. This literary character is reflected in the high style of their poetry, which is generally dense, or even obscure, rather than plain or mnemonic; it is often reflected also in their development of the narrative elements, or their choice of settings. The link with other literature must also be emphasized, however, not least because it has sometimes been suggested that the Egyptian instructions, in particular, embody a distinctive religious, perhaps internationalist ideology.

The only evidence that might support such a suggestion is a tendency among the instructions to speak of 'the god', as though there were only one, which appears to stand in defiance of Egypt's normative polytheism. From this, it has sometimes been deduced that the writers of the instructions were monotheists, or that they were referring to a 'god behind the gods', a creator deity, of whom all other deities were hypostases.[62] The latter idea is actually found with reference to named deities in some other sources; the idea of monotheism in the instructions, however, is rendered incredible by the fact that they often use the names of individual deities also. Such theories have continued to exercise an influence on biblical scholarship.[63] They have now largely been abandoned by Egyptologists, however, who often explain the usage as reflecting the requirement for instructions to meet the needs of different circumstances: 'the god' is whichever deity fits the context of the reader.[64] That explanation is, admittedly, rather unsatisfying, and Jan Assmann has argued that the Middle Kingdom literature does, in fact, develop a new type of theological discourse, somewhat akin to philosophical discussions of the godhead within the context of Greek polytheism.[65]

[62] The issue and earlier theories are discussed in the first chapter of E. Hornung, *Der Eine und die Vielen: Ägyptische Gottesvorstellung* (Darmstadt: Wissenschaftliche Buchgesellschaft, 1971); ET, *Conceptions of God in Ancient Egypt: The One and the Many*, translated by John Baines (Ithaca: Cornell University Press, and London: Routledge & Kegan Paul, 1982).

[63] L. G. Perdue, *Proverbs* (Interpretation; Louisville, KY: John Knox Press, 2000), 15, claims with little qualification, that: 'This deity is a universal being, a deity of creation and all peoples, not merely a national or ethnic deity of a particular people. This monistic, perhaps henotheistic tendency in Egypt, while not monotheism, is more than likely attributable to the universal character of wisdom that transcends the confining boundaries of nationalism.' The idea of an internationalist tendency here goes far beyond anything that has, or could, be claimed on the basis of the texts themselves, and is itself highly improbable, given the general worldview of the Egyptian scribal class; see, e.g. J. Baines, 'Contextualising Egyptian Representations of Society and Ethnicity', in J. S. Cooper and G. M. Schwartz (eds), *The Study of the Ancient Near East in the Twenty-First Century: The William Foxwell Albright Centennial Conference* (Winona Lake, IN: Eisenbrauns, 1996), 339–84; D. O'Connor, 'Egypt's Views of Others', in Tait, '*Never Had the Like Occurred*', 155–85.

[64] So, e.g. Hornung, *Der Eine und die Vielen*. cf. F. T. Miosi, 'God, Fate and Free Will', in G. E. Kadish and G. E. Freeman (eds), *Studies in Philology in Honour of Ronald James Williams: A Festschrift* (SSEA publications 3; Toronto: SSEA, 1982), 69–111: 'The ecumenical convention of using the term *ntr*... permits any Egyptian to comprehend the teachings from the point of view of that divinity who held the dominant position in his or her religious perspective' (84).

[65] J. Assmann, *Ägypten: Theologie und Frömmigkeit einer frühen Hochkultur*, 2nd edn (Kohlhammer Urban-Taschenbücher 366; Stuttgart, Berlin, and Cologne: W. Kohlhammer, 1991), part II; ET (of first edition), *The Search for God in Ancient Egypt*, translated by David Lorton (Ithaca: Cornell University Press, 2001).

Be that as it may, however, the 'god' terminology cannot be used to peel the instructions away from the rest of Egyptian literature or culture, as the product of some group or school of thought that maintained a distinct identity over the centuries. In all important respects, indeed, instructions seem to reflect the backgrounds from which they each emerge, and there are no grounds for believing that they somehow transcended place and time to comprise a continuous, international movement. It is important to emphasize this, because their cultural underpinnings are not always clear in individual works, especially those most interested in daily life: for every *Amenemope*, with its frequent, explicit references to Egyptian deities and ideas, there is an *Any*, which more often presumes them quietly. However universal an instruction may seem, in fact, we are unlikely to understand its original purpose if we neglect its original context, because instructions do not derive their meaning and presuppositions from some body or source independent of the culture and society in which they were written. It is vital to bear this in mind, as we turn to Proverbs 1–9.

2

Proverbs 1–9 as an Instruction

If we take the father–son address as the key indicator that a work is
'instructional', then there can be little reason to doubt that Proverbs
1–9 is an instruction. Its many references to paternal advice, and its
presentation of the father as a real speaker, go far beyond the sort of
mere allusion that we sometimes find elsewhere.[1] It is more difficult,
however, to say whether the writer of Proverbs 1–9 was consciously
writing an instruction, and, if so, what he would have understood
that to mean for his work.

1. ACCESS TO INSTRUCTIONS

Many of the instructions discussed in the last chapter are known
from only one or two copies, and probably never achieved wide
circulation; others, notably the bulk of the Demotic works, had
probably not yet been composed when Proverbs 1–9 was written. It
is possible that some or all of the remainder were available to the
author of Proverbs 1–9, but even if he could obtain copies, he still
faced the problem of then reading them. It must be recalled that most
of these instructions were written in languages and scripts that
would have been known to very few Jews: it is highly improbable
that our author could have dipped into Sumerian or Middle
Egyptian works as the fancy took him, while even Late Egyptian
and Akkadian must have been relatively unusual accomplishments

---

[1] As when Qoh. 12:12, for example, offers a passing address to 'my son'.

for a Jewish writer.[2] Although indirect literary influence is possible, and a degree of oral transmission conceivable, we certainly cannot assume that the writer of Proverbs 1–9 would have had access to some broad corpus of foreign instructions.[3]

Famously, there is one Egyptian work which may have been rather more accessible than the rest: the *Instruction of Amenemope*.[4] This

---

[2] Carr, *Writing*, 156–8 speculates that scribes may have received a 'two-track' education, 'focusing on texts in the local language and another, more exclusive educational track focused on education in a foreign language and a highly limited corpus of foreign language texts'. This idea is based on the knowledge of Aramaic by officials in 2 Kgs. 18: 26, and it is no doubt true that certain royal functionaries would have achieved practical competence in the *lingua franca* of their time. It is hard, however, to see why this should have extended to other languages (the officials in 2 Kings are notably not depicted as inviting the Rabshakeh to speak in Akkadian), or why such language learning should have involved the enculturating, literary elements of education. *Contra* Carr, the situation is hardly comparable to either Amarna or Ugarit, and the evidence he presents is wafer thin. With less sophistication, it is often simply stated, without even any inherent probability, that, e.g. 'Within the monarchic or colonial courts, employers would have required their trained scribes to know several languages'; cf. J. L. Berquist, *Judaism in Persia's Shadow: A Social and Historical Approach* (Minneapolis: Fortress, 1995), 165–6.

[3] Fox, *Proverbs 1–9*, 19, argues that there would have been many opportunities for Egyptian texts to be translated during the period of Egyptian domination in Palestine, before the existence of the Israelite states. We should note, however, not only that the Amarna Letters point to Akkadian being the medium through which Egypt and the city-states communicated, making it unnecessary for scribes to learn each other's languages, but also that the general evidence for Egyptian cultural influence at this time is very limited. The Egyptians made no obvious attempt to assimilate subject peoples in this region to Egyptian culture, and those peoples show little sign of seeking to imitate Egyptian *mores*. Scribal practices at Ugarit, and the use of Akkadian, suggest that Mesopotamian literature is potentially more likely to have exercised an influence. In any case, however, we are speaking about a period long before any possible date for the composition of Proverbs 1–9, and there is no evidence, direct or indirect, that Egyptian literature was being widely read and preserved during the intervening centuries. At a later date, texts may have been available via the diaspora communities, and I am inclined to think that this is a more probable route.

[4] The link between Proverbs 22: 17–23: 10 and *Amenemope* was first recognized in A. Erman, 'Eine ägyptische Quelle der "Sprüche Salomos"', *SPAW* 15 (1924), 86–93, tab. VI–VII. Noting a number of close parallels between sayings in this part of Proverbs and admonitions in *Amenemope*, Erman concluded that it was necessary to suppose that there must have been some relationship between the two works, and suggested that a Jew in the Egyptian diaspora during Saite or Persian times must have produced a Hebrew adaptation of *Amenemope* that was later cannibalized by the collectors of Proverbs. The result was a series of parallels to the content of the Egyptian work, which bore no trace, however, of that work's structure and order. Erman's general thesis is still widely accepted, although subsequent scholars have

New Kingdom instruction has many points of correspondence with Prov. 22: 17–23: 10, and may have exercised an influence elsewhere in Proverbs.[5] There are good grounds for believing, therefore, that some version of the work was known and available in translation; if so, then our writer may have been familiar with it. Any other sources of inspiration, however, are likely to have been more local. As we have seen, *Ahiqar* is probably a Syrian work, and it may reflect a broader tradition of instructional composition in Syria and Palestine. How far this extended is difficult to say, given our chronic shortage of literature extant from the area, but some clues may be found elsewhere in Proverbs: the book does include other instructional texts than chapters 1–9, not only in 22: 17–24: 22 but, more formally, in 31: 1–9.

It is not a straightforward task, however, to establish the significance of this material. We do not even know whether 31: 1–9 is of Jewish origin: it is said to be the words of King Lemuel of Massa, taught to him by his mother,[6] but Lemuel is not the name of any known Jewish monarch, while Massa was probably located outside

---

often preferred an earlier date; objections that Proverbs might, instead, have influenced *Amenemope* can no longer be sustained. See R. J. Williams, 'The Alleged Semitic Original of the Wisdom of Amenemope', *JEA* 47 (1961), 100–6. Most recently, B. Schipper, 'Die Lehre des Amenemope und Prov 22,17–24, 22: eine Neubestimmung des literarischen Verhältnisses', *ZAW* 117 (2005), 53–72, 232–48, suggests a late eighth- or seventh-century BCE date for transmission of *Amenemope*. His arguments, however, amount to little more than a recognition of Egyptian strategic interests in Palestine at this time.

[5] Objections to direct influence have focused usually upon the possibility of a shared source that is no longer extant, as suggested by I. Grumach, *Untersuchungen zur Lebenslehre des Amenope* (Münchner Ägyptologische Studien 23; Munich and Berlin: Deutscher Kunstverlag, 1972), or upon the idea that the resemblances between the two texts are too general to be significant, for which see J. Ruffle, 'The Teaching of Amenemope and its Connection with the Book of Proverbs', *Tyndale Bulletin* 28 (1977), 29–68, and cf. J. Krispenz, *Spruchkompositionen im Buch Proverbia* (Europäische Hochschulschriften Ser. 23, 349; Frankfurt: Peter Lang, 1989), 129–31; Whybray, *Composition*, 132–4. However, the conventional position that Proverbs depended in some way upon a version of *Amenemope* has been defended by D. Römheld, *Wege der Weisheit* (BZAW 184; Berlin and New York: de Gruyter, 1989), and more recently by J. A. Emerton, 'The Teaching of Amenemope and Proverbs XXII 17–XXIV 22: Further Reflections on a Long-Standing Problem', *VT* 51 (2001), 431–64.

[6] Teaching by a mother, rather than a father, is not unprecedented, but is sufficiently unusual to raise the possibility that the introduction in 31: 1 alludes to some familiar story or tradition that is now lost to us.

Palestine. This points to a foreign origin, but since Massa is also mentioned in 30: 1, in connection with another section of Proverbs, it is possible that the place had some traditional significance, which led to the fictional setting there of Jewish works. To complicate matters, there are also some Aramaic expressions in 31: 1–9 which may imply an origin abroad, but these are not found consistently, and it is possible that they are better interpreted as signs of a late date, of dialectal influence, or even of a deliberate attempt to make the text sound foreign.[7] We certainly cannot jump to the conclusion that this short work must reflect some much wider local tradition, and the other instructional material in 22: 17–24: 22 is plagued by even more fundamental questions of unity and origin.

Despite the many foreign instructions that we have, then, Proverbs 1–9 stands rather isolated, with little likely access to foreign texts, and no compelling evidence that there was any strong domestic tradition of writing instructions. There is certainly enough evidence for instructions in Israel to suggest that the author would have known about the genre, and that his work is, therefore, self-consciously and not coincidentally an instruction.[8] It is far from being the case, however, that we can assume him to have had a wide knowledge of foreign compositions in the genre, let alone to have been immersed in Egyptian ideas or motifs.[9]

---

[7] In 31: 2–3, we find the Aramaic word בר, and the plural form מלכין; there are, however, no further Aramaisms in verses 4–9; indeed, the Hebrew plural למלכים appears twice in verse 4.

[8] Probably rather later, the book of Tobit reflects a continuing knowledge of the genre: chapter 4 has an instructional speech by Tobit, given when he believes he is about to die. The influence of *Ahiqar* is certainly to be seen on the work as a whole, but the instruction is in a different style, and is not based on that work; equally, Proverbs 1–9 does not seem to have been a primary influence, despite some focus on warning against exogamous marriage.

[9] The more general influence of Egyptian education and culture on Israel is difficult to assess. Carr (*Writing*, 85–90) summarizes the evidence, but includes, e.g. the use of hieratic numerals, and old ideas that David's officials may have been Egyptian, on which see *EIW* chapter 7. There can be no doubt that Israel inherited Egypt's papyrus-and-ink technology, and an alphabetic system based ultimately on Egyptian writing, but it is also clear that these were not drawn directly from Egypt. Nili Shupak's semantic comparisons of 'educational' vocabulary are cited frequently as evidence for the modelling of Israelite education on Egyptian, but where they do not simply reflect the undoubted influence of *Amenemope*, or perhaps of other literature, it is hard to see the significance of some of these

Even were our author to have had a whole library of Egyptian texts spread out before him, however, and to have known more about instructions than we could ever know, the effect upon his composition is likely to have been limited. Not only does the evidence from abroad suggest that the genre imposed little constraint upon the form or contents even where instructions were common, but it also points to instructions having their roots in their own local and historical contexts. This is an important point. We can be reasonably certain that the authors of works like *Any* or the untitled Insinger instruction were quite conscious of their works' generic identity, and had probably read at least some earlier instructions; both those texts, indeed, show a strong interest in the very nature and authority of instruction. What they do not appear to have done, however, is to model their ideas or content on previous literature in a way that would make detailed knowledge of that literature wholly determinative for a contemporary reader's understanding of them. To take a loose analogy, if we were to try to read Proverbs 1–9 solely in the light of the foreign instructions, rather than the Jewish context in which it was composed, this would be like reading the *Aeneid* solely on the basis of the Greek epic tradition while ignoring its context in Roman literature and thought.

We need, then, to ensure that we keep in mind the Jewish literary and religious context within which Proverbs 1–9 was composed, and to which its original readers belonged,[10] while seeking to identify

comparisons. How telling is it, for instance, that the Hebrew and Egyptian terms for teaching can also be used of physical punishment, that both use terms for 'lacking sense', or that both associate learning with the ear? The examples of the 'hot' and 'cool' tempered who appear in Proverbs may more probably speak to literary influence, but the association of heat with anger is a biblical commonplace anyway, and cool-temperedness only appears once (17: 27 Kt). On the other hand, there is in each language and body of literature a great deal that has no equivalent in the other. See especially N. Shupak, *Where Can Wisdom be Found? The Sage's Language in the Bible and in Ancient Egyptian Literature* (OBO 130; Freibourg: Universitätsverlag Freiburg Schweiz, and Göttingen: Vandenhoeck & Ruprecht, 1993); and 'The "Sitz im Leben" of the Book of Proverbs in the Light of a Comparison of Biblical and Egyptian Wisdom Literature', *RB* 94 (1987), 98–119. The literary evidence is much harder to judge, but (setting Proverbs aside), there is little to suggest widespread or profound Egyptian influence on early Jewish literature and thought, or, in fact, any generally deep Jewish interest in, or knowledge of contemporary Egypt.

[10] Of course, in practical terms this means looking to the other biblical literature, which is our principal point of access to that context, and the matter is thus complicated by numerous questions of date. The best-known study of links with

those ways in which comparison with other instructions may prove fruitful. An obvious starting point is the instructional setting, which marks the affinities of the work.

2. PARENTAL INSTRUCTION IN PROVERBS 1–9

In Proverbs 1–9 we are left in no doubt that the contents are supposed to be the words of a father addressing his son, in the traditional style of an instruction. Indeed, in chapter 4 this father not only draws a comparison with the time when his own father taught him—perhaps thereby evoking the sort of chain of transmission envisaged in *Ptah-hotep*—but also goes on to declare explicitly that he has now given instruction to his son. Lest there be any lingering doubt that he is a real speaker and not a disembodied authorial voice, he proceeds to illustrate his advice in chapter 7 with events that he claims to have witnessed through his window.[11] If our survey of the foreign literature suggests that an admonition addressed by a father to his son would have been associated with the instruction genre in the ancient world, then it seems more than probable that Proverbs 1–9 would have been identified as an instruction by ancient readers.

That said, the presentation of instruction is rather more compli-cated in Proverbs 1–9 than in other instructions. The instructional setting, for instance, is portrayed as something beyond a single act or speech, and the presentation even gives scope for various mentions of the mother's contribution (e.g. 6: 20), a rarity in other works.[12] More

---

that literature is A. Robert, 'Les Attaches Littéraires Bibliques de Prov. I–IX', *RB* 43 (1934), 42–68; 172–204; 374–84; *RB* 44 (1935), 344–65; 502–25. Robert does not address himself to the issue of date until the last section of his work, and something similar is true of G. Baumann, *Die Weisheitsgestalt in Proverbien 1–9: Traditions-geschichtliche und theologische Studien* (FAT 16; Tübingen: Mohr-Siebeck, 1996), the most sympathetic to this approach among recent studies. I am less inclined than either to use such links as a criterion for dating, but am likewise unwilling to discuss date before examining any of the content. Accordingly, the context must remain somewhat ill-defined at this stage.

[11] See the annotated translation, at 7: 6.

[12] See *EIW*, 15; the principal reference is Šuruppak 259–60. Also, J. Day, 'Foreign Semitic Influence on the Wisdom of Israel and its Appropriation in the Book of Proverbs', in Day *et al.*, *Wisdom*, 55–70, especially 66. On the implications for

generally, where other instructions commonly present their words as a single testimonial speech, the father–son instruction in Proverbs 1–9 is placed in a broader context of ongoing parental and other instruction.[13] The instructional setting familiar from other works is retained, then, but generalized and extended.

A. The Solomonic Attribution

Despite the portrayal of the father as a real character, Proverbs 1–9 is also vaguer than most other instructions about its setting. As we have seen, it is usual for ancient instructions to specify the name of the father who is offering instruction, and we might reasonably expect, therefore, to be told the identity of the father-figure in Proverbs 1–9. At first sight, in fact, an attribution does seem to be present: 1: 1 declares what follows to be 'the sayings of Solomon, son of David, king of Israel'. The relationship between this title and Proverbs 1–9, however, is not clear-cut.

The secondary, editorial nature of the system of attributions employed in Proverbs as a whole is unquestionable: no work ever went independently under the heading 'also sayings of Solomon' (25: 1) or 'also sayings of the wise' (24: 23), titles that refer back to previous titles.[14] This fact does, however, support taking 1: 1 to have been a part of chapters 1–9 before its inclusion in the larger

historical understandings of the maternal role, see the cautious assessment in J. E. McKinlay, *Gendering Wisdom the Host: Biblical Invitations to Eat and Drink* (JSOTS 216; Gender, Culture, Theory 4; Sheffield: Sheffield Academic Press, 1996), 101–10. The fact that generic convention is involved in the parental presence should make us wary of over-emphasizing the family setting as a historical *Sitz im Leben*, as do, e.g. Carole Fontaine, 'Wisdom in Proverbs', in L. Perdue, B. Scott, W. Wiseman (eds), *In Search of Wisdom: Essays in Memory of John G. Gammie* (Louisville, KY: Westminster/John Knox Press, 1993), 99–114, especially 101–3, and Claudia Camp, 'Woman Wisdom and the Strange Woman: Where is Power to be Found?', in T. K. Beal and D. M. Gunn (eds), *Reading Bibles, Writing Bodies: Identity and the Book* (Biblical Limits; London and New York: Routledge, 1997), 85–112. The latter claims that the wisdom tradition was 'basically composed of the teachings of the mothers and fathers of Israel' (91).

[13] Elsewhere, it is only in ᶜ*Onkhsheshonqy*—with its exceptional circumstances—that we find instruction portrayed as a process rather than a single speech.

[14] See R. B. Y. Scott, 'Wise and Foolish, Righteous and Wicked', in *Studies in the Religion of Ancient Israel* (SVT 23; Leiden: Brill, 1972), 146–65, especially 150.

work. Three titles describe what follows them as 'sayings of Solomon', and we might expect the second of these, in 10: 1, to be 'also sayings of Solomon', as in 25: 1. It lacks the 'also', however, and seems rather to be presented as the first Solomonic attribution. The simplest explanation for this is that the superscription in 1: 1 was added after the system of attributions was already in place. That it was not just added to cover the whole book, furthermore, might be suggested by the apparent contradiction between an overall attribution to Solomon and the attribution of particular sections to other individuals.[15]

On the other side of the argument, however, we might also expect any attribution to fit the contents better. In the first place, if Solomon is supposed to be the father offering instruction, then the son is presumably Rehoboam, and the depiction of this king in the biblical literature could hardly be taken as an affirmation of the instruction's worth. Furthermore, given the feelings about 'foreign women' in Proverbs 1–9 (which we shall discuss later) it seems unlikely either that Solomon, notorious for his relationships with foreign women, would be warning his son against them,[16] or that Rehoboam's mother, Naamah the Ammonitess (cf. 1 Kgs. 14: 31), would have been considered a suitable teacher (cf., e.g. Prov. 1: 8). We should not overlook the fact, furthermore, that 1: 1 is followed in 1: 2–6 by a short block of material often regarded as secondary. For the title of an instruction to be separated from the main instructional speech is not actually

---

[15] The issue of the superscriptions is clearly relevant to the broader question of whether Proverbs 1–9 was actually supposed to function as a prologue to the rest of the book, the case for which has been put most forcefully among recent commentators by Baumann, *Weisheitsgestalt*. The idea is an attractive one, and it offers an explanation both for the lack of correspondence to the subsequent superscriptions and to the notoriously mysterious 'seven pillars' of 9: 1 (taking those to be the seven sections of the book). If Proverbs 1–9 does currently serve as a prologue, however, I think that this is an editorial rather than a compositional matter. While some links exist with material in the other sections, the number of these is small, and the direction of influence unclear; it would be difficult to maintain that Proverbs 1–9 presupposes the presence of the other sections. At most, therefore, it is not so much a prologue as a free-standing, introductory essay, but I think it is more likely to have enjoyed an independent existence when first written.

[16] J. Blenkinsopp, 'The Social Context of the "Outsider Woman" in Proverbs 1–9', *Biblica* 72 (1991), 457–73, especially 457, notes the significance of the fact that, 'in a composition attributed to Solomon the foreign woman...presents the greatest obstacle to the acquisition of wisdom', and suggests that the work is presented as 'a cautionary instruction of Solomon based on his own experience'.

uncommon, but in these verses the aim of the instruction is said to be the betterment of men in general, and of specific groups in particular: while this may be the actual aim of some instructions, it is not the avowed aim of any, and it sits unhappily beside the address to a single son in the appeals. If this material is editorial, then so may be 1: 1.[17]

In the end, there is no secure basis on which to decide whether Proverbs 1–9 was originally attributed to Solomon. The convention of the genre suggests that it would have been attributed to someone, and no other names are on offer. Solomon, in fact, would fit much better as the addressee of the instruction, rather than the father, but in the absence of any evidence to support the tempting speculation that this was originally the case, then we have to leave the question open.[18] As things stand, if the father is supposed to be Solomon, then the attribution carries little obvious meaning for the text, and is strangely disconnected from the biblical account of that king.[19]

---

[17] There is nothing in verses 2–6 that must be tied specifically to the themes or language of chapters 1–9, and there are some similarities with the sayings in 9: 7–10, which clearly do not belong in their present position. It is tempting to speculate simply that the two sets of sayings originally bracketed chapters 1–9, perhaps at a stage before the absorption of the work into Proverbs. The issue is probably more complicated than this, though, not least because 1: 5 appears to interrupt a sequence of purpose clauses, which themselves resemble a series of sayings at the beginning of *Amenemope*. Verse 6 has done most to persuade commentators that these clauses are inappropriate as an introduction, since the understanding of חידתם as 'their riddles' has led to the assumption that the writer here views wisdom literature in terms of formal puzzles for interpretation. The word does not really have such a precise connotation, though, and in Psalm 78: 2, for example, is used to refer to the recitation of quite unmysterious events in history. See the annotated translation at 1: 6, below. In Prov. 1: 6, then, there may be nothing more than a recognition that wisdom literature may be obscure and require interpretation. This in itself need hardly force us to take the section as secondary, and ultimately it is possible to say only that it may be either an original, editorial comment on the text, alerting readers to its subtlety, or a secondary comment.

[18] The idea of Solomon as addressee is developed at length in J. E. Miles's enjoyable *Wise King—Royal Fool: Semiotics, Satire and Proverbs 1–9* (JSOTS 399; London and New York: T&T Clark International, 2004). Miles sees a satirical critique of Solomon running through the work, with YHWH playing the role of father. He shows that some of the work can be read in this way, but offers no very compelling reason why it should be.

[19] Claudia Camp, in *Wise, Strange and Holy: The Strange Woman and the Making of the Bible* (JSOTS 320; Gender, Culture, Theory 9; Sheffield: Sheffield Academic Press, 2000), 144–86, argues for connections of a rather different sort between Solomon and Proverbs, emphasizing the recurrent elements of foreignness in the account of his reign, and seeing links between Wisdom's house, the structure of Proverbs, and the Temple.

B. Instruction by Other Characters

We might also say, though, that the father–son setting is itself sometimes disconnected from the father. The first indication of this comes in 3: 11–12, where the father's appeal calls on the son to heed not his own but God's teaching, and compares God himself to a father.[20] At the beginning of chapter 4, the father then describes the instruction given to him by his own father, and effectively becomes the son who is addressed. In chapter 8, furthermore, it is the turn of Wisdom to offer instruction (8: 10), using terms similar to those used by the father, and actually addressing her 'sons' (8: 32). It seems unlikely that all of this is just carelessness: the writer is apparently playing with the most basic convention of the genre, and shifting the roles of the characters around. This peculiarity can be understood as belonging to a more general feature of the text. Where most instructions content themselves with the father's speech, and occasionally a reply by the son, Proverbs 1–9 offers speaking parts to several characters. Since the father is apparently the speaker throughout, these characters are speaking within his speech: he is essentially telling stories about them. Perhaps deliberately, though, the boundaries are blurred at points, as in those cases where the father recalls the words of his own father, or Wisdom addresses her 'sons'. The overall effect is to give a much greater integration between narrative and teaching than is found in most instructions: general advice is illustrated by stories, or lent colour by speeches and settings.

It is important to note, despite this, that the degree of action is severely limited in most cases: the characters speak more than they move, and their activities are usually connected with their speeches. In 1: 10–19, for instance, the sinners entice the son, and talk about what they are going to do, but do not actually act; in 1: 20–33 and in chapter 8, Wisdom speaks out from various places, but otherwise does nothing. Even in the relatively dynamic chapter 7, the narrative elements all lead up to or flow from the speech in verses 14–20. Only in chapter 9 do we find some real action, with Wisdom's building of

---

[20] It is just possible that the character of Solomon may have some relevance to the idea of God as father here: in 2 Sam. 7: 14, God promises to David that he will himself act as a father to David's successor.

her house and preparation of food, but even that is described tersely as a background to her speech; the other woman in that chapter does nothing more than sit and call out. It would be misleading to say, then, that the work uses moralistic tales for its teaching: the focus throughout is upon speech.

The significance and inter-relationship of these speeches will be a key concern later in our study. For the moment we are concerned with Proverbs 1–9 as instruction, and here the presentation of the speeches may be seen in a rather interesting light. Firstly, recalling the parental appeals so characteristic of the father's speech that frames them, we can observe that the other characters make their own appeals. In particular, they want their listeners to come with them or turn to them—be they the sinners in 1: 11, the 'foreign woman' in 7: 18, Folly in 9: 16, or Wisdom in 8: 34–5 and 9: 4. If not issuing actual invitations, the characters at least demand attention to their words, as in 1: 20–33; 4: 4–5; and 8: 32–3. The only speech to lack such an invitation, or at least an implicit appeal, is the son's short confession in 5: 12–14. The father is not the only speaker demanding the attention of his audience, then: his characters are also calling out for such attention, and thereby echoing him. If the instruction is, broadly, a speech telling the son what to do, then in Proverbs 1–9 that speech reports a variety of other voices with their own, often very different suggestions.

If the speeches answered each other, we might see this in terms of dialogue or conflict, especially as the speeches are sometimes juxtaposed. The only reactions, however, are those of the father himself, warning against the words of the sinners and the woman. The characters occupy separate cameos, explicitly linked only by the framework of the instruction. This is even true in chapter 9, where the contrast between Wisdom and Folly is evident, but reflected in no interaction between the two: the presentation is split-screen, not confrontational.

We are dealing neither with a series of parables, then, nor with a dialogue like that in the book of Job. Instead, the instructional speech includes reports of other speeches, each, as it were, with its own instructions. The report of past instruction in chapter 4 therefore merely epitomizes a technique found across the work—and a very unusual one at that. There are no known instructions that report separate, substantial speeches within the father's speech, and it is difficult to find close parallels in any ancient literature.[21] The writer seems to be employing an approach that is highly uncommon and may be quite original.

In short, Proverbs 1–9 possesses the instructional setting indicative of an instructional composition. Elsewhere, that setting is generally portrayed as a single speech, attributed to a specific individual, although sometimes used as the basis for an extended narrative or a dialogue. Here, however, we are given a framework of ongoing parental teaching, not certainly attributed to a specific individual, within which others offer invitations, or even give their own instructional speeches. Identities are not fixed but blurred, so that God, the father's father, or even personified Wisdom can occupy the role of instructing parent. This is instruction, but not as we know it.

3. UNITY AND STRUCTURE

What is odd must also be regarded as suspicious, and it should come as no surprise that the majority of modern commentators have doubted the basic unity of Proverbs 1–9. The work is commonly viewed as a series of short instructional presentations, to which have been added other materials (often identified especially with the passages relating to personified Wisdom). Views differ as to the original relationship between the instructional presentations, but many scholars have considered them to be an anthology or collection, rather than a distinct composition; even within that camp, however, there is considerable disagreement about the nature and extent of any redactional activity on the part of

---

[21] Perhaps the nearest equivalent lies in the use of fables. Several of these appear in *Ahiqar* (e.g. 118–23), and feature brief conversations between animals. Such fables do not generally include speeches of any length, however, and are not normally used in instructions. *Ahiqar* has links with the Mesopotamian sentence literature collections, which sometimes do include fables. In Egyptian literature, the 'speech within a speech' is a not uncommon device outside instructions, and is famously taken to extremes in the *Story of the Shipwrecked Sailor.*

the anthologist(s).[22] There is, then, no single hypothesis, but three considerations have played a particularly important role in the discussion. The first is the undisputed fact that Proverbs 1–9 is divided into separate parts by the repeated 'parental appeals', in which the son, addressed directly, is exhorted to heed instruction. Apart from minor quibbles about the identification of particular appeals and parts, the questions raised by this relate to the second consideration, the nature and inter-relationship of the individual sections distinguished in this way. Here, assumptions about form and genre come into play, and it is commonly asserted or assumed that the instruction genre compels us to understand the sections in a particular way. The third, rather different, consideration is of unity or disunity in the thought of the work, frequently with particular regard to the ways in which wisdom is conceived or presented. On the basis of this consideration, it is often argued that the sections of the work, whatever their original relationship, have been supplemented with material that differs in its outlook, possibly in the course of a long process of transmission and adaptation.

Although biblical scholarship has largely moved away from a presumption that texts are composite until proven innocent,[23] it is

---

[22] Some do not even go so far as seeing an anthology in any meaningful sense. We have already noted that Lang, *Die Weisheitliche Lehrrede*, sees Proverbs 1–9 in terms of the Egyptian miscellanies; cf. his later *Wisdom and the Book of Proverbs: An Israelite Goddess Redefined* (New York: Pilgrim Press, 1986), 15–16: 'We are not dealing here with a consciously constructed literary work, but just a collection of didactic poetry, a collection of brief discourses for use in teaching, a reading text that serves as a source book for teachers. The teachers did not have to follow a prescribed sequence. No passage presupposes another. Some parts are almost identical in content and may be exchanged readily. Apparently, it has been left to the teacher's discretion how to organize the material in actual classroom use.'

[23] There are still exceptions. A. Müller, *Proverbien 1–9: Der Weisheit neue Kleider* (BZAW 291; Berlin and New York: de Gruyter, 2000) offers an unapologetically old-fashioned approach, which nevertheless produces a very original result. According to Müller, the work is built around a kernel consisting of an introduction in 4: 10–27 and 5: 21–2, where an opposition between the righteous and the sinner is established, with what is left of the teaching itself now in 6: 1–19. This has undergone what he calls a 'formative redaction', to create what is essentially the present work, with some later expansions finishing the task. The analysis is meticulous, and the conclusion intriguing, but no compelling reason is offered for understanding the material this way round: it is manifestly simpler to explain the distinctiveness of 6: 1–19 as a result of that section being secondary, rather than to take it as original, and the rest as secondary.

still perfectly proper to suggest that unusual complexity may have arisen from redactional activity rather than compositional ambition. Indeed, it would be very difficult to deny that Proverbs 1–9 has undergone at least some supplementation and textual corruption, and it is not my intention to do so. However, in assessing the original import and meaning of a text, there would seem to be a significant gulf between viewing it as a single composition, to which some slight alterations have been made, and taking it to be, in effect, the disjointed work of many hands.

In practice, the gulf is not always so wide. Arndt Meinhold's commentary, for example, takes Proverbs 1–9 to have been created from separate works through the careful interweaving of materials around ten *Lehrreden*, but argues for such intensive and sophisticated redaction that he might almost as readily be speaking of a composition *de novo*.[24] Two other recent commentators seem to be treading much the same path, albeit more casually. Richard Clifford believes that ten separate instructions have been juxtaposed to speeches by Wisdom, which elevates them to a metaphorical level and broadens their audience.[25] Leo Perdue, conjuring with impressive confidence a detailed picture of the post-exilic context, states that 'The theological and ethical materials found in Proverbs 1–9 probably derived from several school settings in the early half of the Persian period: a temple school, family guilds, and civil academies.'[26] He then goes on, however, to say that 'the sages who produced it possessed remarkable literary skills', and to talk of the 'literary positioning of the poems' about Wisdom around the ten instructions 'to form a literary *inclusio* that reconstitutes in the elegance of didactic poetry the themes and language present in the instructions'.[27] Little

---

[24] A. Meinhold, *Die Sprüche*, vol. 1: *Sprüche Kapitel 1–15* (Zürcher Bibelkommentare 16.1; Zürich: Theologischer Verlag, 1991), 43–6. Fox comments that 'This hypothesis is ... self-defeating, for an intricate design such as he proposes would (if persuasive) argue for single authorship rather than for compilation' (*Proverbs 1–9*, 325).

[25] R. Clifford, *Proverbs: A Commentary* (OTL; Louisville, KY: Westminster / John Knox Press, 1999), 2.

[26] L. G. Perdue, *Proverbs* (Interpretation; Louisville, KY: John Knox Press, 2000), 61. His ideas about the context are elaborated more fully in 'Wisdom Theology and Social History in Proverbs 1–9', in Barré, *Sister*, 78–101.

[27] Perdue, *Proverbs*, 62–3.

particular justification is offered for these latter analyses: the idea that the text is built around ten separate instructions seems rather to be taken for granted, but both Clifford and Perdue, like Meinhold before them, clearly wish to attribute to the redactors a creative activity that effectively allows us to treat Proverbs 1–9 as a single composition, while calling it a collection. In which case, we might reasonably ask just what it is that compels them to presume that the work must have been, at heart, a collection.

The answer certainly lies in the first two of the considerations outlined above. Before we examine those in more detail, however, it is important to note that not all issues of unity can be resolved at this stage of the discussion. Michael Fox's commentary, for example, argues that Proverbs 1–9 was composed originally as a series of ten 'lectures' with a prologue, to which have been added five 'interludes' by different authors; most of these interludes (6: 1–19 is the exception) concern the figure of Wisdom.[28] The ten lectures are taken to represent a unified composition that has been supplemented, so Fox's basic reconstruction is not the same as those already mentioned, and his case rests essentially upon the third of our considerations, that of unity in thought and presentation. Something rather similar is done by Rolf Schäfer in his recent monograph, where he identifies twelve of what he terms *Lehrgedichte*, along with an introduction.[29] These, he believes, originally constituted an independent collection, which has undergone a theological reinterpretation, principally through the addition of secondary material. We cannot really address such ideas properly until we have looked in detail at issues of outlook and content. At this point, let us confine our discussion, therefore, to the question of whether the parental appeals, taken together with what we know of ancient instructions, should compel us to regard Proverbs 1–9 as a collection.[30]

[28] M. V. Fox, *Proverbs 1–9: A New Translation with Introduction and Commentary* (AB 18A; New York: Doubleday, 2000), 324–30. See also his 'Ideas of Wisdom in Proverbs 1–9', *JBL* 116 (1997), 613–33.

[29] R. Schäfer, *Die Poesie der Weisen: Dichotomie als Grundstruktur der Lehr- und Weisheitsgedichte in Proverbien 1–9* (WMANT 77; Neukirchen: Neukirchener Verlag, 1999).

[30] We may also note in passing, though, that even Fox's measured conclusions owe something to assumptions in this area, since he argues (*Proverbs 1–9*, 325) that 'The author (or the literary tradition behind him) took the defining elements of the

A. The Parental Appeals

We may begin with the issue about which there is the least substantial disagreement: the parental appeals. Essentially, these consist of a direct address to the son, calling on him to heed or obey the instruction, and they thereby embody in themselves the instructional, father–son setting. The appeals have no have no single form, however, and it is difficult to isolate any basic 'appeal form' without performing radical surgery upon the text. In part, this is because some of the appeals are very closely integrated with the material that follows them, acting in chapter 2, for instance, as the protasis to a long conditional clause. More importantly, though, the appeals give no impression that their author was concerned to apply some fixed formula.[31]

There is an exception to this general variety. Three appeals (5: 7; 7: 24; 8: 32) all begin with the same stich: ועתה בנים שמעו־לי ('And now, sons, listen to me'). Their similarity of form, their address to 'sons' rather than 'son',[32] and their explicitly resumptive nature distinguish these three apart as a group, raising the suspicion that they may not have the same function as the other appeals. Setting aside this special group, it does seem clear, as many commentators have observed, that the appeals each mark and introduce a new section of material. Another structural characteristic lends weight to this view: the

ancient genre of instruction and introduced them into each literary unit, making each lecture a complete instruction.' In his 'Ideas of Wisdom' (cf. also *Proverbs 1–9*, 45–7, 324–5), he spells out a three-part form for each 'lecture' (tripartite exordium, lesson, conclusion), which he takes to be the general form of Egyptian instructions.

[31] Whybray's complaint (*Proverbs*, 23)—about the inexplicable use of variations and synonyms across the appeals—only has any force if one has reason to believe that all the appeals should be the same. I do not think that we need resort to a rhetorical classification of them into sub-groups, as attempted in G. D. Pemberton, 'The Rhetoric of the Father in Proverbs 1–9', *JSOT* 30 (2005), 63–82, let alone take the work as a whole to be a collection of rhetorical exemplars designed for teaching.

[32] It would be unwise to make too much of the singular/plural distinction by itself, since there is great scope for textual confusion here. Among the other appeals, though, only 4: 1 has 'sons', and that appeal lies in a somewhat confusing section where the father reports the words of his own father, using a parental appeal to introduce what is, effectively, yet another parental appeal. If the readings are all original, then it seems probable that the singular/plural usage is intended to mark a distinction.

sections marked out by appeals tend to end with quatrains, either with synonymous parallelism throughout, or, more distinctively, with contrasting synonymous couplets.[33] These clues to the structure would greatly simplify analysis of the text but for one problem: although the appeals each introduce a new section, it is not clear that each new section is introduced by an appeal.

Taking the appeals as introductory, and ignoring the special group of three resumptive appeals, we end up with the following sections:

1: 8–33
2: 1–22
3: 1–10
3: 11–20
3: 21–35
4: 1–9
4: 10–19
4: 20–27
5: 1–6: 19
6: 20–35
7: 1–9: 18

There are clear disparities of length here, but that need not matter in itself, as we have no particular reason to suppose that the sections must be of uniform size. A more significant issue is the lack of continuity within some of the sections, which might more naturally lead us to subdivide them. Two sections stand out in this respect: 5: 1–6: 19 and 7: 1–9: 18. In the former, there is a clear break at 6: 1,

---

[33] For quatrains with synonymous parallelism, cf. 3: 19–20; 4: 8–9; 5: 22–3; 6: 34–5. For quatrains with contrasting couplets, see 1: 32–3; 2: 21–2; 4: 18–19. This is a strong tendency, rather than a fixed rule, probably reflecting a desire to end poetic units with a flourish, which would explain why antithetical couplets appear in 8: 35–6, which ends a poem but does not precede an appeal. It is noteworthy that 3: 33–4 have a quatrain, but not 3: 35, and that the form of 3: 9–10 may be constrained by other factors, which we shall examine later. Schäfer, *Die Poesie der Weisen*, seeks to establish, as a different formal characteristic, 'daß die formale Gemeinsamkeit aller Lehrgedichte in Prov 1–9 in einem *dichotomischen Korpus* besteht' ('That the common formal ground of all the instructional sayings in Proverbs 1–9 consists in a dichotomous core') (8), and he accordingly isolates bipartite structures, more convincingly in some cases than in others. The two elements of each stand in a relationship that, he claims, is analogous to that involved in poetic parallelism, and similarly variable (especially 254–5).

where the text begins with a direct address to 'my son' and a conditional clause like that of 2: 1. The clause makes no reference to the instruction, though, and cannot really be taken as part of a parental appeal, while the material that follows in vv. 1–19 is miscellaneous, and reminiscent more of the sayings added to the 'Words of Agur' in chapter 30 than of anything else in chapters 1–9. Because of this distinctly different character, 6: 1–19 are taken by almost all modern commentators to be a secondary insertion, and this conclusion is probably sound.[34]

The absence of any introductory appeal after 7: 1 is more puzzling, since chapters 8 and 9 seem both to have distinctive contents and structure. This has been a consideration for commentators who believe that the original work, partitioned by appeals, must have been supplemented. However, other possibilities exist. To take the latter problem first, chapter 9 sets the figure of Wisdom, personified as a woman, in deliberate contrast with the 'woman of Follies', with both women issuing invitations to the ignorant. Secondary material may indeed have complicated the picture: Wisdom's speech is interrupted by verses 7–10, which have no counterpart in the other woman's speech, and which introduce a radical change of subject; if not secondary, these verses are probably misplaced. The chapter as a whole, though, would appear to be quite in line with the themes and ideas of chapters 1–8, to the extent that it may even be a summarizing conclusion. In that case, the lack of a parental appeal might be explained by the role of the chapter as a conclusion rather than a normal section. The lack of an appeal at the beginning of chapter 8 is less problematic, especially if we set that absence alongside the similar case in chapter 1: on both occasions, a speech by Wisdom follows other material without any parental appeal to mark a break. This similarity suggests the possibility that no break was intended, and that 1: 8–33 and 7: 1–8: 36 are supposed to be single sections—a possibility that we shall explore fruitfully in a later chapter.

There are several loose ends here, but from a preliminary examination, it does seem apparent that there are no formidable obstacles to taking the parental appeals as section headings, and thereby dividing the work into the following sections:

[34] See the annotated translation, below.

[Introductory material?]	1: 1–7
Section I	1: 8–33
Section II	2: 1–22
Section III	3: 1–10
Section IV	3: 11–20
Section V	3: 21–35
Section VI	4: 1–9
Section VII	4: 10–19
Section VIII	4: 20–27
Section IX	5: 1–23
Section X	6: 20–35
Section XI	7: 1–8: 36
[Conclusion]	9: 1–6, 13–18

This list corresponds broadly to the normal subdivision of the work by modern commentators, so that the start of almost every section here corresponds, for instance, to the start of each of Fox's 'lectures'. The exception is at 3: 11, which I take to be an appeal beginning a new section, but many commentators do not.[35] The specifics of the division are not especially important in themselves, although they do raise some interesting issues.

B. The Parental Appeals and the Instruction Genre

The real question is whether we are looking at a repeated structural device within a single composition, or at a feature shared in common by a series of separate compositions. The issue of genre is important

---

[35] Interestingly, the MT marks this as a new section. I do not regard the number of sections as important, but the number eleven does correspond to an interest, observable elsewhere, in pseudo-acrostic structures, so is no more inherently unlikely than the usual ten. Schäfer's twelve *Lehrgedichte*, in *Die Poesie der Weisen*, are contained in (i) 1: 8–19; (ii) 2: 1–4, 9–15, 20–2; (iii) 3: 1–3b, 4, 21–4, 35; (iv) 4: 1–4, 5b–6, 8–9; (v) 4: 10–19; (vi) 4: 20–7; (vii) 5: 1–6, 8–13; (viii) 5: 15–20; (ix) 6: 20–1, 23–6; (x) 7: 1–22b, 23b–23c, 25–7; (xi) 8: 5–12, 13b–21, 32–3, 35a, 36b; (xii) 9: 1–6, 13–18. He does not, therefore, put a division in chapter 3, but does divide chapters 7–8, and (more unusually) chapter 5. Other scholars have also seen more than ten units; Franz Delitzsch, for example, found fifteen (although three of these were in 6: 1–19); see his *Biblischer Commentar über die poetischen Bücher des Alten Testaments*, vol. 3: *Das Salamonische Spruchbuch* (Leipzig: Dörffling & Franke, 1873), ET, *Biblical Commentary on the Proverbs of Solomon*, translated by M. G. Easton (Edinburgh: T&T Clark, 1874–5).

here—perhaps decisively so. The most famous formal argument for
an anthology of instructions in Proverbs 1–9 was put forward many
years ago by Norman Whybray, whose contention was that the
parental appeals are necessarily an *introductory* form in instructional
literature, so they cannot be used to head subsections; the divisions
they mark must therefore be separate works.[36] Any similarities of
theme between those separate works would then be explicable as
general features of the instruction genre, as special interests of the
context within which Jewish instructions arose, or as the very basis
for the anthologization of these particular instructions. If one accepts
the supposition that instructions must conform to a fairly rigid
shape, as set out by Whybray, then this is a powerful argument, and
it was influential in its day.[37]

The main problem with it, as we have seen, is that instructions
really do not have a fixed form, and accordingly, parental appeals are
by no means a necessary element. When they do appear in
instructions, moreover, while it is often at the beginning, it is not
infrequently at other points instead, or as well, with at least one work
using them to mark separate sections.[38] It is probably true that

[36] See R. N. Whybray, *Wisdom in Proverbs: The Concept of Wisdom in Proverbs 1–9*
(SBT 45; London: SCM Press, 1965). The basic opinions which he expressed there
were essentially reiterated in his more recent commentary, *Proverbs* (NCBC; Grand
Rapids, MI: Eerdmans, and London: Marshall Pickering, 1994), 23–149, and also in
The Composition of the Book of Proverbs (JSOTS 168; Sheffield: Sheffield Academic
Press, 1994), 11–61. The appeals are important to his theory, as they are used to
provide the only external verification for what is otherwise a circular argument, in
which a development of wisdom ideas is proposed on the basis of secondary
materials, whose secondary nature is apparent from their relationship with later
stages of this proposed development. Without being able to call on his idea of a
'model' instruction, with a fixed type of appeal in a fixed position, Whybray can only
resort to much vaguer claims that there are different ideas about wisdom present in
the text. Fox summarizes it well: 'Whybray's procedure is procrustean. He assumes
that the instructions—though supposedly by different authors—were extremely
uniform to start with. Then he pares down the instructions until they all fit a
preconceived primitive mold by excising virtually everything that seems to him to
be redundant or emphatic or to change the topic' (*Proverbs 1–9*, 322).

[37] Interestingly, an appeal to instructional form appears as a component in the
very different hypothesis of Müller, who identifies, and validates, his original kernel
(see above) as 'eine fast klassische Weisheitslehre' ('an almost classical wisdom
instruction') (*Proverbien 1–9*, 294).

[38] Introductory appeals stand as independent units at the head of Šuruppak,
Šube'awilum, Amenemhet, the *Instruction by a Man for his Son*, and *Amenemope*.
Two fragments from Mesopotamia that are probably prologues to instructions also

Proverbs 1–9 has picked up the use of such appeals from other instructional material, but there is no reason to believe that it was using some fixed and inflexible convention. Instructions simply do not have that sort of formal consistency, at least in their foreign manifestations, and they give no basis for the radical divisions and excisions that Whybray goes on to perform on Proverbs 1–9, in an attempt to align the text with some 'model' instruction.[39]

There is another, more positive point about genre to be made here. Anthologies and collections are themselves a type of literature, and are very widely attested in the ancient world. We have seen that some instructions (*Ahiqar*, for instance) can themselves, indeed, be collections of short sayings or of much more miscellaneous material, presented within the customary narrative setting. The various collections may include excerpts from instructions; what we never find anywhere, however, is an anthology of instructions.[40] There are two good reasons for the lack of such collections. The first is rather obvious: instructions are generally just too long to be collected in this way. Consequently, anthologies of instructions were never likely to become an established literary genre. While instructions are clearly not required to conform to any particular length, to take the individual sections of Proverbs 1–9 as separate instructions is to suggest that Judaism uniquely spawned a whole tribe of pygmy

contain such appeals, as does a fragment possibly from a New Kingdom instruction, *Amennakhte*, of which only the prologue is extant; cf. G. Posener, 'L'Exorde de l'instruction éducative d'Amennakhte (Recherches littéraires, v)', *RdE* 10 (1955), 61–72. (The fact that only the prologue appears in the several texts found so far raises the suspicion that there may only have been a prologue, used for copying.) There are also, though, parallels to the repetition of appeals: *Šuruppak* repeats its whole prologue, and a section from the first chapter of *Amenemope* is twice repeated at the end of subsequent chapters. In some works, moreover, appeals are first introduced only at a later stage of the work: *Any* has a single appeal part of the way into the work, while the early Egyptian instructions of *Kagemni*, *Ptahhotep*, and *Merikare* all have appeals in their closing sections or epilogues.

[39] The actual use of appeals in foreign instructions is also of significance for Müller's conclusion that Prov. 4: 10–27 is the original introduction to the oldest kernel of the collection, which he argues through comparison with the beginning of *Amenemope* and Prov. 22; cf. see Müller, *Proverbien 1–9*, 293.

[40] The Book of Proverbs itself anthologizes instructions with other materials, of course, but is not an anthology of instructions. The closest we come otherwise is, perhaps, the copying together of *Ptahhotep* and *Kagemni* in Papyrus Prisse, or the use of extracts from instructions in the Egyptian miscellanies.

instructions; that these instructions uniquely shared a common set of interests and themes; and that they were uniquely collected together to form an anthology of instructions. While none of that is impossible, it is hardly a case that can be built on the back of comparisons with the foreign texts.

The second reason that we do not find collections of instructions derives straightforwardly from the nature of the genre: instructions provide a framework, not specific form or content. While it is conceivable that someone might have wanted to put together a collection of the instructional speeches by different individuals, moreover, the idea of collecting instructions by the same 'instructor' runs against the normal understanding of the instructional speech as a one-time-only testimonial speech. Proverbs 1–9 certainly breaks this convention, as I have already suggested, but it does this by moving away from the normal setting. Scholars like Whybray, who wish to portray it as a collection on the basis of supposed instructional norms, must address the fact that, so far as we can speak of such norms at all, the normal length and the normal understanding of the genre meant that it was *not* normal to collect instructions together into a single work.

In short, a comparison with the use of parental appeals in other instructions offers no secure basis for assuming that Proverbs 1–9 must be reckoned a series of individual instructions, and certainly does not suggest that it must be an anthology. In fact, it is interesting to note that similar appeals do seem to be used structurally, albeit in a rather different way, within another instructional section of Proverbs, where the possibility that they mark separate works may be ruled out.

That other section, 'The Words of the Wise', lies in 22: 17–24: 22. Although it is presented as a single section now,[41] this material may have been created through the amalgamation of earlier texts, as is the case in some other parts of Proverbs.[42] Whatever its compositional history, though, the structure of the work has been variously assessed, with different commentators finding different sections and methods

---

[41] The normal superscription is lacking, but the next heading at 24: 23 claims that what follows is *also* sayings of the wise, suggesting that 22: 17a stands in place of a title.

[42] See chapter 2 of my *Early Israelite Wisdom* on the evidence for amalgamation within the sentence literature collections.

of organization.[43] In this text too, however, parental appeals seem to play a significant role, and to provide some basis for analysis. The first such appeal is part of the work's heading at 22: 17, and the next is at 23: 12; the intervening material is the section commonly linked with the *Instruction of Amenemope*. From 23: 12 to 23: 28, however, appeals become much more frequent, to the extent that each separate piece of advice is apparently preceded by a commendation of wisdom or instruction.[44] The material in 23: 29–24: 12 is very mixed,[45] and there are no further appeals until 24: 13. This final appeal introduces three prohibitions and closes with a (somewhat obscure) warning to fear God and the king, all linked by the theme of retribution. No consistency of theme or form is apparent in 22: 17–24: 22 as a whole, and it would be hard to describe any overall structure. However, the appeals in 22: 17 and 24: 13 do both seem to mark distinct subsections, with the former distinguished by its links with *Amenemope*, and the latter by its theme. The distinctiveness of 23: 12–28, on the other hand, lies in its almost obsessive use of appeals as separators. But if there is no systematic use of appeals, as in chapters 1–9, this later part of Proverbs does at least seem to show an awareness of their potential as section markers.[46] There is a close thematic relationship between 23: 12–28 and chapters 1–9, and we

[43] For example, Whybray, largely following Niccacci, has viewed 22: 17–23: 11 as a single instruction, with an introduction in 22: 17–21 followed by ten sections (22: 22–3, 24–5, 26–7, 28, 29; 23: 1–3, 4–5, 6–8, 9, 10–11), and then regards the sayings that follow as miscellaneous additions. See Whybray, *Composition*, 132–45; A. Niccacci, 'Proverbi 22.17–23.11', *LA* 29 (1979), 42–72. Plöger, by way of contrast, views 22: 17–24: 22 as a collection of admonitions in three parts (22: 22–23: 14; 23: 15–35; 24: 1–22), with, again, an introduction in 22: 17–21. See O. Plöger, *Sprüche Salomos (Proverbia)* (BKAT 17; Neukirchen: Neukirchener Verlag, 1984), 265–84.

[44] See 23: 12, 15–16, 19, 22–3, 26. The appeals include a direct address to 'my son' in verses 15, 19, and 26.

[45] 23: 29–35 describes the numbness and disorientation brought on by wine, making heavy use of rhetorical questions and similes. This is followed by a single short admonition in 24: 1–2, which is in turn followed by a series of indicative sayings about wisdom (24: 3–7) and two short sayings about the planning of evil in 24: 8–9, which may hark back to the initial admonition. We then find a remarkable piece of advice about behaviour in the 'day of adversity', which seems to be concerned with divine knowledge and justice (24: 10–12).

[46] We hardly need add, of course, that the section gives few grounds for taking appeals necessarily to mark separate works; while this might be true of 22: 17 and 24: 13, it would be an obvious absurdity to make this assumption in 23: 12–28. A thorough examination of 22: 17–24: 22 is impractical here. I would suggest that

cannot rule out the possibility that it has drawn on our text in this and other respects. However, it does demonstrate beyond reasonable doubt that, in Israel as elsewhere, such appeals may be resumptive and structural, and need not be regarded as the introduction to independent works.

C. Conclusions

All these considerations weigh heavily towards the view that the argument from form for disunity has little real weight, even when examined in its own terms: comparison with other instructions does not compel us to take Proverbs 1–9 as an anthology, or even as a series of disconnected units; if anything, the repeated parental appeals would appear to reflect an essential unity of structure. It is questionable, though, whether we should even be trying to argue the case in such terms. Setting aside the specific case of the instruction genre, we must be wary of pushing the whole concept of generic convention too far. It is true that in the ancient world, as in the modern, a few types of writing imposed very specific constraints, such as line length or metre. It is also true, however, not only that the number of such genres has always been small, but also that some flexibility is almost always expected. We do not waste our time trying to restore the missing parts of Shakespeare's twelve-line sonnets, and have long since come to terms even with the prose poem, so it is difficult to see why some commentators have been so insistent that biblical writers must have conformed to rigid, predetermined templates, turning their compositions into a sort of painting-by-numbers exercise.

Perhaps the most useful by-product of Whybray's work on Proverbs 1–9 has been to demonstrate just how much one does have to strip away before the idiosyncrasies of the work have been wholly

---

22: 17–23: 11 is to be viewed as a unity, but also that the structural consistency of 23: 12–28, and the strong thematic unity of 24: 37 and 24: 13–22 show these to be single units. The 'my son' addresses of verses 13 and 21 frame the last of these, and it is conceivable that 24: 1–2 and 8–9 are intended to form an *inclusio* around vv. 3–7, although their theme is very different. The key problem is not so much the unity of particular groups of sayings here, but the relationship between those groups: can one legitimately say, for instance, that 23: 29–35 pick up the theme of 23: 19–21, or connect the references to envy of the wicked in 23: 17; 24: 1–2; and 24: 19–20?

removed, and more moderate analyses are obliged to accept some of the peculiarities in the work's presentation of instruction, even if they do not always note them as such. It takes some real work to remove not just the appeals by wisdom and the portrayal of God as instruct-ing father, but also the mentions of the mother, and the father's father; even then, one is left with the problem of instruction presented as a process. It is doubtful that the writer of Proverbs 1–9 would have known that some instructions had been interested in the very nature of instruction almost since the inception of the genre, and he could not have foreseen the radical subversiveness of the Insinger work in this respect. Whether we attribute his own interest in this to generic awareness, however, or to a more immediate creativity, the resulting peculiarities of presentation should not drive us to conclude that Proverbs 1–9 cannot be a 'proper' instruc-tion. They should certainly not in themselves, moreover, lead us to divide or dissect the text in search of something more 'normal'. If that is true with consideration to the genre itself, it is doubly true with regard to such occasional and erratic conventions as the parental appeals. We cannot use its generic affiliations to prove the unity of Proverbs 1–9, but attempts to use them to prove its disunity are mistaken in both fact and method.

4. INSTRUCTION AND POETRY

Last, but perhaps most importantly, the genre of Proverbs 1–9 has considerable implications for how we should approach the style and content. Early critical commentators were, on the whole, quite impressed by the style of Proverbs 1–9, and it could be said of the discourses, for instance, that they are 'neither of a symmetrically chiselled form nor of internally fashioned coherence, but yet are a garland of songs having internal unity, with a well-arranged mani-foldness of contents'.[47] Subsequently, however, the association with

---

[47] Quoting Easton's often elegant translation of Delitzsch, *Spruchbuch*; see ET vol. 1, 14. Similarly, e.g. C. H. Toy, *A Critical and Exegetical Commentary on the Book of Proverbs* (ICC; Edinburgh: T&T Clark, 1899). See also R. Smend, 'The Interpretation of Wisdom in Nineteenth-Century Scholarship', in Day *et al.*, *Wisdom*

foreign instructions—the *Sitz im Leben* of which was taken to be the schoolroom—lent weight to existing suspicions that this literature was pedagogical, and this was all too often understood in terms of instructions being simple textbooks, geared to pragmatism.[48] This, in turn, fostered an attitude among many commentators that was inimical to reading Proverbs 1–9 (or any other instruction) as poetic, except at some superficial, mnemonic level,[49] and that attitude has done much to shape more recent scholarship. If a text is purposefully didactic, the reasoning runs, then it must, correspondingly, be trying to be lucid: any apparent opacity must be the result either of secondary redaction, or simply of a failure on our part to understand what is being said. As William McKane put it in his commentary:

> The Instruction... does not aspire to be literature and it sacrifices imaginative outreach to pedestrian clarity... the concern of the instruction is above all to be clear and to leave nothing to chance or doubt.[50]

When it has proved impossible to sustain such a description for a particular passage, as is very often the case in Proverbs 1–9, then

---

in Ancient Israel, 257–68, who notes (261) the opinion of Davidson, that Prov. 1–9 is 'one of the most remarkable and beautiful things in Hebrew literature'.

[48] The association of wisdom literature with pedagogy does predate the recognition of precise links with Egyptian literature; cf. especially A. Klostermann, 'Schulwesen im alten Israel', in N. Bonwetsch *et al.* (eds), *Theologische Studien: Theodor Zahn zum 10. Oktober 1908* (Leipzig: A. Deichert'sche, 1908), 193–232. The difficulties involved in saying anything precise about schools in Israel, however, meant that awareness of those links strengthened the supposition of such a context immeasurably. The pedagogical character of the Egyptian texts continues to be asserted as an unqualified fact by some biblical scholars. For a recent example, see E. Sevenich-Bax, 'Schule in Israel als Sitz der Weisheit', in M. Fassnacht, A. Leinhäupl-Wilke, S. Lücking (eds), *Die Weisheit—Ursprünge und Rezeption: Festscrift für Karl Löning zum 65. Geburtstag* (Neutestamentliche Abhandlungen n.s. 44; Münster: Aschendorff, 2003), 59–77, especially 66–7.

[49] Writing on the subject of alphabetic and name/sentence acrostics, W. M. Soll, 'Babylonian and Biblical Acrostics', *Biblica* 69 (1988), 305–23, makes an important general point against the common supposition that biblical texts are poetic because poetry is easier to remember: 'Once a poem employs any form of word-patterning, subsequent attempts to memorize it may rely on the pattern, but such reliance does not mean that the author employed the pattern for a mnemonic purpose... One cannot even say that rhymed (or acrostic) poetry is always easier to memorize than blank verse, since ease of memory also depends on the poem's vocabulary, its length, and the strength of the impression it makes on the mind' (321). For a contrary recent view, see Carr, *Writing*, 128–9.

[50] W. McKane, *Proverbs*, 317–18.

some scholars have simply ripped that passage from its context and treated it as an addition, or as an earlier work hijacked by the unimaginative instructors.[51] This is not a good way to approach poetry.

It is, of course, notoriously difficult to judge the original 'literariness' of any work without explicit statements of the author's intentions—not least because the presuppositions of readers can so strongly influence the depth and richness of what they find in a text. Some objective approaches are possible, and have been applied, though often unsystematically, to other instructions. When, for example, Miriam Lichtheim says of *Amenemope* that 'it abounds in rare words, elliptic phrases, and allusions whose meaning escapes us', she is using factual data to support her view that the text is high literature.[52] The very substantial number of scribal errors found in texts of that work may suggest, moreover, that it proved something of a challenge even to Egyptian readers, and thereby support her contention that its language was far from plain. Although extreme, *Amenemope* is not an isolated example of this tendency: rare and obscure vocabulary is a mark of many other instructions, while a leaning towards figurative speech is found in most of the later Egyptian texts, perhaps especially the Brooklyn Papyrus. That tendency is not confined to Egypt, furthermore, and the Aramaic *Ahiqar* makes considerable use of figurative techniques, few of which add any clarity to its message. If we accept that difficult language, obscure vocabulary, and figurative speech are marks of literary ambition, then it is hard to deny that many instructions seem to be very ambitious indeed. It is hard, however, to quantify such aspects of language, and this is especially true in the context of biblical Hebrew texts, of which we have such a limited corpus. It would be pointless, therefore, to undertake some detailed study of the vocabulary in Proverbs 1–9 in the hope of somehow proving it to be high literature,

[51] So Bernhard Lang, for example, feels quite able to separate the 'wisdom poems' in chapters 3 and 8 from their context without giving any justification beyond their 'poetic quality' and 'beauty', which makes them stand out from the rest of Proverbs (*Wisdom*, 16). Lang also cites with approval the views of Mary Ellen Chase, who contrasts these poems with 'the monotonous style' elsewhere, and who thinks that they 'reduce the drab notions of the other sages to dust and ashes'; M. E. Chase, *The Bible and the Common Reader* (New York: Macmillan, 1944), 239–40, cited in Lang, *Wisdom*, 16.

[52] *AEL*, vol. 2, 147.

although those who have read it in the original may need little persuading that it shows no interest in plain speaking.

All the same, it is important to give the lie to the old fallacy that instructions are concerned principally with the clear expression of their content. The literary quality of their compositions should not, of course, be taken to mean that the ancient writers were indulging in some effete and artificial elevation of form and style over meaning. Fine expression was inextricably linked with the presentation of truth in the ancient world, and beauty of language, not simple lucidity, was the goal of those texts that sought to embody some truth.[53] This is the 'perfect speech' with which *Ptahhotep* is concerned, and, in a Jewish context, it is probably the reason for Qoheleth's careful arrangement of sayings (Qoh. 12: 9–10). Self-conscious stylism, then, although it may not be confined to instructions in the ancient world, is often integral to their expression and purpose. We should not be surprised, therefore, if the instructional Proverbs 1–9 shows signs of literary ambition: everything we know about the genre points to the probability that it should do so.

In short, if we are to give weight to its association with the instruction genre, that association should lead us to read Proverbs 1–9 as sophisticated poetry, not as a school textbook, and when we turn to its figurative language in the next chapter, we shall find plenty of internal evidence to support such an approach. In the meantime, however, I wish to focus briefly upon some other material that illustrates just how elaborate a style the work can adopt at times, and which also relates back to the question of unity addressed above.

A. The Structure of Proverbs 2

Meinhold describes chapter 2 as a *Lehrprogramm* for Proverbs 1–9 as a whole,[54] and it is certainly true, at least, that many of the key motifs

---

[53] J. Tambling, *What is Literary Language?* (Open Guides to Literature; Buckingham and Bristol, PA: Open University Press, 1988), 68, notes that the deprecation of high style is essentially a modern phenomenon: 'The scientifically-orientated, post-Renaissance world in its positivism has privileged "truth" as something "mathematically plain," and needing, therefore, no demonstration.'

[54] Meinhold, *Sprüche*, 43, 62.

My son, if you accept my words,
and treasure up my commandments with you,
so as to bend your ear to wisdom,
and turn your heart to understanding
—yes, if you call out for insight,
and cry for understanding,
if you seek it like silver,
and hunt for it like hidden treasure,

Then will you understand the fear of
Yahweh, and find knowledge of God.
For it is Yahweh who gives wisdom:
from his mouth are knowledge and
understanding.
He saves up prudence for the upright,
a shield for those who walk in integrity,
To guard the paths of justice,
and preserve the way of his godly.

To deliver you from the way of evil,
from a man who speaks perversity,
Those who abandon straight paths
to walk on ways of darkness,
Those who take joy in doing evil—
they delight in the perversity of evil—
Whose paths are twisted,
and are crooked in their routes.

Then will you understand rightness
and justice and equity—every good path.
For wisdom will enter your heart,
and knowledge be pleasant to your soul;

Resourcefulness will stand guard over you,
understanding will watch you:

To deliver you from the strange woman,
from a foreign woman who has polished
her words,
She who abandons the companion
of her youth,
and has forgotten the covenant of her God.
For her house reaches down to death,
and her paths to the shades:
None who go to her returns,
and they never reach the paths of life.

So you will walk on the way of the good,
and keep to the paths of the righteous,
For the upright will inhabit the land,
and those with integrity stay in it;
But the wicked will be cut off from the land,
and the treacherous torn away from it.

that appear elsewhere in the work appear also in this section. In particular, it is striking that we encounter for the first time here the 'strange' or 'foreign' woman, who is to play such a prominent role from chapter 5 onwards, and that the chapter makes extensive reference to the imagery of ways and paths that is, as we shall see, strongly characteristic of Proverbs 1–9. Indeed, Fox has gone so far as to say that the presentation of behaviour as a path 'is the *ground metaphor* of Prov 1–9 . . . that unifies its teachings'.[55] I do not wish to

---

[55] Fox, *Proverbs 1–9*, 128.

pre-empt later discussion by examining the themes and imagery here in detail, but it does seem likely that chapter 2 is intended to condense or foreshadow major interests or motifs. It is not, then, simply a random sample of text, but probably comes as close as anything to epitomizing Proverbs 1–9 as a whole.

Syntactically, Proverbs 2 is arguably the longest sentence in the Bible. It is structured (as shown on the preceding page) as a single condition, with a protasis in the first four verses picked up by extended apodoses. The structure here seems fairly clear, although there has been much debate about nomenclature and details: the poem has six stanzas, the middle four of which form two pairs. The first stanza expresses the basic condition through two protases, the first of which is extended. The next two stanzas are apodoses to the condition, each claiming that fulfilment of the conditions will result in understanding of something, and explaining that this will offer protection. The following two stanzas then each promise deliverance from someone who speaks in a certain way, and who has abandoned something. Finally, the last stanza claims that fulfilment will enable or involve walking on the 'way of the good', and contrasts the fates of the righteous and the wicked.

The symmetry within each pair is established by repetition of the key terms and motifs. The length of the stanzas is fairly consistent, moreover, with eight stichs in all but the third and sixth stanzas. These have six stichs each, and there is a slight imbalance, therefore, in the first pair. This may suggest that a distich has been lost, which would not be surprising in such a repetitive text. It more probably, though, reflects another stylistic trick, with the first line of the fourth stanza serving a double, Janus-like duty as the last line of the third, and establishing a transition between the two pairs; it has verbal parallels with both the last line of the second stanza and the first line of the fifth. The writer may have been motivated to use this trick by a different poetic concern: the poem as a whole is a pseudo-acrostic, with its 22 lines reflecting the 22 letters of the Hebrew alphabet, and the central stanzas beginning with the first and middle letters of the alphabet. Twenty-two line, pseudo-acrostic poems are not uncommon in the biblical literature, and eleven line poems are also found; naturally, a poet seeking to divide them into stanzas of equal size would be confronted by a mathematical problem, and the approach taken here seems a clever one.[56]

Although the broader techniques employed are individually commonplace, such thoroughgoing symmetry and patterning is very unusual in extant Hebrew verse. Syntactically, of course, there is a price to be paid. The basic sentence here is something like: 'If you receive my words, then you will understand the fear of YHWH, which will deliver you from the way of evil, and so you will walk on the way of the good.' Each element of that sentence has been expanded in some way, however, to create whole stanzas, and the writer has created an entire poem out of a conditional sentence, in a way that is compositionally sophisticated but syntactically grotesque. The possibility that this structure could have arisen through secondary supplementation appears remote. In the first place, the overall course of the poem is dictated from the outset, by the presentation of the parental appeal as the protasis for a condition, and if the basic elements of what follows had not been in place originally, then this would have been a very short section indeed. It is also difficult to envisage a process of supplementation leading to the parallel wording of the stanzas or to the pseudo-acrostic length, unless, of course, we

---

[56] The general structure of this chapter is widely recognized, although scholars differ in their precise delineation of the stanzas; see especially P. W. Skehan, 'The Seven Columns of Wisdom's House in Proverbs 1–9', *CBQ* 9 (1947), 190–8, especially 190; and his *Studies in Israelite Poetry and Wisdom* (CBQMS 1; Washington, DC: Catholic Biblical Association of America, 1971), 9–10, 16. R. E. Murphy, in *Proverbs* (Word Biblical Commentary 22; Nashville: T. Nelson, 1998), 15, notes that this structure is a strong indication of the chapter's unity, and therefore properly rejects attempts to portray it as composite or to excise material as secondary. Such attempts include those by Maier to see verses 5–8 and 21–2 as secondary, and especially Michel's attempt, in the style of Norman Whybray, to trace historical layers in the chapter, reflecting changes in the wisdom tradition; cf. C. Maier, *Die 'fremde Frau' in Proverbien 1–9: Eine exegetische und sozialgeschichtliche Studie* (OBO 144; Freibourg: Universitätsverlag Freiburg Schweiz, and Göttingen: Vandenhoeck & Ruprecht, 1995), 90; and D. Michel, 'Proverbia 2: ein Dokument der Geschichte der Weisheit', in J. Hausmann and H.-J. Zobel (eds), *Alttestamentlicher Glaube und Biblische Theologie: Festschrift für Horst Dietrich Preuss zum 65. Geburtstag* (Stuttgart: Kohlhammer, 1992), 233–43; similar conclusions are reached by Müller, *Proverbien*, 52–73, although his stated grounds are compositional. Whybray himself, of course, viewed the structural elements as evidence in themselves for the chapter's disunity, seeing the original content of the instruction in verses 16–19, and referring to the chapter's 'constant, wearisome repetition of the same thoughts' (*Proverbs*, 50).

just write these off as the products of over-zealous analysis on the part of many different commentators.[57]

B. Proverbs 1: 10–19

The best reason to accept that we have chapter 2 in more or less its original form, however, is the fact that it merely takes to an extreme some techniques that are found elsewhere in Proverbs 1–9. So, for example, it is interesting to compare an earlier passage, the father's warning against the blandishments of sinners in 1: 10–19, which also involves the abnormal extension of a conditional clause. The basic structure here is very simple, and becomes clear if the sinners' speech is omitted:

My son, if sinners tempt you,   If they say,...

don' t succumb,   My son, do not walk on the way with them
                                          —hold your foot back from their paths.

The father presents his advice in the form of two conditional clauses, each advising rejection of the sinners, and each including an address to 'my son'; the second of these marks the return to the father's own words. The speech of the sinners is itself interrupted in a similar way, with the list of their intentions placed between the two invitations to join them; we might say that this list is a unit within a unit within a unit. The sinners' intentions are then picked up in the father's speech, with his declaration that their deeds will backfire on them. Again, this arrangement, with its strange internal symmetry, does little to enhance the clarity of the message: the second conditional sentence in the father's speech is only completed after the sinners have spoken, which is as awkward syntactically in Hebrew as it would be in English. It is possible that the line 'For their feet...blood' is an addition,[58] but there are no grounds for supposing that the sinners' speech is secondary or misplaced; we must conclude, therefore, that the writer has deliberately imposed this structure for stylistic reasons, probably at the expense of clarity.

[57] As Fox puts it (*Proverbs 1–9*, 128), 'it is improbable that the tightly knit structure...would have resulted from multiple intrusions'.
[58] See the annotated translation.

C. Conclusions

Proverbs 1, then, offers a foretaste of what we are going to find in Proverbs 2: the prolongation of a conditional clause, and the subjugation of syntax to style. We shall see other examples as we proceed, but it is surely reasonable at this stage to accept that the complexity of Proverbs 2 is both original and deliberate. This is important as an indication of the sort of literary ambitions that we might expect of an instruction, and as a warning against expectations of plain speaking in the work as a whole. There are also implications in this for the issue of unity. As I mentioned at the beginning of this discussion, Proverbs 2 has links to many other parts of Proverbs 1–9 in terms of shared interests and motifs. The apparent unity of the chapter, therefore, is itself a strong argument for the basic unity of the work as a whole, or at least for the coherence of the parts that incorporate those interests and motifs.

5. SUMMARY AND CONCLUSIONS

In the last chapter, we saw that the instruction genre is something rather more complicated than it is often made out to be, and that instructions share little more in common than a poetic, literary character, and a particular narrative setting. This chapter began by accepting that Proverbs 1–9 should be considered an instruction, but with the caveats that its author's experience and understanding of the genre might be rather different from our own, and that we should not, in any case, take its association with the genre to render other aspects of its background and context unimportant. We went on to observe that the work presents instruction in an unusual way, portraying it as a process, rather than as a specific event, and attributing instruction to various different characters. This led us to the question of unity, and to an assessment of claims that Proverbs 1–9 is not an instruction, as such, but rather a collection of instructions, brought together, redacted and supplemented to create the work we now possess. Two of the considerations that underpin such claims were examined in detail: the division of the work into sections by repeated parental appeals, and related assertions about the proper form of instructions. Through this discussion I put forward an outline of the work's structure, but could find no compelling reason to accept that Proverbs 1–9 must be an anthology; generic considerations, indeed, appeared to tell against such a characterization. Finally, we turned to the question of style, where an examination based on chapter 2 affirmed that Proverbs 1–9 does indeed seem to possess the belletristic character that we might expect of an instruction (and not the sort of didactic clarity that is often, quite falsely, attributed to the genre). This examination also offered some further support for the basic unity of the work.

Except in this last discussion of style, the arguments presented here have been rather negative ones: much of the chapter has been about what its affiliation to the instruction genre does *not* tell us about Proverbs 1–9. That is, perhaps, inevitable, given the determination of many biblical scholars to take a genre that actually places few constraints on inclusion as being highly prescriptive instead. A more positive evaluation of what the author was trying to do must await further discussion. Similarly, at this stage it is impossible to go beyond a rejection of formal arguments *against* unity and to propose arguments *for* it. Here, though, it is not a simple matter of returning to the discussion at a later point: while we await the invention of a time machine, the only way to demonstrate basic unity is to show that a reading of the text as a single work produces, on balance, the most satisfactory and coherent result, and to leave the rest to Occam. As we go on to examine the key themes and motifs that run through most of chapters 1–9, I do not intend to keep pointing out that each is evidence for unity, but trust that the compositional implications will be taken as read. We shall, however, return to some of the specific claims that have been made for incoherence in the text's thought or presentation.

3

Theme and Imagery in Proverbs 1–9

Our consideration of the genre of Proverbs 1–9 has already led us to
characterize it as stylistically ambitious, but we have so far avoided
detailed discussion of what might be considered the work's most
distinctive feature, its elaborate and extensive use of figurative
language. Such usage tends to confirm, of course, the high-literary,
poetic character that we have already taken to be typical of instructions, but Proverbs 1–9 appears to go much further than most in this
respect. Just how far it does go, however, is difficult to determine,
since all too quickly we run up against problems of distinguishing the
figurative from the literal. If this is merely difficult when we are
dealing with simple metaphors, it can become an almost intractable
problem when we are trying to assess the extent to which the work
employs other devices. The purpose of this chapter, therefore, is
not straightforwardly to identify particular references as literal or
figurative, but rather to examine the ways in which figures and motifs
are linked and deployed across the work. It will be my contention
that Proverbs 1–9 develops an elaborate and distinctive set of motifs,
and that the significance of some elements only becomes clear
through a recognition of their place in this.

1. FIGURATIVE LANGUAGE IN PROVERBS 1–9

Let us, however, start with some basics. Poetic language is often,
of course, characterized by the intensified use of figurative
devices found in other types of discourse, and such devices play an

important role in Proverbs 1–9. The most obvious examples are probably the similes and comparisons used at many points in the work. In 1: 17, for instance, the behaviour of the sinners is contrasted with the wariness of birds, and in 1: 27 the coming of panic likened to a storm. In 4: 18–19, the ways of the righteous and wicked are similarly likened to light and darkness, while the woman in 5: 4 is bitter as wormwood and sharp as a sword. In 6: 27 and 30–1, rhetorical questions are used comparatively, and 7: 22–3 uses a series of similes to liken the young man's fate to that of animals facing death helplessly. These sorts of figures are employed frequently and explicitly. It is important to be aware that their use may convey more than just the stated comparison—linking the woman to a sword, for instance, tells us about more than simply her sharpness—but their presence is generally undisputed and unproblematic.

Many of the metaphors in the work are used similarly, so that instruction and teaching in 1: 8–9, for example, are said to be a garland and pendants (cf. 3: 22), just as God in 2: 7 is a shield, wisdom in 3: 18 a tree of life, and the wife in 5: 18 a 'lovely hind'. More often, though, metaphors are used without such direct declaration, as in the many references to 'paths of justice' and the like. Perhaps the most interesting and characteristic usage lies in the author's creation of short scenes or images, based around metaphorical identifications. In 1: 18, for example, the sinners are depicted as figuratively lying in ambush for their own lives, an image based on a reversal of their stated intentions. Some such images depend on previous identifications, as when the wicked stumble on their dark path, in 4: 19, or when the son is invited in 3: 3 to bind loyalty and faithfulness about his neck (cf. 6: 21), which is an apparent reference to the pendant metaphor used of instruction previously (the author adds an additional image here, of writing on the writing tablet of the heart; cf. 7: 3). At other times, a metaphor is more self-contained, but still extended beyond its initial significance: the very obscure water imagery in 5: 15–18 furnishes the most notorious example.

Such metaphorical usage is sometimes bizarre and exaggerated, as when the woman in 6: 25 is able to capture men with her eyelids, or in 5: 3 drips honey from her lips. More realistically, it often takes the form of personification, or else assumes some degree of personification.[1] The latter is illustrated by 8: 34, for example, where men are depicted waiting at the gates of Wisdom's house. (Even were we to suppose that the writer actually considered Wisdom to be a real, living, talking being, it is unlikely that he believed her to be living down the street.) Elsewhere, concepts are regularly enabled to act or to be treated as though human: in 2: 11, for instance, discernment and understanding are able to stand guard, while loyalty can forsake one in 3: 2 and instruction escape in 4: 13; more aggressively, sins in 5: 22 can ensnare their perpetrator, and, more passively, wisdom and insight can be called sister and friend in 7: 4. It seems clear, furthermore, that the writer feels free to slip in and out of his different figures as required, and 6: 20–3 provides a graphic example of this: parental teachings are first to be tied around the neck as pendants, and are then apparently personified as guardians and companions, before finally being described as lights, linked to the way of life.

Even at this very basic level, and without a tedious listing of every last instance, it would seem difficult to deny that Proverbs 1–9 is, at least, very well supplied with figurative language. It also seems clear that the work contains relatively sophisticated, extended metaphorical language. The important question, however, is just how far down this figurative path Proverbs 1–9 actually travels.

A. Characters and Personification

We have already considered 1: 8–19 in respect of its style and syntax, and it will be recalled that in this section of the work the father envisages his son being invited to join a band of 'sinners', who lie in wait for the innocent as robbers. Many commentators take this section quite literally, as a warning against trying to acquire wealth through violence,[2] although it seems unlikely that this is really the limit of its scope. Even allowing that muggers and bandits posed a

---

[1] The use of personification as a device is examined in detail by Claudia Camp, in chapter 7 of her *Wisdom and the Feminine in the Book of Proverbs* (Bible and Literature Series 11; Sheffield: Almond, 1985). She offers the succinct definition that it 'personalizes the impersonal' (213).

[2] So, e.g. Fox, *Proverbs 1–9*, 85–6, and Perdue, *Proverbs*, 77 takes this as enforcement of the existing social order through avoidance of 'brigands and revolutionaries'.

more everyday danger in the ancient Near East than in the modern West, it seems odd that the first advice offered to the son should be to avoid a criminal career—especially when the topic is never touched on directly again. When we observe, furthermore, that the robbers' invitation is couched in terms similar to those used by other speakers—the seductress in chapter 7 and Wisdom in chapter 9—it becomes tempting to suppose that something rather more complicated is going on.[3] Be that as it may—and we shall explore the issue later—it is important to note that these robbers are not real people. The father is not saying, 'Steer clear of young Ronnie Biggs and his mob', or even simply offering a straight admonition against becoming a criminal, but is hypothesizing a situation in which unnamed robbers—*any* robbers—might invite his son to join them. The speech in this section is, then, a typical invitation, attributed to a type: these robbers stand duty for the whole class of robbers or violent men (and perhaps for something more), while their speech represents the temptations of sin in some more general way, not just a form of words. With the characters and their invitation in this section, then, the father is exemplifying a potential temptation that the son may face at some point, and this is illustrative or figurative, rather in the way that a parable is.

If we turn to the other characters who issue invitations, then it seems likely that similar considerations apply to the dangerous woman who speaks in chapter 7. The case of Wisdom, however, is rather different: where the sinners and the women may be viewed as 'types', or representatives, this can hardly be true of Wisdom in the same way. At a stretch, we might just envisage some broader class of wise women, who jostled for space at the roadside with the various robbers and wicked seductresses of the writer's home town, but Wisdom is not portrayed as a typical member of such a class.[4] Rather,

---

[3] So, e.g. Clifford, *Proverbs*, 38. As Newsom says, 'it seems scarcely credible that the advice should be taken at face value as career counseling. It is much more likely that this depiction of brigands is a metaphor for something else'; see C. A. Newsom, 'Woman and the Discourse of Patriarchal Wisdom: A Study of Proverbs 1–9', in P. L. Day (ed.), *Gender and Difference in Ancient Israel* (Minneapolis: Fortress, 1989), 142–60, especially 145.

[4] This is not to say, of course, that the presentation of Wisdom is not informed by perceptions of human women, an issue explored in detail by Camp, *Wisdom and the Feminine*. She does, in fact, see links with the wise women of 2 Samuel, among others

she is the embodiment of a concept or quality, who can be variously portrayed, in the space of a few verses, both as a woman with physical form and emotions,[5] and as a skill or power enabling others (cf. 8: 14–21). For good reason, it is no longer widely held that the text is intending to portray an individual or entity who was believed to have physical form,[6] and it seems likely that we are dealing basically with a figurative personification—albeit one that many scholars consider to have been shaped by existing mythological or other ideas. In that case, the depiction of Wisdom is more elaborate than, but entirely coherent with the smaller-scale personifications that we have already noted in the work. Indeed, in such places as 3: 16, where she has hands, or 4: 9, where she can adorn the son with a garland, Wisdom is the subject of figurative personification even outside the major passages (1: 20–33, 8: 1–36, and 9: 1–6, 11) in which she appears as a woman who makes speeches.

It would be wrong to place too much emphasis on the fact that Wisdom apparently embodies a concept, while the villains of chapters 1 and 7 are types or representatives. Although they do not interact directly with each other, there are strong connections between all these characters. Chapter 9, moreover, presents us with a character who is almost certainly a further personification, directly parallel to Wisdom, but who is surely supposed to be linked also with one of our types. This is the character described as the אשת כסילות,

(120–3), having earlier argued that these figures reflected a real class, in 'The Wise Women of 2 Samuel: A Role Model for Women in Early Israel', *CBQ* 43 (1981), 14–29 (on which, see *EIW*, 78). See also S. Schroer, 'Wise and Counselling Women in Ancient Israel: Literary and Historical Ideals of the Personified *HOKMÂ*', in A. Brenner (ed.), *A Feminist Companion to Wisdom Literature* (Sheffield: Sheffield Academic Press, 1995), 67–84.

[5] F. Mies, '"Dame Sagesse" en Proverbes 9: une personnification féminine?', *RB* 108 (2001), 161–83, considers the femininity of Wisdom in Proverbs 1–9 to be overplayed by scholars, and often to reflect no more than grammatical necessity. Mies goes too far, but her general point is valid, and should caution us against investing too much in this aspect of the imagery. Similar issues are raised in Scott Harris, *Proverbs 1–9: A Study of Inner-Biblical Interpretation* (SBL Dissertation Series 150; Atlanta: Scholars Press, 1995), 159, n. 6.

[6] Some ideas, however, never quite die. P. Sacchi, *The History of the Second Temple Period* (JSOTS 285; Sheffield: Sheffield Academic Press, 2000), 387, claims that, 'the wise men of the Zadokite period already believed in a presence of God among human beings that was to be fully realized only through the mediation of a more or less hypostasized Wisdom'.

'woman of follies,' in 9: 13; even if we do not delete אשת as a gloss, and simply call her Folly (the 'plural' form is parallel to the designation of Wisdom as חכמות in 9: 1), 'we are constrained by context,' as Fox puts it, 'to understand this "foolish woman" as the personification or embodiment of folly rather than as a human fool'.[7] A counterpart to Wisdom in both designation and action in this chapter, she is clearly supposed to be an alternative or antithesis to her. She also, however, bears more than a passing resemblance to the 'foreign woman', who has earlier been described at various points, and who has herself already spoken in chapter 7. The most obvious point of contact between them is the fact that Folly's dinner guests are said to be in Sheol (9: 18), while the foreign woman's house is the way to Sheol in 7: 27 (indeed, 5: 5 suggests that she is walking there herself). Both women, furthermore, are perhaps described using the unusual term המיה (7: 11; 9: 13, if we accept the text as it stands), and both certainly issue invitations to the innocent, offering illicit pleasures. This woman in chapter 9, then, is a personification, like Wisdom, but she is associated, possibly even identified with the type of woman portrayed in chapters 5–7.[8]

There are also points of contact between the woman of chapter 7 and the sinners of chapter 1, who invite the uneducated to partake of their own illicit gains. In the only further reference to Sheol in Proverbs 1–9, those sinners compare themselves to the underworld, swallowing their victims.[9] Like the woman in chapter 7, moreover, they 'lie in wait' (1: 11 נארבה, 1: 18 יארבו; cf. 7: 12 תארב),[10] and their invitation to 'come!' uses the same word as hers (לכה, in 1: 11, 7: 18. Wisdom, in 9: 5, uses לכו). Finally, in both 1: 17 and 7: 23, the father's commentary on the characters employs distinctive imagery from the trapping of birds. At the very least, there seem to be grounds for

---

[7] Fox, *Proverbs 1–9*, 300. It seems appropriate to call her Folly, therefore, even if this is not a literal translation of the Hebrew as it stands.

[8] In her recent work, Claudia Camp has denied that the foreign woman should be understood in terms of a simple type: she 'does not represent any particular real women or class of women'; 'Woman Wisdom', 93. It might be more accurate to say she embodies several different types, as we shall see later, but I doubt that she is the virtual personification of evil apparently envisaged by Camp.

[9] Although Sheol is not mentioned directly, there is another reference to the underworld in 2: 18, again in connection with the foreign woman.

[10] The imagery of Prov. 23: 26–8 is strikingly reminiscent; cf. p. 133 below.

taking these 'bad' characters to be connected with each other: there are similarities between the portrayals of the sinners in chapter 1 and of the foreign woman of chapter 7, and also between the portrayals of that woman and of Folly in chapter 9. These links are reinforced, of course, by the fact that all of these characters, like Wisdom, are given speeches of invitation. In each case, moreover, the speech is juxtaposed to a speech by Wisdom, and, as we noted in the last chapter, no parental appeals separate the speeches into sections: structurally, at least, we are offered them as pairs.

In the light of both the links between the characters and the positioning of their speeches, it does seem that we should reckon with something more complicated going on here than just a series of separate, figurative vignettes. We are apparently being invited to consider all these characters and speeches together somehow. Before doing so, however, I want to look briefly at another way in which Proverbs 1–9 develops and extends a rather different sort of imagery.

B. Path Imagery

We have already mentioned in passing that Fox calls the portrayal of behaviour as a path the 'ground metaphor' of Proverbs 1–9, by which he means 'an image that organizes other perceptions and images and conveys a way of perceiving the world'.[11] He is not the first or only scholar to attribute such importance to this imagery, and that is hardly surprising, given both its prominence in the first part of the work and the clear exposition of the motif in 4: 10–27.

Although the imagery pervades other material, the key passages can be identified quite straightforwardly. In chapter 1, the son is warned against 'walking in the way' with the sinners, and admonished to keep his foot back from their path (1: 15). In chapter 2, God is presented as a protector of those who walk on 'paths of justice', (2: 8) while acceptance of instruction will protect from those who have abandoned straight paths for crooked ones (2: 13, 15, cf. 19) and enable understanding of 'every good path', so that the son will ultimately 'walk on the way of the good and keep to the paths of the righteous' (2: 9, 20). In chapter 3, acknowledgment of God will

---

[11] Fox, *Proverbs 1–9*, 129.

straighten the son's paths (3: 6), wisdom's paths are pleasant and peaceful (3: 17), and keeping wisdom will enable the son to walk safely without stumbling (3: 23, 26). These ideas are brought together in chapter 4, where the father claims to have taught the 'way of wisdom' and to have led his son in 'straight paths', promising him that he will be able to walk without obstruction and admonishing him to avoid the path of the wicked. In 4: 18–19, the paths of the righteous and wicked are described and contrasted in terms of light and darkness, and the chapter finishes with an appeal for the son to walk with his eyes straight ahead, never swerving from his path.

The presentation of the path imagery in chapter 4 is the fullest expression of the motif, and the work thereafter shifts its focus to the foreign woman and to Wisdom. The initial description of the woman includes the fact, though, that she has in some way left the path of life, and is wandering down to Sheol without knowing it (5: 5–6), while 5: 21 famously observes that 'a man's ways are before the eyes of YHWH', and 6: 22–3 promises that instruction will lead the son as he walks, and in some sense be the 'way of life'.

It seems hard to escape the conclusion that this imagery is important to the writer, and that it goes far beyond the common figurative use of 'ways' that Hebrew shares with English and many other languages.[12] Indeed, it seems likely that the imagery is based around an idea of very specific 'good' and 'bad' paths, as detailed in chapter 4, and Norman Habel, in the first major study of this imagery in Proverbs 1–9, attempted to reconstruct the picture that the author had in mind, arguing that a 'polar contrast' between two paths, the way of wisdom and the way of the wicked, is central to a basic set of symbols in the work.[13] Individuals are expected to commit themselves to one way or the other, and their choice leads them ultimately to either life or death at the end of the path. Each path, moreover, has its own characteristics: the way of wisdom is depicted

---

[12] The Hebrew usage has been scrutinized in great detail by M. P. Zehnder, *Wegmetaphorik im Alten Testament: eine semantische Untersuchung der alttestamentlichen und altorientalischen Weg-Lexeme mit besonderer Berücksichtigung ihrer metaphorischen Verwendung* (BZAW 268; Berlin, New York: de Gruyter, 1999).

[13] N. Habel, 'The Symbolism of Wisdom in Proverbs 1–9', *Interpretation* 26 (1972), 131–56. Habel's article actually only focuses directly on the path imagery in the first part of its first section (135–9).

as straight and clear, open and honest, while that of the wicked is devious, dark, and dangerous.

Habel's understanding of the imagery was influenced by his acceptance of William McKane's analysis of Proverbs, which categorized material in terms of a development from secular-wisdom thought through to a religious, Yahwistic type of wisdom. Correspondingly, Habel believed that it was possible to discern development and reinterpretation within the path imagery: guidance along the path of wisdom was provided by wisdom and instruction in the earliest strata, but later by Yahweh, and reinterpretation of the same symbols thus provided continuity within a context of changing ideology. McKane's classification, however, has many weaknesses, and is not, therefore, a strong foundation for Habel's ideas of development. These ideas are difficult to maintain in any case, since Yahweh is never said to offer guidance, and his role is apparently to protect (cf. 2: 8; 3: 6, 26; 5: 21). Guidance is provided solely by parental teachings (6: 22–3), and it is very difficult to claim that divine guidance is presumed at any stage.

More importantly, although he made a valuable contribution by drawing attention to the importance of the path imagery, it is not clear that Habel adequately described that imagery. In particular, it is hard to isolate just two paths, let alone any 'polar contrast' between them. On several occasions, paths of a single type are described in the plural: wisdom, for example, has 'ways' in 3: 17 and 8: 32, as do the sinners in 1: 19 and the woman in 5: 6. It is hard to understand why the author would do this if he wanted to establish the idea of two specific and opposite paths. If there is a conscious depiction of two such paths, moreover, then other aspects of the usage are equally confusing. On several occasions, an individual's 'way' is clearly not a predetermined route: thus the woman in 5: 6 is headed for Sheol, but through the wandering of her ways, and in 5: 8 one is supposed to 'keep one's way' from the woman. These are not preordained routes, but the directions that individuals take: footprints, as it were, rather than footpaths.[14]

---

[14] The problem is recognized by Fox (*Proverbs 1–9*, 129–31), who thinks, however, that there are two forms of the path metaphor, one with many paths, reflecting individual courses, the other envisaging only two paths, or types of path—the way of life and the way of death. He emphasizes that 'In spite of the importance of the TWO PATHS dichotomy, the author does not picture life as a landscape with two highways

Indeed, it seems better more generally to understand the usage in Proverbs 1–9 in such terms: what constitutes an individual's way is not a set path, to be walked by others, but rather the direction which he or she, as an individual, takes. Where the paths seem to be named routes, like the 'paths of uprightness' in 4: 11, it is easier, in fact, to take the expressions as adjectival: this would be a quite normal way of saying 'upright paths' in Hebrew. Chapter 4, in which the path imagery is very prominent, spells out most clearly what the writer seems to have in mind. The second section in the chapter, 4: 10–19, begins with a claim by the father that he has taught his son the wise way and led him on upright paths, so that he will be able to walk freely. Now he is to avoid the path of the wicked, turning away from it and passing on (4: 15). In the next section, the son is advised to look directly forward, and to avoid swerving to the right or left, turning his foot away from evil. In both these sections, evil, or the 'way of the wicked', is clearly envisaged in terms of turning off a path, rather than choosing an alternative path. In the section that follows, 5: 1–23, the woman's wanderings, which will take her to Sheol, are associated with her failure to 'pay attention to' the path of life: the vocabulary here echoes that of 4: 26, where the son's walking straight ahead is described.

Such references suggest that individuals are set on the right course by instruction, and are expected to maintain this course without deviation, which would, by its nature, take them into the way of the wicked. The characteristics of the righteous and wicked paths are also described in chapter 4: the former is unobstructed, and grows ever lighter; the latter is dark and treacherous (4: 12, 18–19). This presentation is consistent with the many other metaphorical references to ways and paths in Proverbs 1–9. By following the route upon which he has been set by instruction, or that commended by wisdom, the son may expect life and happiness, and will enjoy divine protection. Turning aside from this route, he will find only darkness and death.

running through it, and instead has a much more complicated map in mind' (130). This seems too elaborate: we are asked to envisage a plurality of paths, which are capable of classification into two types, but which are also integrated with a separate depiction of paths that 'refer to whatever type of life one chooses' (129). Fox's motivation is apparently to maintain a link with the 'Way of Life' imagery found in some Egyptian literature.

In short, we find a pervasive path imagery in the first half of Proverbs 1–9, but this revolves around the idea of walking straight rather than following a predetermined route. Although wisdom and instruction can point one in the direction of life and happiness, the danger is presented as lying not in the pursuit of a specific different path, but in wandering or turning aside.

C. Characters and Paths

We have noted a particular emphasis on the path imagery in the earlier part of Proverbs 1–9, with the references most concentrated in chapters 2–5. That would seem to suggest that it is somewhat separate from the speeches and presentations of Wisdom and the other characters in chapters 1 and 7–9. However, the path imagery is associated with the idea of speech in several places, most notably in 4: 24–5, where the rejection of 'crooked' speech is tied to walking straight ahead. The same Hebrew word is used to describe the 'crookedness' of the paths on which the men of perverted speech walk in 2: 12–15, while 5: 1–6 contrasts the foreign woman's smooth speech with her wandering ways. Such connections, along with scattered references to the path imagery among the depictions of the characters, suggest that it would, in fact, be a mistake to regard these as quite separate sets of imagery, developed in isolation from each other.

If we look more closely, we find that the distribution of the path imagery is related not so much to the separation of the work into sections as to the voices we are hearing. Wisdom does refer to paths (8: 20 is an obvious example), but it is the father (or in chapter 4, perhaps, the father's father) who makes most use of the imagery, and this use extends into the places where he is commenting on the bad characters and their speeches, such as 1: 15, 19; 5: 5–6; and 7: 25–7. The bad characters themselves, on the other hand, do not make direct reference to the path imagery in their speeches, and it seems to be this that affects the apparent distribution of the motif. Why they should avoid it is an interesting question, but for the moment let us focus on another issue: if the bad characters do not speak directly about the significance of ways or paths, does that mean that reference to the path imagery, in connection with those characters, is confined only to the father's commentary on their speeches?

In fact, it seems that the imagery does appear within the various cameos, but that it takes a rather different form. The best illustration of this is provided by the narrative that precedes the woman's speech in chapter 7. As the action begins in 7: 7–9, the father describes seeing a young man—one of the simple—passing along the street, but then turning off it at the corner to follow the road leading to the woman's house. Having turned aside, he goes into ever greater darkness. The woman, meantime, is wandering the streets, and lying in wait 'at every corner' (7: 10–12). This build-up to the speech in 7: 14–20 is, we may note, as long as the speech itself, and it seems to be characterized not only by constant reference to roads and streets, but also by allusions to turning aside and to corners. It is difficult to find any obvious narrative purpose for all these references: why are we told about the young man's route? What is the significance of the fact that it becomes progressively darker and darker after he has turned towards the woman's house? While we must be wary of seeking to find significance in every last detail of the poetry, it is hard to resist looking back at 4: 18–19, where the path of the righteous, in contrast to the dark path of the wicked, is described as being like the dawn, growing progressively brighter and brighter until the day has fully broken. It does not seem unreasonable to suppose that some antithesis is intended between a path that grows brighter like the dawn and one, a little later, that grows darker like the dusk. Although less striking and distinctive, the youth's turning aside and the woman's predilection for street corners may also be intended to evoke the turning-aside motif that we have already observed. If this is indeed the case, then it would seem that the imagery associated with the characters here imports and, one might say, realizes the imagery associated elsewhere in the work with paths and ways.

The narrative settings for the other speeches are less clearly defined, but 1: 20 and 8: 2 both put Wisdom in or beside the street,[15] like the woman of chapter 7, and the twin cameos of chapter 9 each

---

[15] This is not, of course, to suggest that a metaphorical implication is the only one here: it is also important that Wisdom in 1: 21 and 8: 3 speaks at the city gates, where public speakers probably held forth; cf. Lang, *Wisdom*, chapter 3.

involve an invitation to turn aside from the road (9: 4, 16)—with Folly's distinguished by the fact that she is addressing those who are already going 'straight on their way'. The depiction of the robbers in chapter 1 is the only presentation to lack any explicit physical setting, but then it would seem redundant to point out that those who set ambushes do so at the roadside. In short, all the settings involve roads, implicitly or explicitly, and in a work that displays a strong interest in the figurative use of ways and roads, it seems unlikely to be a coincidence that the speeches of significant characters are associated with them in this way.[16] Before trying to assess the meaning of this association, however, we need to establish a clearer idea of the ways in which the characters actually function within Proverbs 1–9, and that involves considering the nature of their speeches.

2. THE SIGNIFICANCE OF THE IMAGERY

Having sketched out the extent and interrelationships of the principal imagery, we need next to try to understand its significance. Some important aspects of the interpretation must await a consideration of the context within which Proverbs 1–9 would have been read, and there are parts of the work that we have hardly mentioned yet. Despite its importance, therefore, an interpretation of the imagery is not an interpretation of the work as a whole, although it does, as we shall see, raise some interesting questions about how the 'literal' material is to be read.

A. Seduction and Speech

So far we have noted that the speeches by Wisdom correspond to speeches by other characters, but have not explored their content beyond observing that all involve invitations of some sort. However, the nature and interrelationship of these invitations is important in

---

[16] Baumann, *Weisheitsgestalt*, 72 notes the position of Wisdom at the crossroads, and wonders whether there is a metaphorical indication here that humans are being forced to choose between the ways of Wisdom and the woman.

itself, and was the subject of J. N. Aletti's 'Séduction et parole en Proverbes I–IX', one of the most significant and perceptive studies of these chapters.[17] Aletti's principal contribution in this article was to observe not only that the speeches are paired but that they are all presented as enticing: the problem they present is the need to choose between them. To understand this crucial point, it might be helpful to review, briefly, what offers are actually being made, and how these are presented.

In 1: 10–19, as we saw above, the son is warned against sinners who might entice him to join them. Their offer in itself contains no disincentive to doing so. On the contrary, it holds out the prospect of easy money in a society that, we should recall, saw nothing wrong in the accumulation of wealth per se. These robbers portray themselves as, like Sheol, immensely more powerful than their victims, so that there would be little danger; they also, very reasonably, offer their potential recruit an equal share of the proceeds.[18] The invitation, then, does not reveal the dangers that acceptance would involve, and it is left to the father to spell these out. Much the same is true of the woman's speech in 7: 14–20, where the seductress is at pains to point out that there is no man at home, so as to minimize any fear that accepting her invitation would be dangerous. Like the robbers, she offers something desirable and safe: it is the father, again, who has to warn of the hidden risks.

In neither case does the character deploy any weapon other than their words. The woman might be dressed attractively (7: 10), but it is her speech and not her physical charms that she uses to attract the young man, cajoling him 'with her great persuasiveness, with the smoothness of her lips' (7: 21).[19] These are, of course, the qualities against which the father had already warned in earlier descriptions (cf. 2: 16; 5: 3, 24; 7: 5). Since there is no detailed narrative in

[17] Published in *VT* 27 (1977), 129–44.

[18] Newsom, 'Woman', 145 draws out further the ways in which the speech is given an 'egalitarian subtext', and the sinners are presented as the son's peers, in contrast to his relationship with the father.

[19] Of course, the speech itself promises other benefits. R. O'Connell, 'Proverbs VII 16–17: A Case of Fatal Deception in a "Woman and the Window" Type-Scene', *VT* 41 (1991), 235–41, especially 237–9, makes the interesting observation that there may be deliberate ambiguity involved in the woman's description of her bed, with both erotic and funerary associations attached to the promised linen and spices.

1: 10–19, no strong argument can be based on the robbers' use of speech alone, but the verb used, פתה, emphasizes that they attract recruits through what they say.[20]

Wisdom's counterparts, then, offer dangerously tempting invitations through their speeches, and reveal nothing of the risks involved—perhaps being unaware of them themselves (cf. 5: 6). Wisdom can only respond with her own speeches, and her own promises. In chapter 1 she warns of the dangers ahead for those who ignore her, and in chapter 8 she presents her credentials as evidence that it is her speeches and invitations that the simple should accept. Throughout, though, she works with the disadvantage that she cannot offer the immediate rewards and gratifications offered by the other characters, nor any proof beyond her word that what she does offer is better.

What Aletti rightly perceives here is that the reader, or the 'son' in the narrative, is not supposed to be able to distinguish the beneficial offers made by Wisdom from the dangerous invitations, the 'perverse speech', of the other characters. The author, indeed, goes so far as to use some of the same imagery and terminology for both of the female characters: each may, for instance, be 'embraced' (cf. 4: 8; 5: 20).[21] He has also made some surprising use of vocabulary, as when the woman's seductions in 7: 21 are called her לקח, literally her 'instruction'—this is the term used of the father's teaching in 4: 2, and it is never used pejoratively elsewhere. The purpose of all this is apparently to emphasize that the problem presented by the bad characters is not that of the temptation to do wrong so much as the recognition of what *is* wrong: they force their hearers to discern true speech from false speech. The individual cannot make a choice based on what is actually offered (both Wisdom and the sinners offer

---

[20] For some typical uses, cf. 1 Kgs. 22: 22; Ps. 78: 36. The verb appears in Prov. 16: 29, which is so like the scenario presented here that a direct relationship seems probable.

[21] Aletti's conclusions have been taken further by Gale Yee, ' "I Have Perfumed my Bed with Myrrh": The Foreign Woman (*'iššâ zarâ*) in Proverbs 1–9', *JSOT* 43 (1989), 53–68. Yee points out some other interconnections between the characters and speeches, and in particular between the sinners of chapter 1 and the seductress of chapter 7, who both 'lie in wait', and who both employ similar 'Come let us…' expressions. Yee also goes further than Aletti in suggesting that Wisdom is herself portrayed as a potential lover.

wealth), nor on any superficial appearances. What they require is an informed, intelligent understanding of the situation and the consequences.

If Aletti is right, and I find his arguments very persuasive, then the point of the contrast between Wisdom and the woman is not merely to demonstrate the superiority of Wisdom over the foreign woman. The individual—assumed to be male and thus vulnerable to the attractions of both—cannot easily tell them apart. The real point is that both Wisdom and the woman address their speeches to the simple—that is, the uninstructed (cf. 1: 22; 7: 7; 8: 5; 9: 4, 16), and that protection against the woman is afforded by heeding instruction (2: 1–22; 5: 1–6; 6: 20–4; 7: 1–5). It is the instructed who can recognize true and perverted speech, and the contrast is thus associated with the strong emphasis on instruction elsewhere in Proverbs 1–9.[22] The teaching that the father offers is presented as a way of distinguishing right from wrong, the beneficial from the dangerous.[23]

B. Speeches and Settings

Aletti's study holds its focus on the speeches, and he does not take account of the path imagery, which, as we have already seen, may be linked to the portrayals of the characters. Doing so does not substantially affect the conclusions he draws, but it does offer a more rounded view of the presentation. In particular, it seems likely that we are supposed to understand what is going on in a more visual way: the characters do not simply try to attract, but physically to lure

---

[22] LXX 2: 16–17 actually replaces direct reference to the woman, and warns against κακὴ βουλή, 'bad counsel', which has 'abandoned the teaching of youth'. J. Cook, 'אשה זרה (Proverbs 1–9 Septuagint): A Metaphor for Foreign Wisdom?', *ZAW* 106 (1994), 458–76, sees in this a reference to the Jewish idea of the 'bad inclination'; see also his *The Septuagint of Proverbs: Jewish and/or Hellenistic Proverbs? Concerning the Hellenistic Colouring of LXX Proverbs* (SVT 49; Leiden, New York, and Cologne: Brill, 1997), 135–8.

[23] Newsom, 'Woman', 147, puts it less positively: 'Far from valuing the plurality of discourses that intersect a culture, Proverbs 1–9 seeks the hegemony of its own discourse. If one has internalized a discourse, one is insulated from, or as the text more polemically puts it, protected from other voices.'

the uninstructed in their direction. In the case of the bad characters, this would seem to imply that their task is simply to turn their victims aside, off the straight path.

The introductory narrative in chapter 7, however, suggests something more complicated. The youth there has already turned aside when he encounters the woman who seduces him, and has already walked into the deepening darkness that bodes so ill for his future. We might say, indeed, that the woman in this chapter merely finishes the job, and seals his fate. A problem is also posed by Wisdom's invitation in 9: 4; she is surely not supposed to be inviting the simple to 'turn'. If the uninstructed are apparently going in the wrong direction anyway, then the bad characters seem redundant, and it is not clear how accepting the wrong sort of invitation will change anything for their victims. Conversely, if those who are invited to turn aside by Folly in 9: 16 are going 'straight on their way' despite being uneducated, the role of Wisdom also seems unnecessary.

The path imagery associated with the characters, then, seems to demand that we see the uneducated youth as something more than just a sort of blank slate. To be uneducated is not to lack a path, and to lack instruction is not to be stationary. Rather, the uneducated have to be seen as essentially random; they may be travelling the right way or the wrong way, straight or crooked, but their direction is not fixed. The role of the characters, in that case, is to remove this randomness, and to direct those who accept their invitations. Since 2: 19, furthermore, seems to declare that an acceptance of the foreign woman's invitation is final and irreversible, with no possibility of regaining the paths that lead to life, it may be that we are supposed to see the acceptance of an invitation as something that one does only once, irrevocably.

Without placing too much weight on the details, then, it does seem that we can offer a slightly fuller account of the ideas sketched by Aletti, by giving more consideration to the path imagery used in connection with the speeches. It appears that for Proverbs 1–9, the default setting for a human is to wander through life without particular direction, taking routes that may be harmful or beneficial. Whatever way one goes, however, there is a probability that one will receive an attractive invitation, delivered either by Wisdom or by another character: Wisdom and her counterparts actively seek out the uneducated to deliver such invitations to them as they pass by. It is possible to reject or ignore an invitation, but to do so is to pass up an opportunity to set oneself on a road to guaranteed prosperity and life; to accept the wrong invitation, on the other hand, is to condemn oneself to the dark road that leads to death. Choosing between the invitations is no easy matter, not least because the bad characters may be unaware themselves that they are offering something deadly; indeed, the reason that they do not mention good and bad paths may simply be that they are unaware of the situation. To accept an invitation, then, is a dangerous lottery—unless one has properly received the instruction which enables one to distinguish good invitations from bad.

C. Adultery and the Foreign Woman

It is not difficult to see that much of the material in Proverbs 1–9 corresponds to this emphasis on the importance of instruction: this is notably the theme of both the parental appeals and the extended appeal in chapter 2, and it is only within chapters 3 and 5–6 that we find substantial stretches of text where the focus is apparently elsewhere. We shall look at chapter 3 later, when we consider the question of what exactly Proverbs 1–9 considers instruction to be. Chapters 5 and 6, however, raise some important questions about the relationship of the imagery, and of the associated emphasis on instruction, with material that seems more concerned with specific, day-to-day matters.

After the long discussion of paths in chapter 4, chapter 5 begins with a warning against the foreign woman, who has previously been introduced in 2: 16–19, but has not otherwise figured up to this point. The parental appeal in 5: 1–2 is a short one, and the following description, although phrased as an explanation, is directly linked to it only by the catchword 'lips'. The description itself, in 5: 3–6, presents elements with which we are now familiar: the woman has smooth, attractive speech, but is actually dangerous, and unknowingly leads the way to death. In 5: 7, as later in 7: 24, a resumptive appeal follows, warning against approaching her, but this then leads into a much longer discussion (5: 9–23). To go near the woman is to risk giving life and honour to strangers, experiencing deep regret at the end of life; the putative speech of one ruined this way is included (5: 12–14), and here the regret is all about not having heeded instruction. We are then offered, in 5: 15–17, an admonition based around water imagery, which is obscure, but which is probably to be interpreted, in line with what has preceded it, as advice to keep one's efforts for those who are one's own, and not for strangers.[24] The imagery is continued into 5: 18–20, where the advice is to love 'the wife of your youth', and to avoid the foreign woman. Finally, 5: 21–3 warn that God watches all paths, and that the wicked will be trapped by his own wrongdoing, dying for his folly and lack of discipline.

In 6: 20–35 we are offered something that seems rather similar (and the placement of 6: 1–19 between these two sections is often adduced as evidence of its intrusive, secondary character). Here there is a longer parental appeal, promising that instruction will protect, especially from the persuasive foreign woman (6: 20–4). That woman is not to be desired, and capture by her is to be avoided, we are told in 6: 25, but the explanation offered this time is rather different. Again, the text is difficult, but there seem to be two parallel sections, 6: 26–9 and 6: 30–5, each emphasizing the seriousness of adultery, and the inevitability of punishment. The first notes that a prostitute seeks only food, but a married woman seeks the very life of a man; the second, that a thief is not despised for seeking to satisfy his own hunger, but is punished nonetheless, and forced to pay compensation: the adulterer, on the other hand, will be dishonoured, and unable to buy his way out.[25]

Both of these sections are closely aligned with the broader portrait of the foreign woman, and there is no reason to doubt that we are dealing with the same character who appears in chapters 2 and 7. Here, however, we are not simply told that she is deadly dangerous; rather, the consequences of involvement with her are spelled out in terms of the effect upon one's life before it is lost. These are rather different in each section. In chapter 5, there is no obvious reference to adultery—at least as it is understood in biblical terms. The man

---

[24] See the annotated translation.
[25] How far the death penalty was actually applied is a matter for conjecture; cf. Crenshaw, *Education*, 198.

may already be married, to the 'wife of his youth', but this does not preclude involvement with an unmarried woman (perhaps even without divorcing his wife, although that may be assumed), and the fact that he subsequently labours 'in the household of a foreigner' would seem to suggest that he does, in fact, marry the foreign woman. The issue in this section is not the punishment for adultery, but the loss of authority and honour to the strangers and foreigners with whom the woman, presumably, belongs. In chapter 6, on the other hand, although it is not explicitly stated that the foreign woman is married, the consequences of adultery, that is, sex with the wife of another man, do seem to be identified as consequences of involvement with her. There would appear to be some contradiction between these outcomes in chapters 5 and 6, not least with regard to the marital status of the woman.

The woman's assertion in 7: 19 that 'there is no man at home', is an odd way of referring to the absence of her husband, and although she is probably supposed to be married, that section as a whole shows no particular interest in her marital status. No reference at all is made to it in chapter 9, when the woman, as Folly, invites the simple to dine. Most commentators see in 2: 17, however, an explicit statement that she is, in fact, an unfaithful married woman. This involves taking the 'companion of her youth', whom she has abandoned, to be her husband (cf. 'the wife of your youth' in 5: 18), and the 'covenant of her god' to be a marriage covenant. The language is, in fact, strikingly close to that of Mal. 2: 14, where God does not accept sacrifices from the priests because he had 'stood witness between you and the wife of your youth, to whom you have acted unfaithfully, although she is your companion and the wife of your covenant'. The links to that passage are very important, but let us merely note here that the reference in Malachi is not to adultery but to divorce. In Prov. 2: 17, it does indeed seem likely that the woman is supposed to have been married, but the language can quite readily be understood to suggest here, too, that she is divorced.[26] The significant thing in this

---

[26] She is a 'forsaker' (participle) and 'has forgotten' (perfect): the Hebrew does not demand that we translate 'who forsakes ... and forgets' and the past tense is at least as likely. Note also, that in Jer. 3: 4, where Israel is portrayed as a divorced wife, addressing God as her ex-husband, she calls him 'companion of my youth', using the same term (אַלּוּף) as here.

verse is not her current status, but the fact that the text takes no trouble to define that status precisely. More generally, indeed, the important point in all of this is that Proverbs 1–9 shows much interest in the persuasiveness of the foreign woman, but rather little interest in her marital status: she is dangerous whether married, single, or divorced.

There is a marked tendency to read all the material about the foreign woman in the light of chapter 6, as though the warnings there are a key to understanding the character as a whole. On such a reading, the foreign woman as a type represents adulteresses, and the warnings against her are, therefore, warnings against adultery. There is a danger here, however, of allowing the tail to wag the dog. If we accept that this character is supposed to be a counterpart or antithesis to personified Wisdom, what does that make Wisdom, and why is Wisdom not correspondingly described in terms of chastity?[27] Why, for that matter, is the character consistently described as 'strange' or 'foreign', rather than simply as an adulteress, and why is there so much emphasis on her speech rather than her marital status? We shall return to the question of just what it is that the foreign woman does represent. For the moment, the important point is that however literal and practical some of the material may seem, we must be wary of prioritizing it simply for that reason, and ignoring the figurative aspects of the context in which it stands. This is especially true, perhaps, when that material represents such a small proportion of the work.

If we read 6: 20–35 carefully, it is not, in fact, an admonition against adultery. The exhortations are specific: following the promise that instruction will give protection 'from the woman of evil, from the smoothness of the foreign woman's tongue', the son is exhorted not to desire her, or to allow her to capture him. When the explanation begins, the obscure 6: 26 continues with this theme: the dangerous woman is a hunter. Much the same is true in chapter 5, where, after the warnings about her deadly persuasiveness in 5: 3–6, the basic admonition is to avoid her. Similar sorts of preamble

---

[27] cf. Camp, 'Woman Wisdom', 99: 'If some version of the "whore" is in a sense on one side of Proverbs' polarity, it is curiously not the virgin on the other.' Camp argues instead for an opposition between controlled and uncontrolled sexuality.

and advice characterize the advice in chapter 7, although they are arranged around the narrative there (7: 5, 25). In each case, the warnings are explained in a different way, but it is important that we do not confuse those explanations with the advice itself. The admonitions themselves are consistently against involvement with the woman, not against particular behaviour, and the explanations, less consistently, spell out a range of consequences that may ensue from entanglement with her. This advice, then, is very much bound up with the broader themes of the work, not just with advocating sexual morality.[28]

D. Wisdom and the Woman

A more general point arises from our discussion about adultery. If there is any foundation to Aletti's scheme, or if we are to see any significance to the pairing of the characters and their speeches—even just within chapter 9—then it is questionable whether we should be trying to assess the nature of any single character without reference to the others.[29] This is relevant, of course, to the considerable efforts that have been made to identify Wisdom or the woman individually in very specific terms. Wisdom has not only been viewed as a divine hypostasis, for example, but as a goddess in her own right; the woman has also been seen as possibly a deity, or at least as a sacred prostitute. It is not my intention to discuss such identifications in detail, not least since none has won any general acceptance, but it is important to say a little about the presuppositions and consequences of such hypotheses.

---

[28] It is worth noting that in chapter 9 the woman does not explicitly offer sexual favours at all, although some scholars have seen sexual connotations in the idea of stealing, and McKinlay, *Gendering*, 57, also asserts that 'the motif of food from harlots has a long history', although she does not spell out what links lie in the presumably lengthy chain between Proverbs and her cited example of Enkidu. Lang, *Wisdom*, 108, suggests, on little evidence, that this is a prostitute's coded language for sex.

[29] So Fontaine, *Smooth Words: Women, Proverbs and Performance in Biblical Wisdom* (JSOTS 356; London and New York: Sheffield Academic Press, 2002), 93, writes: 'the consideration of Woman Wisdom apart from her twin, Woman Stranger, is not a tenable working method. Both characters are bound up together, displacing and inverting the features of the other.'

It is not difficult to find points of contact between our characters and other figures or phenomena, and Clifford may be right, for instance, to draw attention to the 'type-scene' of a goddess offering herself to a young man,[30] or Boström to see significance in 7: 20's apparent reference to the moon.[31] It is very difficult, however, to say whether such links are simply coincidental, or whether they do actually represent conscious or unconscious influences on the portrayals. The one thing of which we can be fairly certain, in fact, is that much more than this is needed if we are to establish an identification, rather than just an influence. If Wisdom is essentially to be identified with *Mꜣꜥt*, say, as Kayatz would have it,[32] then we might be able to overlook the preponderant lack of correspondence in minor details, provided the identification fitted, and shed light on Wisdom's role in Proverbs 1–9, which it does not. The pursuit of trivial and superficial resemblances might help to set us on the path to an identification, but it accomplishes little in itself: possible influences from the depiction of *Mꜣꜥt*, from the self-proclamations of Isis, from Asherah, or from the worship of some hitherto unknown Canaanite goddess, constitute at most a footnote to the portrayal of Wisdom,[33] if they

---

[30] Clifford, *Proverbs*, 27.

[31] G. Boström, *Proverbiastudien: Die Weisheit und das fremde Weib in Spr. 1–9* (Lunds Universitets Årsskrift, N.F. I.30.3; Lund: Gleerup, 1935), 124–7.

[32] The link has also been affirmed by, e.g. Othmar Keel, *Die Weisheit spielt vor Gott: Ein ikonographischer Beitrag zur Deutung des mesaḥäqät in Sprüche 8, 30f* (Freibourg: Universitätsverlag Freiburg Schweiz, and Göttingen: Vandenhoeck & Ruprecht, 1974). His student, Silvia Schroer, states as a fact that 'within the Israelite symbol system personified Wisdom corresponds almost exactly to the Egyptian goddess Maat'; *Die Weisheit hat ihr Haus gebaut: Studien zur Gestalt der Sophia in den biblischen Schriften* (Mainz: M. Grünewald, 1996); ET, *Wisdom Has Built Her House: Studies on the Figure of Sophia in the Bible*, translated by Linda M. Maloney and William McDonough (Collegeville, MN: Liturgical Press, 2000), ET 3.

[33] Baumann, *Weisheitsgestalt*, 25, concludes a lengthy survey of attempts to identify Wisdom as a goddess or to find a mythological background by noting, rightly I believe, that, 'Es ist bisher nicht gelungen, eine einzige altorientalische Parallel- oder Vorbildgestalt für die personifizierte Weisheit plausibel zu machen... Es lassen sich für bestimmte Einzelaspekte der Weisheitsgestalt in Prov 1–9 Ähnlichkeiten zu altorientalischen Göttinen nachweisen. Dabei bleibt zunächst offen, ob es sich lediglich um Parallelen oder aber um Vorbilder handelt.' ('It is not currently possible to identify any individual ancient Near Eastern figure as a parallel or model for personified wisdom... For particular, individual aspects of the portrayal of wisdom in Proverbs 1–9, it is possible to detect similarities with ancient Near Eastern goddesses. For the time being, though, it remains an open question whether this is

cannot answer such questions as why she invites the uneducated to turn to her, why finding her will earn the favour of YHWH, and how she is the antithesis of both the robbers and the foreign woman. The identification of any single character needs to be a step in the direction of interpreting the imagery and characterization as a whole, not an end in itself.

Life becomes simpler, in this respect, if the characters are lifted out of their context, and we noted earlier that it is not uncommon for the depictions of personified Wisdom to be treated quite separately.[34] To do this is, of course, largely to deny that there is any significant pairing of characters and speeches, or at least to regard such a scheme as a secondary, redactional creation—and that brings us back to the question of unity.

E. Imagery and Unity

The two areas on which we have concentrated in our review of the imagery—the characterizations and speeches on the one hand, and the path imagery on the other—each point to an essential continuity in Proverbs 1–9. The links between the characters, the juxtaposition of their speeches, and the explicit representation in chapter 9 of an antithesis that is implicit elsewhere, all seem to point to unity at what we might call a structural, organizational level. The path imagery, with its own antithesis between good and bad ways, indicates unity by its very pervasiveness, as well as by the fact that it appears to involve some cross-referencing between different sections. Each area involves the use of coherent and distinctive motifs, and there are points at which the two seem to function together. If none of this proves unity, it does surely, at the very least, provide a way of reading

simply a matter of parallels, or rather of models.') The issue is also surveyed by J. Hadley, 'Wisdom and the Goddess', in Day *et al., Wisdom in Ancient Israel*, 234–43. On proposals to link Wisdom with Asherah, see J. Day, *Yahweh and the Gods and Goddesses of Canaan* (JSOTS 265; London and New York: Sheffield Academic Press, 2000), 66–7.

[34] B. L. Mack, 'Wisdom Myth and Mytho-logy: An Essay in Understanding a Theological Tradition', *Interpretation* 24 (1970), 46–60, raises analogous questions about this in the sphere of theology: account must be taken of the '*configuration* and function of wisdom *within Judaism*' (51).

Proverbs 1–9 as a single composition, and place the burden of proof on those who prefer to dissect it.

We observed in the last chapter that formal criteria, based on understandings of the instruction genre, offer little support for viewing Proverbs 1–9 as a composite work, and it is in the area of imagery and characterization that most other arguments against unity root themselves. Some of these arguments appear to show little more than that there is no pleasing some people: supplementing his arguments from form, for example, Whybray takes some of the very similarities that we have assumed to show unity as evidence of the opposite, on the basis that no author would indulge in so much repetition.[35] To be taken more seriously, perhaps, are Whybray's additional appeals to a developmental scheme of ideas about wisdom, against which the various statements in Proverbs 1–9 may be measured to assign relative dates. This finds an echo in other scholarship, notably the work of McKane; as I have argued in detail elsewhere, however, the proposed scheme is not merely unsubstantiated and hypothetical, but almost certainly wrong.[36]

We have already touched on Michael Fox's description of 'wisdom interludes' set secondarily, and probably separately, within the work's basic framework of ten lectures.[37] In part, his argument rests on the absence of parental appeals before Wisdom's speeches, a point that we addressed earlier. Fox also notes, however, that these interludes seem out of sequence,[38] and has problems not only with the fact that while Wisdom walks the streets herself in chapters 1 and 8, she sends out her maids to do it for her in chapter 9, but also with the disappointingly incidental personification of Wisdom in 3: 13–20, and with the brevity of her speech in chapter 9. Furthermore, while acknowledging that it is an aesthetic judgement, he finds the cameo in chapter 9 rather disappointing as a whole, and doubts that it would have been put there by the author of chapter 8. It is difficult

---

[35] For instance, Whybray, *Proverbs*, 24, 50. It is hard, sometimes, to see just what Whybray might have accepted as evidence of unity.

[36] *EIW*, chapter 4.

[37] Fox, *Proverbs 1–9*, 326–9; cf. also his 'Ideas of Wisdom'.

[38] In particular, Wisdom in 1: 20–33 condemns those who have ignored her call before she has actually made it, in chapters 8 and 9, and has a house in 8: 34 before she builds it in 9: 1.

to know how to respond to these points, because they appear to be not so much arguments, as the complaints of a tidy mind. All that Fox says is true, in a way, but it presupposes that the writer of Proverbs 1–9 must share his tastes, ideas and priorities, and that the cameos are supposed to be in chronological or logical sequence.[39]

What would seem to be the more substantial part of Fox's argument appears in his separate essays on the presentations of wisdom in the lectures and in the interludes, and here he represents a more common opinion, that the personified Wisdom of the speeches seems quite different from wisdom elsewhere in the work.[40] Wisdom in the lectures, he argues, is a power, 'an inner light that guides its possessor through life';[41] it protects from the danger of seduction, and has an emotional, as well as an intellectual side, giving not only the ability to tell right from wrong, but the desire to do so. In the interludes, on the other hand, wisdom transcends all this, and is expressed through 'the mythos of Lady Wisdom',[42] a godlike figure who 'symbolizes the perfect and transcendent universal, of which the infinite instances of human wisdom are imperfect images or realizations'.[43] This seems to be at once an oversimplification of the differences and an over-elaboration of the personification. With regard to the former, we might note, for instance, that 3: 19 (interlude, according to Fox) depicts wisdom as a skill or quality of mind (albeit God's mind), not as a 'universal', while it is difficult to see how the exhortation to 'love her and she will guard you', in 6: 6 (lecture), is very different from Wisdom's declaration in 8: 17 (interlude), that she loves those who love her. This is not just nit-picking: there is a substantial overlap of language and attitude,

---

[39] We might note, in this context, the proposal of R. B. Y. Scott, *Proverbs, Ecclesiastes* (AB; Garden City, NY: Doubleday, 1965), especially 16–17, that the poems about Wisdom are by the same author as the 'ten discourses', but may originally have existed separately, since they disturb the sequence of those discourses and 'have a distinctiveness and completeness of their own'. He similarly suggests that chapter 2 must originally have stood at the beginning, and it is apparent that his perception of structural disturbance draws primarily on a largely aesthetic notion of how the text ought to be.

[40] Fox, *Proverbs 1–9*, 346, 347–51, 352–9.

[41] Ibid., 347.

[42] Ibid., 352.

[43] Ibid., 356.

and many possible examples. With respect to Fox's rather grand conceptualization of Wisdom in the interludes, it is hard to disagree that personified Wisdom represents, in some sense, the abstract quality of which each case of human wisdom is a concrete instance. Fox is, however, going much further than that.

There is little sign of a *mythos* in chapters 1 or 9, and when matters do get to that sort of level in chapter 3, wisdom is barely personified at all. Much of what Fox is claiming, therefore, seems to be based essentially on chapter 8, which does indeed present Wisdom as in, but not of humanity and the world. This chapter is the principal assertion of Wisdom's credentials, and it not only lists what she has to offer (in contrast to the more passing pleasures offered by the woman in chapter 7), but also affirms both her longstanding, close relationship with God, and the joy that she takes in humanity. That it has commonly been read as primarily cosmological or mythological seems undeniable, although whether that is what the author intended is another matter. Whatever the reception history, the question we must ask is whether anything here precludes the identification of Wisdom simply as the personification of an abstract concept, and the only point at which we might give an affirmative answer to this question is at 8: 30. There, in a notorious crux, Wisdom appears to assert that she played a distinct role at the creation, either as a craftsman or as a child, playing before God. I have argued elsewhere that she is, in fact, making no such claim, but merely affirming her continuing relationship with God.[44] Be that as it may, however, there is no reading of 8: 30, or of the chapter as a whole, that really requires us to take Wisdom as a transcendent universal, let alone as godlike, and there is nothing elsewhere in Fox's interludes that comes even close.

In the final analysis, it is not clear that what Fox is offering is really an argument at all. He acknowledges links between the lectures and the interludes, and he does not claim that the different presentations are actually contradictory. Indeed, since he believes that the interludes were written to complement the existing series of lectures, he is prepared to allow that the writers of the interludes were willing to juxtapose the different presentations of wisdom, and saw no problem

[44] In 'The Context and Meaning of Proverbs 8: 30a', *JBL* 125 (2006), 433–42.

in doing so. Effectively, then, he is merely asserting that the writer of the lectures would not have done just what he allows that the writers of the interludes actually did.

There is more to be said about the presentation and personification of wisdom in Proverbs 1–9, but for the time being we need observe only that it does not seem to provide any substantial basis for denying the unity of the work. Where those passages that personify wisdom are separated from the rest in modern scholarship, the arguments adduced seem to rest either on hypothetical presuppositions about the development of thought,[45] or on essentially aesthetic judgements, neither of which seems sufficient to override the evidence for an essential continuity between those sections and the rest of the work.

3. CONCLUSIONS

There is no way to prove beyond doubt that Proverbs 1–9 is essentially a single composition. In the work's extensive use of imagery and figures, however, we do find a characteristic that is both distinctive and pervasive. Some elements of this usage, furthermore, seem to constitute or presuppose broader figurative motifs, which embody and reinforce central concerns of the work. In particular, we find a consistent emphasis upon the vital importance of instruction, which is explicit in the parental appeals and the poem of chapter 2, but implicit also in the figurative presentations of the characters and their speeches. Instruction, according to Proverbs 1–9, is what allows one to distinguish Wisdom from the woman, and thereby to win the divine favour that enables long life and prosperity.

---

[45] This is, as already noted, a constituent of Whybray's argument. A more recent example is furnished by Schäfer, *Die Poesie der Weisen*, which asserts (264–5) a distinction between an original, *mᵊ⁼t*-like *Kulturreligion* and a secondary reinterpretation that seeks 'das weisheitliche Denken in den JHWH-Glauben zu integrieren' ('to integrate wisdom thought into Yahwistic belief') (265). Naturally, if one strips the Yahwistic elements from a text on the basis that they are Yahwistic, what remains can be read as non-Yahwistic, but it is hard to see that the process proves anything.

Much of the imagery has a sexual aspect. After the brief appearance of the sinners in chapter 1, picked up, perhaps, in 2: 12–15, Wisdom's rival is consistently female—an alluring seductress. As others have noted, the choice of such imagery says much about the underlying assumptions and intended audience, but it might be a mistake to assume that attitudes to sex and gender are actually the force behind the choice of characters: sex, and sexual solicitation, are the vehicle, not the driver. All the same, the association of such imagery with instruction does seem curious, as does the apparent lack of any clear attempt to describe or define what constitutes proper instruction. At this stage, then, we have a clear idea of the main point that Proverbs 1–9 is trying to make, and of the ways in which the work puts this point across. The details, though, are rather less clear: we do not know what the work takes good instruction to be, or what relevance, if any, the choice of imagery has for the understanding of instruction.

4

Wisdom and the Character of Instruction

As we saw in the first chapter, instructions do not necessarily offer much in the way of practical advice, and overemphasis upon their didacticism has often led to a neglect of their poetic character. All the same, when an instructional work lays as much emphasis as does Proverbs 1–9 on the importance of instruction, we might expect it to tell us what that instruction is. Instead, as we have seen, most of the work is devoted to asserting the need for the uneducated to receive teaching, and not to providing teaching itself.

Where Proverbs 1–9 does touch on aspects of daily life in chapters 5 and 6: 20–35, the real-world components are among the threatened consequences, not within the admonitions, and the actual advice offered there relates directly to the foreign-woman imagery. There are two sections of the book, in 3: 1–10 and 3: 21–35, however, that do seem to offer more specific advice. These employ the path imagery extensively, and there is no good reason to regard them as secondary, but they are not obviously subsidiary to the imagery, and seem genuinely to present teaching for or against particular behaviour. These will be the starting point in this chapter for our investigation into the understanding of instruction in Proverbs 1–9. They will lead us on, however, to explore clues to that understanding within the figurative material also.

1. INSTRUCTION IN PROVERBS 3

We have not really considered chapter 3 in detail up to this point, so it is worth saying a little about its content and position. From chapter

5 onwards, as we have seen, Proverbs 1–9 is dominated by concerns about the foreign woman, set in contrast with Wisdom; the first half of the book, by contrast, is much more miscellaneous. After the preliminary statements, chapter 1 sets the sinners, who speak within the father's speech, next to Wisdom, who here threatens and cajoles more than she tries to allure. Chapter 2 follows, with its long conditional clause, tortured on the rack to produce what amounts to a summary of the work's message and imagery. The two sections of admonitions follow in chapter 3, separated in 3: 11–20 by a section in which the son is exhorted to heed divine teaching, and the importance of wisdom is extolled. Finally, in chapter 4, we hear about the instruction offered by the father's father, and there is a lengthy disquisition on good and bad paths.

It is difficult to know what significance, if any, should be attached to the order of the materials here. Certainly, although they lay the foundations for much of what is to follow, the first two chapters have the feel of party pieces, as much demonstrations of technique as they are introductions to the work. It is only when we reach chapter 3, therefore, that we seem actually to be settling down to the main business, so its position may be more prominent than a simple enumeration would suggest. There is also the rather strange fact that 4: 10–12 seems to suggest that the father believes his work to be done, and his task of instructing complete. Again, we must be wary of putting too much weight on this, but it adds to the suspicion that chapter 3 may be a good place to look for clues to what constitutes instruction in Proverbs 1–9.

A. The Sayings Series of 3: 1–10, 21–35

Proverbs 1–9 tends to employ longer and more complicated admonitions than are usually to be found elsewhere in Proverbs,[1] and while

---

[1] The admonitions in Prov. 22: 17–24: 22 and 31: 1–9 (the sections that also present themselves as parental teaching) show a certain consistency of length. Of the twenty-six admonitions in 22: 17–24: 22, twenty-one have motive clauses, as does one of the four admonitions in 31: 1–9: all but a few of these are four to six stichs long, while the remaining admonitions, without motive clauses, are all two stichs long. The admonitions scattered among the sentence literature collections of Proverbs 10: 1–22:

these long forms are distributed across the work, shorter admonitions seem to be confined largely to particular sections, and are generally found in series. Thus, of the twelve admonitions in Proverbs 1–9 that have two stichs, only those that begin and end the parental appeal of 4: 10–13 lie outside the series 3: 5–10, 25–32; 4: 20–7; and 9: 7–10, 12. There is also a similar, though less marked, concentration of four-stich sayings into series. That is to say, Proverbs 1–9 adopts the constraints upon the length of admonitions that are normal elsewhere in Proverbs only within four short series of sayings. It seems possible that this is a deliberate attempt to conform more closely to established, recognizable forms; at least, it serves to distinguish these series from the surrounding material. One of the series, 4: 20–7, summarizes the general requirements to guard one's heart, avoid perverse speech, look straight ahead, watch one's way, and avoid deviation from one's course. Another, 9: 7–10, 12, gives advice on the proper use of instruction, but may be secondary or misplaced. It is the other two, 3: 5–10 and 3: 25–32, that concern us here.

The first series, in 3: 5–10, consists of just three sayings (5–6, 7–8, 9–10), each four stichs long and consisting of commands followed by a promise, introduced by *waw*. This is an unusual form, and the series is distinctive for that reason. The second series, in 3: 25–32, is part of a longer series of sayings, which extends to verse 35 and includes indicative statements after the admonitions. The admonitory section consists of 'bipartite prohibitions', in which a prohibition is followed by a clause of motive or circumstance; this form of saying is found in instructions from earliest times, very often

16 and 25–9 do not generally exceed these constraints, and include some shorter forms; only 27: 23–7, which may stand at the join between two earlier collections, is substantially longer, with eleven stichs. Elsewhere in the book, among the more miscellaneous sections, there is a much greater diversity of length and form, but even the relatively long 30: 7–9 has only seven stichs, or nine if its introduction is included. Against this background, the length and distribution of the forty admonitions in Proverbs 1–9 is striking. In 22: 17–24: 22, only two of the admonitions (23: 6–8 and 31–5) have seven or more stichs; in the whole of the rest of Proverbs 10–31, moreover, only two more reach this length (27: 23–7 and 30: 7–9), totalling four out of sixty admonitions altogether. In Proverbs 1–9, however, there are twelve admonitions longer than six stichs—some thirty per cent of the total—and their length is attributable not simply to extended motive clauses, but to complicated constructions often involving a number of main verbs.

in series. Here, though, the first and last sayings of the series are quatrains, instead of the normal distichs, while, as an antithetical statement, the motive clause of the last saying provides a transition to the second part of the series in 33–5, which consists of antithetical sayings. Long strings of antithetical statements are found in 10: 1–22: 16, and that collection probably incorporated a work consisting entirely of such sayings.[2]

The sections 3: 1–10 and 21–35, then, both follow their introductory appeals with series of sayings that conform much more closely to the length of sayings elsewhere in Proverbs than is normal in most other sections of Proverbs 1–9. In the second of these sections, moreover, the series uses familiar forms that may regularly have been employed in series elsewhere. In other words, these two sections look much more like the didactic material found elsewhere in Proverbs than does most of the work. This very ordinariness makes them stand out in the otherwise formally idiosyncratic Proverbs 1–9.

Unlike most of Proverbs 1–9, moreover, these sayings also tender practical advice, each on a different area. The first series commends particular behaviour towards Yahweh, with the promise, in return, that one's paths will be made straight, one's body healed, and one's barns filled with plenty. This behaviour consists of trusting, fearing, and honouring YHWH, and the section on wisdom that follows is introduced by an appeal demanding that one should also heed YHWH's instruction. The second series begins with an assurance against panic, since YHWH will give protection, and this ties the series both to its introductory appeal and to the antithetical statements that end it, promising divine favour to the righteous. The prohibitions in 27–31, though, are concerned with behaviour towards other humans: one should not refuse or defer help that is within one's power, plot against one's trusting neighbour, contend with somebody who has done one no harm, or choose the ways of the violent man. This division of the advice into behaviour towards YHWH and towards humans may pick up the promise in 3: 4: 'So you will find favour and understanding, in divine and human eyes.'[3]

---

[2] *EIW*, 24–7.

[3] Meinhold, *Sprüche*, 39, puts this in a broader context: 'Das Besondere des JHWH-Glaubens kommt in Sprüchebuch vor allem dadurch zum Ausdruck, daß die unauflösliche Zweiseitigkeit der Frömmigkeit—hin zu JHWH und gleichzeitig

The very distinctiveness of these sections has sometimes led scholars to regard them as secondary, but there is little reason to reject them. Both, after all, have parental appeals, and both refer to the path imagery, while neither contradicts ideas found elsewhere in the work. It is simpler to regard them as a distinct part of the work, and they may form the kernel of the instruction that the father claims in the next chapter to have given his son. Their actual advice is phrased very generally, and is far less specific than that of the genuinely secondary 6: 1–19; indeed, it might reasonably claim to offer comprehensive coverage of the proper behaviour towards God and towards other humans. This behaviour is commended with a promise of life, health, and prosperity, essentially the promise made by Wisdom, but is not otherwise geared to personal advancement, and its tone is both pious and ethical. In short, there is nothing to forbid the assumption that this advice constitutes the way of wisdom or of the righteous. What I am suggesting, then, is that between the summarizing chapter 2 and chapter 4, in which the father claims to have instructed his son, the writer is sandwiching two series of sayings that embody his own summary of proper instruction. These call on the son to trust and honour YHWH, while helping and behaving well towards other humans.

B. The Description of Wisdom in 3: 11–20

The two series are separated from each other by a commendation of wisdom that seems to interrupt them by introducing another section, complete with its own parental appeal. On closer examination, though, there is something strange about the structure here. That parental appeal, in 3: 11, commends not the father's own teaching, but the teaching offered by YHWH; without its address to 'my son', it

hin zum Mitmenschen, und zwar besonders in Form von Barmherzigkeit und Recht gegenüber den Bedürftigen—, wie sie auch dem Dekalog mit seinen beiden <Tafeln> zugrundeliegt . . . , von Anfang an und immer wieder erwartet wird.' ('The particular character of Yahwistic belief achieves expression in the Book of Proverbs above all through the indissoluble two-sidedness of religious responsibility—towards YHWH, and simultaneously towards one's fellow humans, and most especially in the form of compassion and justice towards the needy—to whatever extent it underpinned the Decalogue, with its two "tablets" . . . it is expected from the outset and repeatedly.')

could easily be a continuation of the preceding series. We have already seen, in 2: 12 and 3: 32 for example, how this writer seems to have a fondness for verses that, structurally, do a double duty and link one block of material to another. That may well be what he is doing here again, so that the sense of 3: 11 makes it a part of the preceding section, while its role as an appeal makes it the introduction to the next.[4] The description that follows is an assertion of Wisdom's benefits and, in verse 19, a presentation of her credentials comparable to chapter 8. If we can see how the section is linked to what precedes, however, it is less obvious why the author has chosen to place it here, between the two sections of direct advice.

The answer probably lies in the explicit links that this section defines between parental instruction, YHWH, and Wisdom. The relationship between these has been outlined already in chapter 2, where reception of the father's words may make the son open to receiving wisdom, and wisdom itself is a gift from YHWH. In chapter 3, the father and personified Wisdom are now linked more poetically to YHWH, but similarly placed on the same side: by making the opening appeal an exhortation to heed YHWH's teaching, the father's instruction is formally associated with divine instruction, and the point is emphasized by the explicit portrait of YHWH as a father; the benefits offered by Wisdom are then described, before Wisdom herself is identified as an attribute of YHWH. This last section, in verses 19–20, both validates Wisdom and emphasizes her relationship with YHWH himself.

Verses 11–20, then, explain why it is important to act properly towards YHWH, in terms of the admonitions to heed wisdom and instruction that are more characteristic of the work: wisdom and instruction are attributes of YHWH, and to enjoy his favour is therefore to reap their benefits. That message is again implicit in the following section, where the safety and dangers—which are elsewhere linked to heeding instruction—are now explicitly

---

[4] The use of catchwords and 'catch-themes' in sentence literature often provides a comparable sort of link between sayings, and sometimes between series of sayings. Prov. 15: 1, for example, is linked to the preceding 14: 35 by the theme of anger, and to the following 15: 2 by the theme of speech. On this technique generally, see *EIW*, chapter 2.

attributed to divine action. This interlude thus serves to integrate the admonitions into the work as a whole.

C. Conclusions

Given the various attempts to find a secular, practical wisdom underpinning Proverbs as a whole, and chapters 1–9 in particular, it seems ironic that what may originally have been the only practical advice in these chapters has a strongly religious character. The religion it advocates, furthermore, is very specifically Jewish, not only in its use of the divine name, but in its reference to first fruits (3: 9).[5] I suggested the possibility, at the beginning of this discussion, that the material in chapter 3 might have a particular significance for any understanding of what Proverbs 1–9 believes to constitute proper instruction. What we find here, in fact, are commendations of piety and proper behaviour towards others, linked by an association of wisdom and teaching with YHWH. Can this be the instruction that protects those who heed it, and enables them to choose Wisdom over the foreign woman? Maybe not in itself, but it is possible that this material epitomizes such instruction.

2. WISDOM AND INSTRUCTION

I earlier emphasized the need to assess instructions primarily within their own cultural contexts, and there should be nothing surprising about the fact that parts of chapter 3 are quite explicitly linked to Jewish piety. In addition, if we allow that our writer (date permitting) had some knowledge of other Hebrew literature, then some interesting links become evident. The most obvious and important of these in chapter 3 is probably to be found in verse 12, with its

---

⁵ Meinhold, *Sprüche*, 76, sees an emphasis on כל, ('all') here, linking this to the specific post-exilic situation of Mal. 3: 6–12, Neh. 10: 36–9; 13: 10–13. Note also the very biblical combination חסד ואמת, 'loyalty and faithfulness', in 3: 3. The terms are frequently used together of divine faithfulness (e.g., Exod. 34: 6 [cf. Ps. 86: 15]; 2 Sam. 2: 6; 15: 20; Ps. 25: 10; 40: 11), and are associated in Prov. 16: 6 with fear of YHWH.

comparison between God and a father. This is strongly reminiscent of Deut. 8: 5: 'Know with your heart that, just as a man instructs his son, so YHWH your God instructs you.'[6] More generally, we may recall that God is elsewhere depicted as a father in Deuteronomy (e.g. Deut. 1: 31; 32: 6), who carries and creates, as well as instructing. It is his instruction that is of interest here, however, and the very term used in 3: 11, מוסר יהוה ('instruction of YHWH'), is found in Deut. 11: 2, where it is used, in connection with the divine statutes, to refer to God's demonstrations of greatness during the exodus and the wilderness wanderings. The word מוסר is picked up and used widely to describe God's teachings or demonstrations in Jeremiah, so this is far from being an isolated instance.[7] Apart from raising the possibility that the writer of Proverbs 1–9 may have been familiar with Deuteronomy (which is likely to have been true of any educated Jew, at least by the postexilic period),[8] this draws attention to a more

---

[6] The verb that Deuteronomy uses for 'instructing' here is from the same stem as the term מוסר ('instruction') used in Prov. 3: 11 (and of parental instruction in 1: 8 and 4: 1), on which see the next note. RSV translates 'discipline', which has too negative a connotation. The same terminology appears in Jer. 35: 12–17, where God invites the Judahites to receive his instruction. Depictions of God as a father are surprisingly uncommon in the biblical literature, and, where they do occur, they rarely portray the relationship in terms of parental teaching. Apart from this verse in Deuteronomy, however, we do find similar imagery in the Isaianic corpus (Is. 1: 2; 30: 9; 54: 13), and it could reasonably be described as an established, if unusual, metaphor. The father–son relationship is elsewhere used particularly for the closeness of Israel's relationship with God (cf. Is. 63: 16; Jer. 31: 20; Hos. 2: 1 [ET, 1: 10]; 11: 1–11; Mal. 3: 17), the duty owed by a child (cf. Deut. 14: 1; 32: 6; Jer. 3: 22; Mal. 1: 6), or the role of God as creator (cf. Is. 64: 7 [ET, 8]; Mal. 2: 10). In two passages from the Psalms (the famous 2: 7 and 89: 27 [ET, 26]), it is seen as the basis for elevation, while Deut. 1: 31 and Ps. 103: 13 employ specific images of parental love and care.

[7] See, e.g. Jer. 7: 28; 17: 23; 32: 33; 35: 13, and cf. Ps. 52: 17; Job 5: 17; 36: 10; Is. 26: 16; Zeph. 3: 2, 7. Without reference to God, the term is used often in Proverbs, generally with reference to parental teaching. See, e.g. 1: 8; 4: 1; 5: 12; 10: 17; 12: 1; 13: 1; 15: 5; 19: 27.

[8] I should make it clear, however, that I do not see the evocations of Deuteronomy here and elsewhere as specific interpretation of that work. There have been some attempts to see Proverbs 1–9 as Midrashic, most famously George Buchanan's article, 'Midrashim prétannaïtes: À propos de Prov., I–IX', *RB* 72 (1965), 227–39, which speaks of 2: 20–7: 3 as 'un exposé midrashique d'un texte, *Deut.*, xi, 18–22, et de son parallèle, *Deut.*, vi, 4–9' (238). While unpersuasive, this is at least attached to known interpretative practices, in a way that Robert's 'Les Attaches Littéraires' is not, with its loosely regulated and much-criticized notion of anthological interpretation. For a general discussion, see also Maier, *Die Fremde Frau*, 72–9; Maier herself takes 6: 20–35

general point about the implications of instruction in later Hebrew literature.

Whatever else it may be, Proverbs 1–9 is religious literature, and even if we acknowledge the possibility that it drew on foreign texts, it is fundamentally still Jewish, Yahwistic religious literature. It consequently operates, to a greater or lesser extent, against an established background of concepts and vocabulary. When, therefore, the work repeatedly advocates adherence to instruction, and when it evokes the Deuteronomic idea of God as instructor, it is hard to believe that the writer would not expect his Jewish readership to see in this a reference to the Torah—a term that we are accustomed to translate as 'law', but which of course literally means 'teaching'.[9]

The writer, in fact, uses this very term, תורה, of the parental teaching in 1: 8 and in 3: 1. In several places he also uses the term מצות ('commandments') even juxtaposing it to תורה in 3: 1; מצות is also used commonly, throughout Hebrew literature, to refer to divine commandments or statutes.[10] It is all very well to say, as Fox does in response to Baumann's similar observations on the matter, that 'these are basically secular words and carry with them no allusion to divine law':[11] the important question is not whether the words *must* refer to the Jewish Law when they are used in a context like this, but whether

to be a Midrashic interpretation of the Decalogue and Shema. More recently, and very differently, Harris, *Proverbs 1–9*, has linked portions of the work with Jeremiah and (very unpersuasively) with the Joseph story, and seen in the links a refashioning and interpretation of the older materials. That, as Delitzsch puts it, 'the whole poetry of this writer savours of the Book of Deuteronomy' (*Spruchbuch*, ET, vol. 1, p. 34), results, I think, not from an attempt to interpret Deuteronomy, or any other text, but from the allusive use of language and citations to incorporate meaning within Proverbs 1–9, and to set up certain resonances.

   [9] So K. A. Farmer, *Who Knows What is Good? A Commentary on the Books of Proverbs and Ecclesiastes* (ITC; Grand Rapids, MI: Eerdmans, and Edinburgh: Handsel Press, 1991), 36, of 3: 1–4: 'It seems clear...that similarities in subject and in forms of expression must have forced early audiences to see some connection between these admonitions in Proverbs and the covenant they believed God had made with their ancestors.'

   [10] See 2: 1; 3: 1; 4: 4; 7: 1, 2. The singular, which is less common in other literature, is used at 6: 20 and 6: 23, both times alongside תורה.

   [11] Fox, *Proverbs 1–9*, 79; cf. Baumann, *Weisheitsgestalt*, 294–300. Baumann complicates matters too much in this instance, I think, by approaching the question in terms of suffixed forms, but it is Fox's constant exclusion in his commentary of common religious meanings that, in cumulative effect, is ultimately less persuasive.

they would have been perceived as doing so by the contemporary readership. We can give no definitive answer to that, but we may at least say that if the writer intended no such allusion, then his close packing of such terms, in the vicinity of references to YHWH, can have done nothing to allay the misapprehension. We might also note that the invitation to write instruction on the 'tablet' of the heart, which follows closely the references to 'teaching' and 'commandments' in 3: 3 and 7: 3, uses the term לוח, most familiar from its use elsewhere to refer to the tablets of the Law.[12]

This matter of understanding not what terms *might* have meant but what they *would* have meant is important, and we shall come back to it later in connection with other terms and motifs. For the moment, though, I want to pursue the possibility that Proverbs 1–9 is actually trying to assert some sort of connection between proper instruction and the Law. This requires us to delve a little deeper into the work's understanding of wisdom.

A. The Function of Wisdom in Proverbs 1–9

Modern Western culture draws a distinction between inherent intelligence and acquired knowledge that would probably not have been recognized in the ancient world. To become wise, one had to learn, and to learn the right things properly was to become wise.[13] Consequently, it is difficult to draw any firm boundaries between concepts of wisdom and discernment, on the one hand, and of

---

[12] For instance, Exod. 31: 18; Deut. 9: 9; 1 Kgs. 8: 9. The expression 'tablet of the heart' itself appears elsewhere only in Jer. 17: 1, where it is said that the sin of Judah is written 'on the tablet of their heart, on the horns of their altars', and there is no reason to believe that it was a common expression. The idea of writing on the heart, however, is also found in Jer. 31: 33, where the Law is to be written on the people's hearts. The image is striking and distinctive, suggesting that there may be some allusion to Jeremiah here, as well as to the tablets of the Law, an issue which we shall explore below. Note that the terms חסד and אמת, 'loyalty' and 'faithfulness', which individually have religious connotations themselves, are used together in Ps. 25: 10, where they describe the paths of YHWH for those who keep his covenant.

[13] The epilogue of *Ptahhotep*, however, does recognize that some are inherently more able or willing to learn than others, an idea that it explores in terms of divine favour (evoking, for modern readers, issues more familiar from later predestinarian theology).

learning on the other. In Proverbs 1–9, this gives rise to a dichotomy not between the wise and the foolish, as found often elsewhere, but between the instructed and the uninstructed. It is the latter, the פתים, who receive invitations from both Wisdom and the foreign woman.[14] Without the benefit of proper instruction, as commended to the son in the parental appeals, the 'simple' are vulnerable to the blandishments of the wicked and may be killed by turning aside (1: 32–3). In her final speech, Wisdom therefore invites them to leave their state of simplicity and live.

This idea crops up elsewhere in the Book of Proverbs: the virtual duplicates 22: 3 and 27: 12 emphasize the inability of the simple to perceive dangers ahead of them, while 1: 4 (although of questionable authenticity) lists giving shrewdness to the simple as being among the book's purposes. More significantly, 14: 18 declares that it is the simple who will acquire folly, while those who have already gained shrewdness will acquire knowledge. This is a strong clue to the broader concept underpinning Proverbs 1–9, for which we have already argued a similar case on the basis of its path imagery: folly is not the natural condition of the uneducated, but something they may acquire instead of wisdom. So it is that we find Wisdom and Folly set beside each other as counterparts, in chapter 9, each offering their own invitations to those who are, as yet, neither wise nor foolish. For Proverbs 1–9, at least, the possession of wisdom is not an accident of birth, any more than is foolishness: wisdom is acquired by making a choice or commitment, informed by instruction.

What does one get for making that choice? In its most basic sense, חכמה ('wisdom') is probably best translated as 'know-how', and the term can be applied to a variety of technical skills.[15] When used in a general way, it indicates knowledge of how to survive and prosper in the world: it is the 'know-how' of living.[16] Such wisdom can be very superficial—a matter of how to behave in the law courts or at table, for example. Inherent even in such superficialities, however, is a deeper concern with the proper basis for behaviour, and this is the

---

[14] See 1: 22; 7: 7; 8: 5; 9: 4, 16.

[15] e.g. Exod. 28: 3; 1 Kgs. 7: 14.

[16] See S. Weeks, 'Wisdom in the Old Testament', in S. C. Barton (ed.), *Where Shall Wisdom be Found? Wisdom in the Bible, the Church and the Contemporary World* (Edinburgh: T&T Clark, 1999), 19–30.

factor most likely to vary between different cultures. In Egypt, for example, proper behaviour is behaviour in accordance with *m3ᶜt*, the principle of social and cosmic order; to behave in harmony with this order is to support it against the force of chaos, but is also to reap personal benefit from doing so. For ancient Near Eastern literature generally, individual prosperity is the result of proper behaviour, and the problem for the individual is simply to recognize what constitutes proper behaviour, and so to gain the knowledge of how to prosper.

The basis for such wisdom in Israel has been much debated, with some scholars positing a concept similar to *m3ᶜt*, and others seeking to isolate an empirical, secular outlook.[17] Beyond noting that neither seems very likely, we need not address the general issue here. Proverbs 1–9 is fairly explicit about what it perceives to be the origin and nature of wisdom: wisdom is something created and established by God (8: 22–3). As an embodiment of skill, it is used by God himself to create the world (3: 19–20); as the skill of survival, it is given by him to humans (2: 6–7). To find wisdom is to obtain divine favour (8: 35), since it enables an understanding of 'the fear of YHWH' and a knowledge of God (2: 2–5; cf. 1: 29). Wisdom, then, is apparently set in the world by God to enable humans to know him and

---

[17] The issues of figurative similarity between Wisdom and the goddess *M3ᶜt*, noted above, have become entwined with wider ideas of world order or inherent retribution in Proverbs, or Israel more broadly, associated with scholars such as Gese, Würthwein, and especially H. H. Schmid, who saw them as a central constituent of 'international' wisdom thought; cf. Schmid's *Wesen und Geschichte der Weisheit* (BZAW 101; Berlin: Töpelmann, 1966). On the idea of world order in Proverbs, see especially the criticisms by L. Boström, *The God of the Sages: The Portrayal of God in the Book of Proverbs* (CB OT Series 29; Stockholm: Almqvist & Wiksell International, 1990), 90–140; Murphy, *Proverbs*, 264–9. The problem with the Egyptian link is that the concept of *m3ᶜt* is not only more complicated than the notion of inherent retribution, but is firmly integrated with other aspects of Egyptian thought. It is hard to imagine how it could be exported, even partially, or find any place in Jewish thought. For a succinct rebuttal, see M. Fox, 'World Order and Maᶜat: A Crooked Parallel', *Journal of the Ancient Near Eastern Society of Columbia University* 23 (1995), 37–48, and cf. also Assmann, 'Weisheit, Loyalismus und Frömmigkeit'. Assmann's work has tended to play up the shift towards a more personal piety in the later New Kingdom, which is an important consideration, but which can be over-emphasized as an argument against the influence of *m3ᶜt* (as it is by Steiert, *Die Weisheit Israels*). Baumann, *Weisheitsgestalt*, 303–11, compares this shift in Egypt with what she perceives to be, in Proverbs 1–9, a synthesis of older deed/consequence-based wisdom with a wisdom more directly grounded in God and piety.

understand his will. Correspondingly, to behave in accordance with wisdom's dictates is to fulfil that will, and to reject them, becoming a fool, is to incur divine punishment.[18]

It is hardly astonishing to find a Jewish book claiming, essentially, that personal survival depends on obedience to the divine will. One very distinctive aspect of the presentation in Proverbs 1–9, though, is the strong emphasis upon the openness and visibility of wisdom. In the so-called sceptical literature, represented by Job and Ecclesiastes, humanity faces the problem that God does not advertise precisely what is needed to survive in his world, or may act in ways that contradict the human understanding of his will and purpose. Proverbs 1–9 does not consider such possibilities: wisdom is portrayed as a woman crying aloud in the street and public places, or sending her maids to issue invitations from the most prominent parts of the city (1: 20–1; 8: 1–3; 9: 3–4). For this writer, as we have seen, the problem is not that wisdom is hidden, but that there are competing voices, presenting their own, false invitations.

Once accepted, wisdom provides protection against these voices: the individual is no longer simple and uneducated. In practical terms, though, acceptance of wisdom involves listening to teaching, and the concept of wisdom in Proverbs 1–9 is so closely tied to the theme of instruction that it can be difficult to separate the two. It seems that the writer starts from the idea that instruction opens the individual to the influence of wisdom (cf. 2: 10), perhaps by awakening a consciousness of the need to 'get wisdom' (cf. 4: 5–7). However, in 6: 20–4, for instance, it seems to be instruction itself that performs the role of protecting and guiding the son, while personified Wisdom seems to offer her own instruction in 8: 33–4. We should probably not, therefore, try too hard to pin down a precise process or sequence: instruction serves, and continues to serve, as a vehicle for wisdom.[19]

---

[18] See, e.g. 3: 33–5, which also explicitly links wisdom with righteousness and folly with wickedness.

[19] M. V. Fox, 'The Pedagogy of Proverbs 2', *JBL* 113 (1994), 233–43, paraphrases Sa'adia Gaon's idea of the sequence: '. . . education has two phases. It commences with the father's teaching and its rote incorporation by the child, but this must be complemented by the learner's own thought and inquiry. Then God steps into the picture and grants wisdom' (242).

This conceptualization of wisdom and instruction may underpin other parts of Proverbs, but was almost certainly not universal, and we should not assume that Proverbs 1–9 is simply tapping into a common pool of ideas. While other writers share the basic understanding that wisdom, in a general sense, is the skill of survival, there seems to be some variety in understandings of its nature, and of the ways in which it may be attained. Although all such understandings are religious in one way or another in the biblical sources, the presentation in Proverbs 1–9 stands out in this respect, emphasizing as it does the closeness of Wisdom to God, and her active promotion of conformity to the divine will. Conversely, although the presentation may be original, we have no reason to presume that the work is consciously putting forward some new, heterodox form of Judaism, and its subsequent influence (which we shall discuss later) counts against early readers having taken it that way. Once more, therefore, we have to ask how this depiction would have been understood by the original audience.

B. The Presentation of Wisdom in Context

As much of the presentation of personified Wisdom in Proverbs 1–9 is poetic and figurative, tied to other aspects of the work's imagery, we should not expect to find close parallels elsewhere to the figure of Wisdom presented in chapter 8, and, more briefly, in 3: 13–18. All the same, it is worth noting that the association of divine wisdom with creation, a characteristic of both these passages, is not without parallel in the biblical literature: Jer. 10: 12; 51: 15 and Ps. 104: 24 all remark on God's use of wisdom in creation, while Job 28: 27 has wisdom established at the time of creation. The description of wisdom as a 'tree of life' in 3: 18, moreover, probably depends indirectly on Gen: 2–3.[20] There is nothing in these descriptions of

---

[20] Newsom, 'Woman', 151, notes that 'Here the two trees of Genesis are condensed into one—knowledge that gives life.' Although the tree of Genesis was later to take on eschatological significance, elsewhere in Proverbs it has a more general poetic sense, as something which gives life or happiness (cf. 11: 30; 13: 12; 15: 4). The metaphor here is probably intended in that sense, rather than as a direct reference to the Genesis account. R. Marcus, 'The Tree of Life in Proverbs', *JBL* 62 (1943), 117–20, suggests,

wisdom which excludes a Jewish background, and there are points of contact with other Jewish literature.

We have seen, however, both that Proverbs 1–9 uses terms for instruction that would probably have been evocative of the Law for Jewish readers, and that wisdom is closely connected to instruction in the work. It is not difficult to see how the portrayal of wisdom as a guide to the divine will might fit into Jewish conceptions of the Law, and such associations between wisdom and Law are certainly important in some later literature. It is less clear, though, that any comparable association is attested before Proverbs 1–9. Furthermore, there is one important element in the portrayal of wisdom that would appear to be incompatible with normal biblical understandings of the Law: wisdom in Proverbs 1–9 is not just older than the Sinai covenant, but older than the world.

It is in Deut. 4: 6 that we find the most important biblical association between the Law and wisdom. Speaking of the laws that he has taught to Israel at God's behest, Moses commands the people to keep them, '. . . for that will be your wisdom and your understanding in the eyes of the peoples who hear all these statutes; and they will say "only this great nation is a wise and understanding people!" '[21]

A proper treatment of this verse would require a more thorough examination of Deuteronomy as a whole than is possible here.[22] The

---

indeed, that any original metaphorical sense has been lost in Proverbs, and that the term merely refers to a remedy or medicine. The usage, incidentally, makes it highly unlikely that we should see here a reference to Asherah or any other deity, however diluted; cf. Camp, *Wisdom and the Feminine*, 197, and contrast, e.g. McKinlay, *Gendering*, 35–6. The extent to which the language is poetic here is indicated by the way in which wisdom can be virtually personified in 3: 16, where she has hands, shortly before transferring to the vegetable kingdom as a tree. Although it would be possible to seek specific origins for the rest of the imagery, it would be a mistake to take any of it too literally as a description. When Kayatz argues that the holding of life in wisdom's left hand echoes iconographic depictions of *Maʿat*, therefore, I would acknowledge the (slender) possibility: I am far from sure, though, that we can thereby identify wisdom with *Maʿat*, any more than we can, or should, try to identify the species of the tree.

[21] Although the word-order is a little difficult, I take רק here to have its common restrictive sense, 'only'. An adversative implication would have no place here, while the 'surely' of RSV would be a highly unusual use of the word. The next verses go on to speak of Israel's uniqueness, and that would seem to be the point here too.

[22] The conjunction of wisdom and Law in Deuteronomy is more commonly portrayed as the consequence of sapiental influence on that work. Blenkinsopp, for instance, notes that 'Exhortations to take heed, to recall the experiences of the past, to

writer is apparently asserting, though, that other nations would perceive Israel's obedience to the Law in terms of wisdom: such behaviour would exhibit an exceptional understanding of how to behave. The following verses enlarge on this by explaining that Israel's God is much closer to his people than are the gods of the other nations, and that its statutes are exceptionally righteous. The Law in Deut 4: 6 is thus presented as something that might be perceived by others as fulfilling the role of wisdom, since it provides guidance that allows the nation to survive and prosper. This is a matter, though, of functional equivalence, not identification: the behaviour engendered by the Law gives an impression of wisdom to outsiders, but that does not mean that wisdom is the Law.

Since there are no other biblical texts that can reasonably be taken to equate wisdom with Law, or which portray the Law in terms similar to those used of personified Wisdom in Proverbs 1–9, we can hardly say that this figure would naturally have been read as a representation of the Law by a contemporary readership. This leaves us, therefore, in the uncomfortable position of having two closely connected concepts in Proverbs 1–9, instruction and wisdom, one of which is described using terminology that would have been strongly evocative of the Law, but the other of which is not. In part, this problem can be eased by resort to a purely literary explanation: the writer has had to create a figure of Wisdom somewhat independent of instruction, in order to implement his scheme of contrasting characters and speeches. While there is doubtless some truth in that suggestion, however, it is rather unsatisfying. Although the imagery is not strictly allegorical, we might expect it, at least in this important matter, to reflect some more precise conceptualization of the wisdom and instruction it so loudly commends.

acknowledge the truth of what is being said, give a character and tone to the book which inevitably call to mind the style of the sages in Proverbs and other sapiental compositions. There can be no doubt that in Deuteronomy the legal and sapiental traditions flow together'; J. Blenkinsopp, *Wisdom and Law in the Old Testament: The Ordering of Life in Israel and Early Judaism* (Oxford Bible Series; Oxford: Oxford University Press, 1983), 100; cf. M. Weinfeld, *Deuteronomy and the Deuteronomic School* (Oxford: Clarendon Press, 1972), part 3, especially 255–6. Issues of dating aside, I think the idea of two traditions converging is much too simplistic. For a more sophisticated approach, see A. Fitzpatrick-McKinley, *The Transformation of Torah from Scribal Advice to Law* (JSOTS 287; Sheffield: Sheffield Academic Press, 1999), especially chapter 4.

There is, in fact, one reference to wisdom's activity—outside the depictions of personified Wisdom—that does evoke a particular idea about the Law found in some literature. In 2: 10, the son is promised that wisdom will enter his heart, and there are a number of references to the Law being in the heart of individuals or the people. Psalm 37: 30–1 provides the most striking parallel to Prov. 2, declaring that the righteous man speaks wisdom and justice; with his God's Law (תורה) in his heart, his footsteps do not slip. In Ps. 40: 9 (ET, 8), the psalmist declares that, with God's Law in his heart, he delights to do the divine will, while in Is. 51: 7, God himself addresses the people as those who know righteousness and have the Law in their heart. These verses seem to envisage a state of obedience and acceptance, and rely on the same imagery as do Ezekiel and Jeremiah in their promises of a new relationship with God, whereby the people will have a new heart, or the Law written upon their hearts.[23] Imagery aside, this is an important idea that reflects an internalization of the Law, so that individuals do not merely obey the precepts, but acquire an inherently 'law-abiding' character.

The idea in these texts of an internalized Law, which is itself rather different from simpler conceptions of a Mosaic covenant, offers a way in which to understand the role of wisdom in relation to instruction. With reference to the imagery of paths and characters in Proverbs 1–9, we observed earlier that acceptance of Wisdom or the foreign woman seemed to be an irrevocable decision, an absolute commitment to a particular direction. Wisdom does not spend her time chasing backsliders, or the woman waste her energy trying to corrupt the wise: both focus their efforts on the uncommitted and uninstructed. Equally, a proper acceptance of instruction, which makes one 'bend one's ear' to wisdom (2: 2), and even seek her out, leads inevitably to an acceptance of Wisdom's invitation. All of this is most readily explained in terms of a process of internalization: receptiveness to instruction brings about a state in which one lays

[23] See especially Jer. 31: 33–4; Ezek. 11: 19–20; 36: 26–7. Whether Deuteronomy itself comes close to this idea is unclear: in 6: 6 and 11: 18, the commandments are to be set 'upon' one's heart, but the context in each case is physical (linked with binding on hands, eyes, doorposts in 6: 8–9; throat, hand, eyes, and doorpost in 11: 18–20), and mnemonic. What is envisaged may be a wearing on the chest, cf. Exod. 28: 29–30. This is itself probably metaphorical, of course, as in Song 8: 6, and, indeed, Prov. 6: 21, but it is a rather different figure from writing directly upon the heart. Deut. 30: 6 uses an alternative image of 'circumcising the heart' to portray internalization.

hold of wisdom, and thereby perpetually enjoys both divine favour and protection from the temptation to turn aside. If instruction is indeed to be associated with the Law, then wisdom may be the way in which Proverbs 1–9 characterizes not the Law, but the condition achieved by those who have internalized the Law.

C. Wisdom, the Fear of YHWH, and Knowledge of God

If there is anything in such a supposition, then it may help to explain the relationship in Proverbs 1–9 between wisdom and the 'fear of YHWH', to which reference is made at various points. Some doubt is often expressed as to whether two of these references, 1: 7 and 9: 10, are original parts of the work, and we shall look at them last. The concept is also found, however, in 1: 29; 2: 5; 3: 7; and 8: 13, always either directly or indirectly in association with wisdom.

Before looking at those verses in more detail, it is important to observe that, although there are many references to fear of YHWH in the biblical literature, it is not clear that we can attach any single, precise understanding to the phrase.[24] Foreign analogies suggest that its origins may lie in a sense of awe at the numinous, and a few biblical examples suggest that real fear or terror may be implied.[25] In general, however, the fear of YHWH should probably be understood to imply a relationship of loyal, obedient respect: Mal. 1: 6 suggests that fear is something owed to a master, just as honour is something owed to a father.[26] Obedience is certainly a key part of the emphasis

---

[24] See especially S. Plath, *Furcht Gottes: Der Begriff* ירא *im Alten Testament* (Arbeiten zur Theologie 2.2; Stuttgart: Calwer, 1963); J. Becker, *Gottesfurcht im alten Testament* (Analecta Biblica 25; Rome: Pontifical Biblical Institute, 1965); L. Derousseaux, *La Crainte de Dieu dans l'Ancien Testament: royauté, alliance, sagesses dans les royaumes d'Israël et de Juda. Recherches d'exégèse et d'histoire sur la racine 'yâre'* (Lectio Divina 63; Paris: Cerf, 1970). On the concept within wisdom literature, see R. E. Murphy, 'Religious Dimensions of Israelite Wisdom', in P. D. Miller, P. D. Hanson, S. D. McBride (eds), *Ancient Israelite Religion: Essays in Honor of Frank Moore Cross* (Philadelphia: Fortress Press, 1987), 449–58.

[25] For example, 2 Chron. 20: 29; Ps. 2: 11; 119: 120; Dan. 6: 27 [ET, 26]. On the connection between fear and reverence, see especially M. I. Gruber, 'Fear, Anxiety and Reverence in Akkadian, Biblical Hebrew and Other North-West Semitic Languages', *VT* 40 (1990), 411–22.

[26] cf. Deut. 6: 13, where fear is set beside service.

in Gen. 22: 12, where Abraham's willingness to sacrifice Isaac is taken as proof that he fears God.

It is not surprising, then, that 'fear of YHWH' comes to be used as a way of talking about obedience to the Law. Deuteronomy, in particular, sees it in terms of keeping the statutes and walking in God's ways;[27] it is learned by hearing and studying the Law.[28] Similar ideas are expressed elsewhere,[29] and when the term retains a more general sense of standing in a relationship with YHWH or of straight-dealing,[30] we may reasonably assume that, for some writers, this would have implied obedience to the Law.

Within Proverbs 1–9, the most difficult reference to the concept is, perhaps, in 8: 12–13, where personified Wisdom is describing herself:

(8: 12) I shall establish wisdom:
shrewdness and an understanding of tricks
shall I reveal.
(8: 13) Fear of YHWH (is) hatred of evil:
pride and arrogance and the way of evil and speech full of perversions
I hate.

Many commentators take the second verse here to be wholly or partly secondary; we may note, however, not only that both 'way of evil' and 'speech full of perversions' echo the vocabulary of 2: 12, but also that the distinctive structure of verse 13 is very similar to that of verse 12: in each verse, a short sentence is followed by a list and then a final verb, with that verb taking the preceding members of the list as its object (the original Hebrew word order is reflected in the English translation above).[31] In any case, the apparent intrusiveness of the first line in verse 13, which is the main reason for regarding it as an

---

[27] See Deut. 5: 29; 6: 2, 24; 10: 12; 13: 5 [ET, 4]; 28: 58.

[28] See Deut. 4: 10; 17: 19; 31: 12–13. Fear of YHWH is also acquired, according to Deut. 14: 23, by eating one's agricultural tithes at the central sanctuary; this is a rather obscure suggestion, which may be meant to indicate that piety will be acquired through exposure to the Temple.

[29] See, e.g. 1 Sam. 12: 14; 2 Kgs. 17: 28, 34; Ps: 55: 19; 112: 1; Qoh. 12: 13.

[30] *EIW*, 101.

[31] A number of commentators feel that 8: 13 interrupts the flow of the piece, and intrudes on the list of wisdom's attributes in verses 12 and 14. Such judgements are always rather subjective, but I take verse 14 to belong with what follows (hence the stylistic matches of לי in 14 with בי in 15–16), and verses 12–13 to be an explanation of verse 11.

addition, ceases to be a problem if we recognize this to be part of wisdom's claim to legitimacy. Framed as a statement of fact, or perhaps as a definition, 8: 13a identifies the fear of YHWH as hatred of evil. By listing manifestations of evil, the rest of the verse then goes on to declare, in effect, that wisdom too hates evil, and so aligns the purposes of wisdom with those of the fear of YHWH.[32]

Elsewhere, 3: 7 contrasts fearing YHWH with being wise in one's own eyes, and sets it alongside turning away from evil. This suggests an understanding similar to that in 8: 13—fear of YHWH is to be associated with the rejection of what is bad. The other passages, however, introduce a more complicated way of looking at the concept.[33] The first, 1: 29, equates fear of YHWH with knowledge, and with the advice and reproof offered by Wisdom: it is something that those who have ignored Wisdom have failed to choose. The second, 2: 5, suggests that the fear of YHWH is something to be understood, as a consequence of listening for wisdom and seeking out insight; it is set in parallel, moreover, with knowledge of God, which is to be found in the same way. Here, then, fear of YHWH is not just an attitude—which may be characterized in terms of rejecting evil—but in some way an accomplishment: it has to be learned and understood.

It is difficult to make sense of such a notion, if the fear of YHWH is simply a posture of piety and obedience. It is congruent, however, with the Deuteronomic notion that fear of YHWH is to be learned and taught, and we find some rather similar language, furthermore, in Is. 11: 2, where the 'shoot from the stump of Jesse' will receive the spirit of YHWH, which is 'the spirit of wisdom and of understanding, the spirit of counsel and of might, the spirit of knowledge and of the fear of YHWH'.[34] In other words, Prov. 1: 29 and 2: 5, along with some other biblical material, appear to view fearing YHWH not just

---

[32] cf. C. R. Yoder, *Wisdom as a Woman of Substance: A Socioeconomic Reading of Proverbs 1–9 and 31: 10–31* (BZAW 304; Berlin and New York: de Gruyter, 2001), 106–7.

[33] So Becker, *Gottesfurcht*, 222.

[34] On links between 8: 12–14 and Is. 11: 1–5, see Baumann, *Weisheitsgestalt*, 91–3. R. B. Y. Scott, 'Priesthood, Prophecy, Wisdom, and the Knowledge of God', *JBL* 80 (1961), 1–15, especially 13, connects the correlation of 'knowledge' and 'fear' of God with Is. 11: 2, taking it to indicate that specifically religious knowledge is implied—that is, 'wisdom to worship God rightly'.

as something which one chooses to do, but as something which one has to comprehend: it is a form of knowledge or skill.

It is surely significant that the fear of YHWH in 2: 5 is set in parallel with the expression 'knowledge of God', which is itself something to be 'discovered'. This expression, perhaps surprisingly, is much less common in the biblical literature, and is most familiar from its use in Hosea, where it expresses the relationship between God and Israel in marital, almost sexual terms.[35] That meaning would seem to make little sense in Prov. 2: 5, however: it is a strange ambition to 'discover' a relationship of intimacy with God, rather than simply to have one. The context would seem to suggest, indeed, that, like the fear of YHWH, knowledge of God in 2: 5 is something that arises from heeding instruction and seeking out wisdom, another accomplishment. Strikingly, the closest parallel to this understanding is to be found in Jer. 31: 34, in the context of the internalization of the Law.[36] Once the Law is written upon human hearts, we are told there, it will no longer be necessary for people to teach each other to know YHWH, as they will all possess such knowledge anyway; knowledge of God, in other words, is a product of the internalization of the Law.

We cannot assume that Jer. 31 was in the mind of the writer of Proverbs 1–9, but the issue here is not, in any case, one of literary dependence. We suggested above that wisdom might be understood in terms of the condition attained by those who have internalized the Law: Jer. 31: 34 suggests that knowledge of God might be one of the things to be attained in such a condition, and Prov. 2: 5 sees knowledge of God as something attained through seeking out wisdom. This proves nothing, but it does demonstrate, at least, that the presentation of wisdom is compatible with ideas espoused elsewhere about the consequences of internalization.[37] Although we lack such a

---

[35] See, e.g. Hos. 2: 22 (ET, 20); 5: 4.

[36] cf. Habel, 'Symbolism of Wisdom', 145. Habel sees this, however, as Yahwistic reinterpretation and reorientation of the text.

[37] It is not clear whether the change within the individual should be viewed as the result of divine action, as in Jeremiah, and the text is silent on the point. Fox, 'Pedagogy', 243, notes: 'This idea of wisdom is a naturalistic counterpart to Jeremiah's concept of the "heart of flesh"... Jeremiah, however, expects God to intervene and effect the change, while the sage of Proverbs 2 believes that education, with God's help, can achieve this rectification individually, in the present'; compare his 'Ideas of

precise analogy, it seems likely that something similar can be said about the fear of YHWH, which is given alongside wisdom as a gift of the spirit in Is. 11: 2, but which is more commonly identified in the Deuteronomic literature as a product of learning the Law: in Proverbs 1–9 it is, similarly, an accomplishment, but one achieved through possession of Wisdom.[38] In other words, what one attains in other literature through internalizing the Law (either by learning or as a consequence of divine action), one gains in Proverbs 1–9 from seeking and possessing wisdom.

Finally, it is worth returning briefly to 1: 7 and 9: 10. Because they lie outside the main structural elements that we identified earlier, it is difficult to make any judgement of their originality on formal grounds, and the second verse, 9: 10, whether it is secondary or not, has almost certainly been misplaced. However, both verses make a strong association between wisdom and the fear of YHWH that is in line with the statements we have just examined. This tells in favour of their authenticity, and we might legitimately regard them, therefore, as opening and closing mottoes for the work. If so, then the link between wisdom, instruction and fear of YHWH is given a very prominent role indeed.

The parallelism in 9: 10 once again associates the fear of YHWH with knowledge of God, or something similar—the expression used (literally 'knowledge of the Holy One(s)'; cf. 30: 3) is strange.[39] The most interesting thing about both 1: 7 and 9: 10, however, is the relationship that they express between fear of YHWH and wisdom. In both cases, English translations generally render 'The fear of the LORD is the beginning of knowledge/wisdom' for each, but the Hebrew varies in both order and vocabulary: יראת יהוה ראשית דעת in 1: 7, and תחלת חכמה יראת יהוה in 9: 10. There has been some debate about

---

Wisdom', 619: 'The wisdom the teacher is seeking to impart . . . resides in the learner as a potential and must be activated by God in order to become the faculty of wisdom.'

[38] On the 'fear of YHWH' in Proverbs 1–9 and Deuteronomy, see Derousseaux, *Crainte*, 327–8.

[39] קדשים has a plural form; if this is not some sort of intensive or honorific formation, it may refer to heavenly beings rather than simply to God (as, e.g. Ps. 89: 8 [ET, 7]). Lang, *Wisdom*, 88–9, improbably believes that all these passages originally referred to 'fear of the gods', and uses the form as support for this view. The expression is unusual enough, at least, to suggest a link of some sort with 30: 3. See the annotated translation.

whether ראשית in 1: 7 means 'beginning' or 'prime part of',[40] and the term is ambiguous. The most common use of the word, though, is to indicate something that comes first in a temporal sense, like the beginning of a season or the first-fruits of a harvest. This is close to the sense of תחלה in 9: 10, which is generally used of the first item in a series, and sometimes of the beginning of a period of time.[41] Especially if we take both verses to be saying essentially the same, then the probable meaning in each is that 'the fear of YHWH is the start of knowledge/wisdom'.

Despite the assertions of some commentators, this is unlikely to mean 'the fear of YHWH is the *basis* of knowledge/wisdom'.[42] Nowhere do we find that meaning for תחלה in biblical Hebrew, and the only place where ראשית might have such a sense is in the difficult Mic. 1: 13 (where, in fact, it is probably temporal). Despite the focus of discussion on 1: 7, it is actually the easier verse to translate, and its implication is probably that the fear of YHWH is the first product of knowledge. The construction with תחלה in 9: 10 implies that wisdom is to be viewed as a continuing state or process, rather than as a simple skill or attribute,[43] and the verse would seem to be suggesting that the fear of YHWH is the first point (in the process or continuing situation) of being wise. In both cases, we are dealing with statements not that wisdom arises from or requires the fear of YHWH, but that the fear of YHWH comes from, or is a part of wisdom.[44] In short, they are stating what I have argued above, which is also implied in 1: 29 and asserted plainly in 2: 5, that the fear of YHWH is something that one gains from wisdom and knowledge, not *vice versa.*[45]

[40] As in, e.g. Deut. 33: 21; Amos 6: 1, 6; Prov. 4: 7.

[41] It is used once, in Is. 1: 26, to mean 'as things were before', but otherwise refers to the first in a series of actions, occasions, or events, or to the beginning of something continuous, like a journey, a reign, or a season (once, in Neh. 11: 17, a liturgy). It cannot mean 'prime part', cf. Becker, *Gottesfurcht*, 215.

[42] So, e.g. Yoder, *Wisdom*, 107; *contra* Becker, *Gottesfurcht*, 216, and Derousseaux, *Crainte*, 324, it is difficult to see how the parallelism with 1: 7b could force that sense in 1: 7. Baumann, *Weisheitsgestalt*, 118–19, confusingly discusses these verses in connection with the meaning of ראשית in 8: 22, where the issue is rather different.

[43] Compare Hos. 1: 2, תחלת דבר־יהוה בהושע: 'the start of YHWH's speaking through Hosea'. Also, e.g. 2 Kgs. 17: 25; Qoh. 10: 13.

[44] We might compare Ps. 119: 34, in which the Psalmist asks God to give him understanding, so that he may (then) keep the Torah.

[45] There are a number of other, similar sayings outside Proverbs 1–9. Of these, Prov. 15: 33 seems to affirm that 'the fear of YHWH is the instruction of wisdom', not 'instruction *in* wisdom', as RSV has it; it also, incidentally, links the fear of YHWH

One might say that the fear of YHWH, then, is almost offered as a reward of wisdom, which seems a little strange if we take it to be simply an attitude towards God, or obedience to the Law. There are some references outside Proverbs 1–9, however, that emphasize its benefits. Proverbs 10: 27, 14: 27, and 19: 23 all portray it as something that extends life and preserves from death, while 22: 4 promises that its consequences will be riches, honour, and life. Outside Proverbs, Is. 33: 6 (interestingly linking it with salvation, wisdom, and knowledge) describes it as God's treasure, and Ps. 34: 10–11 (ET, 9–10) claims that those who fear YHWH want for nothing. The reason is probably simple: as, for example, Pss. 25: 14 and 33: 18 indicate, God forms a special relationship with those who fear him, and protects them; Ps. 34: 8 (ET, 7) even has him assign them a guardian angel. There are plenty of other such references, and it seems clear that, whatever fear of YHWH had come to mean precisely, it was widely regarded as something to be desired and pursued.[46]

D. The Personification of Wisdom

It seems probable, then, that the understanding of the relationship between wisdom and instruction in Proverbs 1–9 is relatively straightforward, especially if we recognize the way in which it draws, at least to some extent, on established ideas. Essentially, the internalization of instruction grants possession of wisdom, which itself grants such benefits as the fear of YHWH. It is not so clear, however, that the author has found it easy to represent this

---

with ענוה, another term that is probably to be associated with obedience to the Law (cf. Zeph. 2: 3), and the same link is made in 22: 4. Psalm 111: 10 says that 'The fear of YHWH is the beginning (ראשית) of wisdom, those doing [it] have good sense', without making clear what the doers are doing, or whether the sense is something they gain from it or already have. The most interesting parallel is in Job 28: 28, where God says to humans, after searching out the elusive wisdom: 'Behold, the fear of the Lord—that is wisdom, and understanding is turning away from evil.' This actually identifies wisdom with the fear of YHWH, but the poem is probably adapting the idea to suit its own message, rather than quoting a common idea. For the many references in Ben Sira, see Becker, *Gottesfurcht*, 214 n. 14.

[46] It is also important to note that this significant concept in Proverbs 1–9 is most unlikely to have been derived from foreign instructions; cf. Plath, *Furcht*, 58–62.

understanding within the figurative framework he has adopted, and this raises some important questions about the personification of wisdom in the work, which has so often been viewed as central to its purposes.

Wisdom appears as a character first in 1: 20–33, following the speech by the sinners, and her name there has the plural form also used in her last appearance (9: 1). She appears in the streets, on top of the city walls, and at the entrance to the gates, advertising herself visibly and publicly. This is something that is re-emphasized on Wisdom's further appearances, in chapters 8 and 9, when her physical location (or that of her maids) is again public and prominent: she is not elusive or hidden, but actively seeks out the uninstructed.

Her speech in chapter 1 proclaims that she has reached out but been rebuffed; those who have rejected her and turned aside face destruction, eating the 'fruit of their way'; they have hated knowledge, and failed to choose the fear of YHWH, acts equated with refusing to listen to Wisdom. In 1: 25 and 1: 30, what they are spurning is described as Wisdom's עצה and her תוכחת, which can be translated roughly as 'advice' and 'teaching' respectively, although the latter, which appears earlier in the speech at 1: 23, can also have implications of arguing, complaining, or exercising discipline; on the other occasions when it appears in Proverbs 1–9 it is associated with מוסר (3: 11, 5: 12, and 6: 23). This characterization of what Wisdom has to say distinguishes her somewhat from the father, and her words from his instruction. 'Advice', also an asset of Wisdom in 8: 14, is something that God may offer (and, indeed, in Ps. 107: 11, the same vocabulary as in 1: 30 is used to describe rejection of God's advice). It is never used directly of the Law, however, and is not attributed to the father in Proverbs 1–9. While the father commends תוכח(ו)ת מוסר in 6: 23,[47] alongside instruction and commandment, תוכחת has no general associations with Law, and is not used absolutely of the father's instruction; rather, it too is associated with God in 3: 11. Wisdom is not, then, offering instruction here, in the way that the father does, but rather the sort of counsel and reproof that can be associated with God.

---

[47] On the reading, see the annotated translation.

The matter seems less clear-cut, however, by the time we reach Wisdom's second speech in chapter 8. Now she is willing to describe what she offers as instruction (8: 10), to echo the language of the parental appeals, even to the extent of talking about herself in the third person (8: 11), and ultimately to deliver her own resumptive parental appeal and address (8: 32–6), which present a contrast to the father's corresponding verdict on the foreign woman (7: 24–7). The instructional setting is, then, more or less retained to the end of the chapter, but the role of the father seems to be subsumed by Wisdom, and the distinction between instruction and wisdom consequently blurred. What may be an attempt to restore that distinction in chapter 9, when it is not Wisdom herself but her handmaids who issue invitations (9: 3), seems only to draw attention to the rather different presentation in chapter 8.

At the poetic and figurative level, this anomaly is probably to be understood largely in terms of the purpose of chapter 8. The speech here is oriented towards a validation of Wisdom over and against the foreign woman. After an initial appeal to pay heed, it begins, therefore, with a strong affirmation that what Wisdom says is true and straight (8: 6–9), unlike the woman's speech. It closes, similarly, with an image of Wisdom's residence and a declaration of her own association with life, which stand in stark contradiction to the description of the foreign woman and her house at the end of chapter 7. The problem for the author is that his two female figures are only opposites in certain respects: one is a liar who seduces the unprepared to sin and death, while the other leads them through truth to divine approval and life. There is no intermediate father-figure on the foreign woman's side, however, and no process of learning or internalization. The process that she represents is a single stage, set against the two stages of preparation and attainment on the other side, which are individually associated with instruction and wisdom. For the two women to be set in direct opposition, then, the author has to combine the attributes of the father together with those of Wisdom herself.

This is done explicitly in chapter 8, when Wisdom speaks as parent, but there is a tension throughout the work between the Wisdom who has to be an active self-publicist, like the foreign woman, and the Wisdom who has to be sought out and found through instruction. The outstretched arm of 1: 24 and the handmaid imagery of chapter 9 probably offer the best clues as to how the author might have understood this at a more theoretical level. The instruction that leads to the attainment of wisdom, through internalizing it, is not independent of wisdom, and so not a human creation designed to give access to an understanding of God. Rather, it is the way in which wisdom itself reaches out to humans, offering them the knowledge they need, and it can be portrayed, therefore, as a limb or servant of personified Wisdom. If we are right in thinking, however, that Proverbs 1–9 intends instruction to be understood in terms of the Law, conventionally understood to have been given by YHWH himself, then this raises further questions about the way in which the figure of Wisdom relates to God. That relationship, in fact, is one about which the text has a great deal to say.

When Wisdom appears in 3: 11–20, the personification is only brief. With no bad character in sight, she is not called upon to speak, and the section is principally concerned to establish her importance. This lies firstly in what she offers—long life, prosperity, and contentment—but secondly in her association with YHWH, who uses wisdom in the creation of the world. The short section within which all this lies is notably introduced by a 'parental' appeal about divine instruction, and it follows the advice about behaviour towards God in 3: 5–10, which itself promises 'straight paths', health, and prosperity. We have already been told, in 2: 6, that wisdom is a gift from YHWH, and that associated concepts come 'from his mouth'. It seems, therefore, that the juxtapositions here are meant to imply that what Wisdom offers is essentially what God offers, and that she is able to offer it because of her association with him.

Similar ideas appear in the lengthier validation of Wisdom that dominates chapter 8.[48] After the initial assertion of her veracity, we are again told what she offers in terms of prosperity and power, although the account of this in 8: 10–21 emphasizes strongly that these gifts are to be associated with righteousness and fear of YHWH.

---

[48] It is helpful to observe that the chapter is apparently divided into four sections (verses 1–11, 12–21, 22–31, and 32–6), with the first expressing Wisdom's direct assertion of her own value, the second outlining her worldly benefits, and the third affirming the antiquity of her relationship with God. The last section, half the length of the others, draws these themes together in an appeal, which commends instruction in terms of the life and divine favour offered by Wisdom.

In 8: 22–31, the subject of the creation is raised again, as a way of asserting both Wisdom's antiquity and her close relationship with God. This culminates, however, in a portrayal of Wisdom delighting in humanity and the world, while retaining her closeness to God, and that is presumably the explanation of her concern to reach out to humans. Chapter 8, therefore, goes further than 3: 11–20 in its affirmation of Wisdom's benefits and credentials, but the two are both making essentially the same points.[49]

Too much can be made of the fact that 3: 19–20 views wisdom as a divine attribute at creation, while 8: 22–31 distinguishes a separate figure of Wisdom. This is a function not of some underlying conceptualization, but of the consistent poetic personification in chapter 8. Judging by the vagueness of 8: 22, indeed, the author has little interest in trying to specify just how such a figure might have come into existence, or in creating an explanatory cosmological framework within which his characters may be understood. We are on our own, then, if we wish to understand just how wisdom in Proverbs 1–9 can at once be a divine attribute or possession, and at the same time have a personality distinct from God. It seems likely, though, that we are dealing with the same sort of idea that allows humans each to have wisdom, while wisdom itself remains a concept that transcends the individual: when the divine attribute of wisdom comes into being, so, simultaneously, does the whole concept of wisdom, the general arising from the first instance of the particular.

Of more immediate relevance to the concerns of Proverbs 1–9 is the question of why wisdom is needed at all, as a concept or figure intermediate between God and humans. Far from being central to the message of the work, Wisdom as an intermediary figure seems somewhat redundant, even obtrusive. The Law, after all, is given by YHWH himself, and it is his will that humans are seeking to understand, so why is an agent required in this relationship? An answer to this might be formulated in terms of the divine transcendence that characterizes the theology of the other biblical wisdom books, and which is arguably a mark of much post-exilic Jewish

---

[49] Without going into the broader question of whether wisdom literature reflects a 'creation theology'—an idea that, I think, requires considerable qualification—I agree with Lennart Boström's general conclusion that 'the creation of the world theme is employed to enhance the status of wisdom'; *God of the Sages*, 83.

writing. In 3: 11–12, however, the author associates YHWH directly with teaching, and so we can hardly assume that he believes him to be above such matters. It seems more likely, in fact, that the personification of wisdom is, in this respect, creating an issue that does not exist in the underlying thought. As we characterized it earlier, wisdom is literally to be conceived of as something that is within humans, an attribute or condition that allows them to discern the good and understand what is required of them by God; it is also, however, as 2: 6 says, something that he gives or proclaims. The concept, then, is of a means by which God offers humans access to his will, and wisdom is therefore *in* humans but *of* God. This is not something that can be sustained once the concept is personified, and although much emphasis is laid upon Wisdom's relationships with humans, on the one hand, and God on the other, her very presence separates the two.

This does not mean that there are two distinct concepts of wisdom in Proverbs 1–9, and we find no deliberate attempt to establish a separate framework that incorporates the personified figure. What it does imply is rather that this personification was not intended primarily to epitomize the actual relationship between wise humans and God, and actually creates problems in this respect. There is, we might say, an important distinction to be drawn between the two statements 'To find wisdom is to find God' and 'To find Wisdom is to find God', just as soon as one starts to consider the role of wisdom/ Wisdom. We have already seen that the same personification leads to some difficulties with respect to differentiating between wisdom and instruction also, and this further problem might, perhaps, fuel a suspicion that the author has not picked an ideal vehicle for expressing what he is trying to say.[50] Why, then, has he used it?

There is little or no evidence to suggest that personified Wisdom was an established figure in Jewish thought before Proverbs 1–9,

---

[50] In particular, I am not convinced that the writer is trying to establish wisdom as something that has an active intermediary role between humans and God. Viewed as a concept, wisdom is essentially a spiritual or intellectual attainment which gives one automatic insight into the divine will, not a messenger service from God; the personification cannot adequately represent this, although the statements of Wisdom's long proximity to God are surely an attempt to reflect the nature of the concept in those terms, but it notably offers no specific alternative model. On attempts to see Wisdom as an intermediary, see especially Baumann, *Weisheitsgestalt*, 42–3; I agree with much of the measured opinion that she offers herself in 291–4.

although it is just possible that she had earlier been used as a poetic figure.[51] We cannot suppose, therefore, that the author was under some constraint of convention or tradition when he chose to use her,[52] but the difficulties that arise from the personification would seem to imply that his presentation is, nevertheless, constrained in some other way. The simplest explanation, perhaps, is that the portrayal of wisdom through the figure of Wisdom, however important and influential it may have become later, was not originally a primary purpose of the work, but was subsidiary to other considerations—that Wisdom, in other words, was not the author's starting point, but was created to match some other element or elements in the presentation. Since the most obvious role of the character is as a counterpart to the foreign woman, it is tempting to suppose, therefore, that the idea of that woman came first.[53] Indeed, as we shall see shortly, there are good reasons to suppose that the foreign woman plays the role that she does in Proverbs 1–9 because of well-established ideas associated with foreign women, and we can also, arguably, view the presentation of her as much more rounded and detailed than the presentation of Wisdom. Whether that is the case or not, the author's decision not only to use a character to represent wisdom, but also to use a personification of the concept, rather than a type like the woman or the sinners, has left him with problems both in correlating their roles, and in dealing with the implications of Wisdom (the person) for wisdom (the concept).[54]

[51] Lindenberger, *Aramaic Proverbs*, 68–70 follows others in seeing a 'hymn in praise of wisdom' in *Ahiqar* col. vii (94b–95); even if this is the case—and extensive reconstruction is required—it is not clear that personification is involved. As it is, the term חכמתה itself is only preserved partially and uncertainly on a separate flake. Kottsieper, *Die Sprache*, 47, restores חכמתם, rather than חכמתה מן, making this a reference to the wisdom of humans, not an abstract concept.

[52] I am also very sceptical of the idea that we are dealing with a 'mythic personification' forced upon writers by a crisis of ideas, and intended to draw wisdom out of the realm of social discourse, as elaborated by Burton Mack, in *Wisdom and the Hebrew Epic: Ben Sira's Hymn in Praise of the Fathers* (Chicago Studies in the History of Judaism; Chicago: University of Chicago Press, 1985), 143–50.

[53] As suggested by, e.g., Blenkinsopp, 'Social Context,' 466–7; R. J. Clifford, *The Wisdom Literature* (Interpreting Biblical Texts; Nashville, TN: Abingdon Press, 1998), 55; Yoder, *Wisdom*, 74–5.

[54] While fully acknowledging the powerful influence of the personification on subsequent literature and thought, I am wary of attributing an authorial intention to many of the implications that have been identified. Gerlinde Baumann, for instance,

3. CONCLUSIONS

We began this chapter by observing that Proverbs 1–9 lays a strong emphasis on the need for instruction, but offers very little instruction itself. After reviewing the content of its precepts, and the way in which it relates instruction to wisdom and the fear of YHWH, we are in a stronger position to explain this peculiarity: the instruction that Proverbs 1–9 wants its readers to accept is neither enumerated nor explicitly identified because the work probably expects those readers to recognize that it is talking about the Jewish Law, the 'instruction' *par excellence*, which is already, after all, in the public domain. That expectation rests in part upon allusions to other literature and the character of its summarizing precepts about proper behaviour towards YHWH and fellow humans. Those are almost redundant, however, in a Jewish religious work that uses such strongly evocative terms as תורה and מצות.

Instruction is, at one level, a process of human teaching, which can be exemplified or summarized in the admonitions of chapter 3. Between the series of admonitions there, however, we are reminded that God also instructs like a father, while the next chapter characterizes the father's instruction in terms of the path imagery used conventionally in connection with the divine 'teaching', that is, the Law. The father's instruction, then, is not crudely identified as the Law, any more than the father is identified as God, but the language and imagery forge a close relationship between them. Something similar has already been implied in the complicated, summarizing poem of chapter 2, where receiving the father's commandments leads to a relationship with God that, in its turn, provides an understanding of God and everything that he values,[55] along with protection on the right paths.

in 'A Figure with Many Facets: The Literary and Theological Functions of Personified Wisdom in Proverbs 1–9', in Brenner, *Feminist Companion*, 44–78, lists a wide range of consequences, and describes the personification in terms of filtering and unifying a previously diverse phenomenon: even if it does all these things, I suspect that many were incidental, or even contrary to the author's intentions.

[55] The terms used in 2: 9 (also in 1: 3), צדק, 'rightness', משפט, 'justice', and מישרים, 'equity', appear together in Ps. 99: 4 (with צדקה for צדק) as divine accomplishments. More generally, צדק(ה) and משפט appear together so often as to constitute almost

This understanding of wisdom and instruction is affirmed by the identification of wisdom as the source for the desirable 'fear of YHWH', but is not very lucidly reflected in the personification of wisdom. Indeed, despite apparent attempts to overcome the difficulties, the very fact of that personification rather confuses the issue, and the author would seem to have adopted it not as a particularly suitable vehicle for his ideas about instruction, but as a necessary component of his imagery. This problem emphasizes, however, the important fact that Proverbs 1–9 is much more than just a prolonged commendation of the Law. Among other things, it apparently elaborates an understanding of legal piety in terms of wisdom, drawing, perhaps, on established ideas about internalization of the Law, and, as we shall see in the next chapter, it relates its ideas to some significant biblical themes. At the same time, however, it is also a very complicated poetic composition, in which the expression of those ideas is tied to, and sometimes confined by, the limits of the language and imagery.

a definitive expression of what God does and what he desires (e.g. Ps. 89: 14 [ET, 15]; 106: 3; Is. 33: 5; 56: 1). Within Proverbs 1–9, the terms are also associated with Wisdom, cf. 8: 20. Ezek. 18: 5–9 offers a description of what it means for a human to do משפט and צדקה, culminating in a general requirement to obey the divine statutes.

5

The 'Foreign Woman' and the
Path Imagery

Earlier in this study I complained about attempts to identify elements of the imagery in Proverbs 1–9 without reference to the work's broader interconnections. After concentrating on wisdom and instruction in the last chapter, therefore, I want to return at this point to a consideration of the figurative context in which they are presented. Since Proverbs 1–9 has invested substantial effort in developing such elements of its presentation as the foreign woman, the path imagery, and, for that matter, the instructional setting, it seems unlikely that these are irrelevant to the work's central concerns. Indeed, they offer alternative approaches to understanding those concerns, and therefore a way of verifying or falsifying the conclusions that we drew from other material in the last chapter. Furthermore, as we saw in the last part of that chapter, there are some reasons to suspect that these elements, far from being subsidiary to the author's expression of ideas about wisdom and instruction, may themselves have influenced and constrained that expression. In this chapter, therefore, we shall look at the ways in which such key elements would have been understood by the original readership—beginning with the distinctive presentation of the foreign woman—before trying to establish what these different elements would have suggested in combination.

1. THE FOREIGN WOMAN

To recap briefly, we have already observed that the foreign woman appears to act as a counterpart to the figure of Wisdom.

The principal elements of the character are established on her first appearance, in 2: 16–19, where she stands alongside 'the man who speaks perversity' as a figure from whom the son needs protection. Most importantly, she speaks persuasively, and this characteristic is at the forefront of the subsequent warnings in chapter 5 and 6: 20–35, where the son is admonished to stay away from her. Chapter 7 recalls the promise of chapter 2 by offering assurance that establishing a relationship with Wisdom will preserve the son from the foreign woman, and then presents a cautionary tale—in which the woman seduces a youth with her seductive speech—before again warning the son to keep away from her. In chapters 5 and 6, the consequences of ignoring such a warning are spelled out in terms of one's efforts going to the household of a foreigner, or by reference to the inevitable penalty for adultery; the broader and more consistent theme, however, is that she leads her victims to their deaths, perhaps unwittingly heading in that direction herself. In chapter 9, a figure with similar characteristics appears as an explicit antithesis of Wisdom, although she is there called Folly, or 'the woman of follies'. It seems probable not only that this figure is to be identified as the foreign woman, but also that the foreign woman is supposed to serve a similar role throughout the work, as a dangerous temptress who lures the unwary from their paths.

A. The Foreignness of the Foreign Woman

Although we have looked in some detail at the role of this woman, we have not so far examined the terms used to describe her. Those employed in chapter 9 are unproblematic, in that they simply make explicit her role in relation to Wisdom, but the terms expressive of her foreignness, used elsewhere, have given rise to much discussion.

Many commentators, and even some translations, have been inclined to play down this description of the woman as 'foreign', or to see it as having some explicit moral connotation,[1] and for that reason it is important to emphasize that the terms used are common,

---

[1] This, as Kathleen Farmer puts it, 'Turns what is basically xenophobia into what seems to be misogyny'; *Who Knows*, 10.

and essentially unambiguous. The two key words are found in the first reference to the woman, 2: 16, where she is זרה and נכריה—'alien' and 'foreign'. The first of these, זרה, is used of her again in 5: 3, 20 and 7: 5, while the second, נכריה, appears in 5: 20, 6: 24, and 7: 5. Although each is used separately, then, they are more frequently found as a pair. This is important, because it helps to define exactly what is meant, but the sense is clear anyway.

Of the two, זרה has the slightly broader meaning: the adjective זר can just indicate a 'third party', as in 1 Kgs. 3: 18 or Ezek. 16: 32, but it generally means anyone or anything that lies outside a defined category or group. So, for example, 'aliens' can be non-priests who approach the tabernacle (e.g. Num. 1: 51), and someone estranged from his family can be called 'alien' (e.g. Job 19: 17). There is no pejorative implication inherent in the use of the term, though, and the closest the word comes to indicating impropriety is in the use of it to describe the unauthorized incense burned by Nadab and Abihu (cf. Lev. 10: 1). When used of people in contexts other than the cultic, it generally just means someone who lies outside the family or the people.

The second term, נכריה, is more precise: נכרי is used, literally or hyperbolically, to describe people who are not Israelite or Jewish (e.g. 1 Kgs. 8: 41).[2] Again, it has no obvious moral implication in itself.[3] Used together with the first term, it retains this normal sense,[4] and

[2] This is true also of the related noun נכר. According to BDB, there is a cognate (denominative) verb נכר, which is used of disguising oneself or pretending not to recognize another (e.g. Gen. 42: 7); HALOT is surely right, however, to connect the references given with the more common, but probably unrelated, נכר ('recognize, acknowledge'); Ruth 2: 10 is, therefore, a pun on the two.

[3] It is important to note that Rachel and Leah are probably not accusing their father of treating them as prostitutes in Gen. 31: 15, as is sometimes asserted. The context suggests, rather, that they are either justifying their departure by the loss of the inheritance due to them and their children (which has removed the family bond and left them in the position that foreign women would occupy in the household), or merely speaking hyperbolically (see below).

[4] For the literal sense 'foreign', when the adjectives are used together, cf. Ps. 81: 10 (ET, 9); Is. 61: 5; Jer. 5: 19; Lam. 5: 2; Obad. 1: 11. In Prov. 20: 16 and 27: 13, where the reference is to giving surety, the 'foreignness' is probably also literal, although it may be an instance of hyperbolic use (the feminine form נכריה in 27: 13, incidentally, is probably a textual error, possibly influenced by the references to the 'foreign woman' in chs. 1–9 and elsewhere).

there is no evidence to suggest that the terms might together have some other implication of marital or social status.[5]

The fact that there has been so much discussion of these words is a consequence not of difficulties in establishing their literal meaning, but of problems in squaring that meaning both with the description of the woman in the text, and with suppositions about the role of the woman. The reference in 2: 17, to her having 'forgotten the covenant of her God' need not be taken to imply either that she is foreign or Jewish,[6] and, more generally, there is no self-evident reference to her ethnicity outside the two words repeatedly used to describe her, except, perhaps, in chapter 5.[7] It is hard to see, on the face of it, what relevance ethnicity or nationality might have to her role in Proverbs 1–9.[8]

B. Admonitions against Women in Other Literature

Such problems have provoked a wide range of responses and identifications. Many commentators have looked to other instructions, where warnings about women are a common enough theme. Although by no means a fundamental and indispensable component of instructions, furthermore, there is a possibility that this theme may have been closely associated with the genre in popular

---

[5] See the annotated translation, at 2: 16.

[6] See the annotated translation, at 2: 17.

[7] Maier, *Die fremde Frau*, takes זרה and נכריה to imply different things, so that 'Die Figur der "fremden Frau" repräsentiert daher ethnisch fremde *und* aus der judäischen Gemeinschaft stammende Frauen' ('The figure of the "foreign woman" thus represents both ethnically foreign women and women originating in the Jewish community') (254), within the context of her understanding that the woman represents a 'literarische Gestalt unterschiedliche Lebenssituationen von Frauen und deren Stellung in der Gesellschaft' ('literary depiction of women's various positions in life, and their place in society') (253). While sympathetic to the overall claim, I think such a double depiction is too precise a way of understanding the text, and that the terms are intended to be virtual synonyms.

[8] cf. McKinlay, *Gendering*, 97. In view of these considerations, I think it would be difficult to sustain in such general terms the view put forward by Ralph Marcus, that the woman is 'a poetic personification of pagan idolatry and foreign culture, contrasted with the Israelite way of life'; R. Marcus, 'On Biblical Hypostases of Wisdom', *HUCA* 23 I (1950–1), 157–71, especially 165.

perceptions.[9] Instructions rarely go beyond straightforward warnings against prostitutes, promiscuity or adultery, but a rather obscure passage in the *Instruction of Any* (16: 13–17) has frequently attracted the attention of biblical scholars.[10] This warns against involvement with a woman who is 'from outside', and certainly has many superficial points of contact with the descriptions of the foreign woman in Proverbs 1–9, not least an association with deadly entrapment. The similarities are not great enough, however, to suggest literary dependence, and we have no other reason to suppose either that *Any* was known to the writer of Proverbs 1–9, or that the theme and description in *Any* were ever picked up in any other instructions.[11] In any case, although attempts have been made to identify the (somewhat unclear) 'outsider' status of *Any*'s woman with the foreignness of the woman in Proverbs, there are too many difficulties in the Egyptian text, and too many differences between the presentations and their contexts, for us simply to interpret Proverbs on the basis of *Any*.[12]

The foreign instructions, then, do no more than suggest that the genre in which he was working may have inspired the writer of Proverbs 1–9 to include warnings against women. Only *Any*,

---

[9] That would explain, for instance, why a Demotic work that seems to parody the genre chose to begin with this subject; see above, p. 20.

[10] Whatever its significance for Proverbs, it is important to note that this passage stands alone in the Egyptian literature, and it is unfortunate that some scholars have generalized from it. Blenkinsopp, 'Social Context', 463, for instance, claims that 'In the moralising didactic literature of ancient Egypt... the *femme fatale* is typically a foreigner, or at least an outsider'—but this is only true of *Any*; Yoder, *Wisdom*, 102–3 similarly bases on it a description of the way in which New Kingdom sapiental literature characterizes women more generally.

[11] A. Depla, 'Women in Ancient Egyptian Wisdom Literature', in L. J. Archer, S. Fischler, M. Wyke (eds), *Women in Ancient Societies: An Illusion of the Night* (Basingstoke: Macmillan, 1994), 24–52, says (49) that 'Woman as "temptress" occurs for the first time in the New Kingdom texts, although the greatest number of references to this theme is to be found in the Graeco-Roman material.' It is difficult to imagine what references she has in mind among those materials, but if it is a motif at all in the Demotic instructions, it is a rare one.

[12] Quack, *Ani*, 212–14, offers a parallel presentation of the lines from *Any* with selected passages from Proverbs 1–9, claiming that 'Diese Zusammenstellung dürfte zeigen, daß sich für jeden Gedanken des ägyptischen Textes tatsächlich eine mehr oder weniger gute Proverbienparallele finden läßt,' ('This synopsis may show that for each idea in the Egyptian text, it is actually possible to find a more or less good parallel in Proverbs') (214), but 'weniger' ('less') is surely the key word here. Quack himself doubts that the author of Proverbs 1–9 knew *Any* directly.

however, offers a warning that is at all comparable to the highly developed imagery used of the foreign woman, and there are no instructions at all that devote so much of their content to warning against women, or elaborate the theme at such length. While it is just possible that our writer had read *Any*, and worked himself into a lather of prurient indignation, our investigations so far suggest that we are dealing with something much more sophisticated than the obsessive repetition of a conventional theme. Furthermore, even if we do accept that Proverbs 1–9 has been influenced by instructional literature, the great variety among the warnings to be found in that literature, against different types of women, offers little clarification of what our writer is trying to say.

There are two other passages in Proverbs that resemble the descriptions of the foreign woman: 22: 14 warns that 'the mouth of strange women is a deep pit: he with whom YHWH is angry will fall there'. Proverbs 23: 27–8, which serves as the motive section for a parental appeal in 23: 26, uses the same words for its initial image: 'For a strange woman [MT: prostitute] is a deep pit, and a foreign woman a narrow well. Moreover, she lies in ambush like a robber, and increases those who are faithless amongst [or: toward] humankind.'[13] There are a lot of points of interest here, especially when the second of these passages describes the consequences of the woman's actions. It is hard to know how to relate them to Proverbs 1–9, however, and 23: 27–8, in particular, may well be drawing on our work. Be that as it may, neither offers significant further information, any more than does Qoh. 7: 26, which refers to a similar woman, or type of woman, without using the נכריה זרה / terminology.[14]

---

[13] There are several difficulties in this verse. MT's זונה is probably an (interpretative?) error for זרה, which almost certainly underlies the curious ἀλλότριος οἶκος of LXX (cf. McKane, *Proverbs*, 390). The term חתף is *hapax* in the biblical literature, but *HALOT* notes that it occurs in the Hebrew of Ben Sira with reference to robbery, and the cognate verb appears in Job 9: 12, perhaps with the sense of snatching something as one passes, hence 'robber'. Finally, בגד, 'to deal treacherously', can be used absolutely, but when it takes an object (the person being betrayed), this takes the preposition ב; since באדם also commonly means 'among humans', the verse is ambiguous.

[14] Although the description is not of a woman, it is worth noting that the description of the treacherous companion in Ps. 55 has a number of points of contact with the presentation of the foreign woman; see especially vv. 21–2 (ET, 20–1).

C. Internal Evidence

Since the parallels in other literature offer such limited assistance, identifications of the foreign woman have tended to draw principally on the evidence presented within Proverbs 1–9 itself. The various suggestions that she is a prostitute (cultic, commercial, or amateur)[15] draw heavily on the account in chapter 7, and run into the immediate problem that there is no reference to such a status in the other depictions of the woman.[16] Even within chapter 7, we are only told that she dresses like one—which may be no more than a statement that she dressed provocatively ('tarted herself up', as they say in my part of the world). The criticism of this view—that it is rooted too much in chapter 7 alone—may also be levelled at Boström's famous identification of the woman as a devotee of Astarte. The more popular idea that she is an adulteress seems to fit the material as a whole rather better (although I doubt very much that chapter 5, at least, is to be read that way). It struggles, however, to explain both the strong emphases on her foreignness and persuasiveness, and the relative lack of emphasis, outside 6: 20–35, on her marital status.

[15] Or even an unpaid one: Waltke (who has earlier called her a 'lustful strumpet') claims that she is 'at heart a prostitute ... [which] here means one who engages in sexual intercourse with no intention of a binding or enduring relationship'; B. K. Waltke, *The Book of Proverbs: Chapters 1–15* (NICOT; Grand Rapids, MI: Eerdmans, 2004), 122, 124. That is, however, just a mischievous use of the term for rhetorical effect. The identification as a cultic prostitute is most famously proposed by Gustav Boström, in his *Proverbiastudien*; all other problems aside, it should be noted that the whole notion of cultic prostitution in the region is currently being questioned very seriously; cf. Camp, *Wise, Strange*, 43–4. The view that the woman is a commercial prostitute is largely confined to earlier commentators (cf. the LXX translations of 5: 3; 7: 5), but has left its mark through BDB (*sub* נכר): 'foreign woman, as term. techn., in Pr, for *harlot* (perh. because harlots were orig. chiefly foreigners)'. More recently, van der Toorn has argued, in 'Female Prostitution in Payment of Vows in Ancient Israel', *JBL* 108 (1989), 193–205, that the woman in chapter 7 needs some money to 'pay her vows', and has to earn it through casual prostitution after her husband has gone away with the money. The idea of casual prostitution, a common enough phenomenon even in the modern world, seems less incredible than the fact that the reader is expected to understand this background story from the text.

[16] We should also recall that the biblical literature shows little general concern with the purchase of sexual services, which would raise questions about why Proverbs 1–9 alone should be so bothered by it.

In view of the problems, some commentators seem to have moved to a more literary or symbolic approach, rejecting or avoiding specific, limiting identifications. That move is to be welcomed, but it does not absolve us of the need to explain aspects of the woman that are clearly important to the text itself. Ironically, I think it is two recent studies that go in the opposite direction, positing a very concrete, historical situation, that point the way most clearly to understanding both the designation of the woman as 'foreign' and the significance of her appearance in Proverbs 1–9.

D. 'Foreign Women' and the Post-exilic Context

Joseph Blenkinsopp and Harold Washington have argued independently that the woman must be understood within the context of the post-exilic campaign against marriages to foreign women.[17] This campaign is described in the book of Ezra (9–10), and mentioned more briefly in Nehemiah (10: 30; 13: 23–7); it also forms the backdrop to the preaching in Mal. 2: 10–16, which we came across earlier in connection with Prov. 2: 17. These accounts, though strongly partisan and possibly viewed through the lens of a later generation, probably do reflect a real controversy in the community of the Return, when a (more or less serious) attempt was made not only to prohibit marriage to those outside the community, but to force men who had already contracted such marriages to dissolve them. The reasons for this may have been tied up with land tenure, an idea pursued at length by Washington, and they were almost certainly part of a broader concern with defining and delimiting the community. In this context, consequently, the idea of ethnicity is both important and confusing: to be within the community was to be a member of the true Israel, to be outside it was to be, in the eyes

---

[17] H. C. Washington, 'The Strange Woman (אשה זרה/נכריה) of Proverbs 1–9 and Post-Exilic Judaean Society', in T. C. Eskenazi and K. H. Richards (eds), *Second Temple Studies*, vol. 2: *Temple Community in the Persian Period* (JSOTS 175; Sheffield: JSOT Press, 1994), 217–42; Blenkinsopp, 'Social Context'. Maier, *Die fremde Frau*, also takes this controversy as a significant background for the foreign woman, while seeing it as only one element in the portrayal.

of the community, a foreigner.[18] Whatever their own beliefs about their ethnicity, then, the women with whom marriage was banned are called נשים נכרזת, 'foreign women/wives'.[19]

This context is important, but not because, in itself, it offers an adequate explanation of the foreign woman in Proverbs 1–9. Blenkinsopp and Washington illustrate some important links, and the concern in Prov. 5, about labour and substance going to the household of a foreigner, may well be explicable in terms of concerns about alienation of property (or individuals, for that matter) from the community. It is hard to see, though, how the issue of adultery in 6: 20–35 fits with the particular issue of foreign wives: the very problem is that the men are married to them, not having illicit affairs with them. Similarly, as Fox notes, the woman of chapter 7 is after a 'one-night stand (7: 18), not marriage'.[20] Rather than it offering a direct explanation, the significance of the post-exilic debate lies, I believe, in two areas.

The first of these is terminology. I made the point earlier that we should be more concerned with what the readership *would* have understood than with what they *might* have understood. If Proverbs 1–9 is a post-exilic work, as the great majority of modern commentators assume, then is it really likely that, on hearing the term נכריה, the original audience would have ignored that word's central significance in a debate that had most probably convulsed the community? Even were it possible that the term could be used of social marginalization, or imply marriage to someone else, these would be, in comparison, obscure alternative senses.

The second area where the controversy is significant for us is the rationale offered within the debate for the rejection of foreign wives. Blenkinsopp and Washington may be doing their job as historians too well, in this respect, looking for the actual motives rather than the stated ones. Whatever the historical or political realities, the

---

[18] The fact that this distinction may actually have been dubious, historically and genetically, is not, of course, evidence that נכריה has a sense other than 'foreign', or that 'foreign' for a post-exilic Jew meant something other than it does to us. Ideas of foreignness, of national or ethnic identity, or even of race, are as much constructs in our modern societies as they were in ancient ones. If we translate as 'outsider', however, and allow this to elide into different concepts of social marginalization or liminality, then we are missing the point.

[19] Ezra 10: 2, 10, 11, 14, 17, 18, 44; Neh. 13: 27.

[20] Fox, *Proverbs 1–9*, 135.

explanations offered in the principal biblical accounts are themselves biblical in character, and pick up what was certainly an existing theme, connected to ideas about apostasy and the reasons for the fall of Israel.

According to Deuteronomy 7: 1–5, the Israelites are commanded to exterminate the nations resident in the land not as a demand of 'Holy War' but because these peoples threaten to corrupt Israel, and to lead the Jews astray from God; intermarriage is especially to be avoided:

When YHWH your God brings you to the land where you are going, to take possession of it, and he clears out many nations from before you—the Hittite, the Gergashite, the Amorite, the Canaanite, the Perizzite, the Hivite, and the Jebusite, seven nations larger and more powerful than you—then, when YHWH your God has set them before you and you have beaten them, you must utterly annihilate them. You shall make no treaty with them and have no mercy on them, and you shall make no marriage alliance with them: you shall neither give your daughters to their sons, nor take their daughters for your sons. For each would turn your child away from me, and they would serve other gods; then the anger of YHWH would be kindled against you and he would destroy you swiftly. (Deut. 7: 1–4)

Verse 5 goes on to command destroying their altars, pillars, and Asherim, as does a similar passage in Exod. 34: 11–16. Here, God promises to drive out 'the Amorites, the Canaanites, the Hittites, the Perizzites, the Hivites, and the Jebusites', and warns against making a covenant with the inhabitants of the land, 'lest it become a trap in the midst of you' (v. 12), and 'when they go whoring after their gods and sacrificing to their gods, [one of them] invites you, and you eat some of their sacrifice, or you take some of their daughters for your sons, and their daughters go whoring after their gods and get your sons whoring after their gods' (vv. 15b–16). The reference to such ideas in Ezra 9 is unmistakable, not least because the first verse anachronistically lists the ancient peoples, merely including a few new names amongst the usual suspects:[21]

---

[21] These, the Ammonite, Moabite and Egyptian, are probably drawn from 1 Kgs. 11: 1–4, on which, see below. Note that Blenkinsopp, 'Social Context', 456 n. 3, with other commentators, takes the references to Ammon and Moab to be secondary in Neh. 13: 23, and it seems possible that there has been an attempt to align that passage with the same material.

The people of Israel, the priests, and the Levites, have not separated themselves from the peoples of the lands according to their abominations,[22] from the Canaanite, the Hittite, the Perizzite, the Jebusite, the Ammonite, the Moabite, the Egyptian, and the Amorite. For they have taken some of their daughters for themselves and for their sons, and the holy seed has become mingled with the peoples of the lands, and the hand of the leaders and officials has been at the forefront of this transgression. (Ezra 9: 1b–2)

Ezra goes on to paraphrase the commandments in verses 11–12, and after lamenting the destruction that has already come upon the nation, suggests that further punishment will ensue from such inter-marriages (13–14); a little later, Ezra 10: 10 likewise talks of them 'increasing the guilt of Israel'.[23]

Sidestepping such points of interest as the idea of a holy seed, or the deliberate association of the current inhabitants of the land with those supposed to have occupied it in ancient times, the most significant point here is the evocation of the conquest commandments in this context. We find this also in Nehemiah 13: 25, where the vow that Nehemiah enforces is surely intended to recall those commandments, and both works are probably drawing on an earlier idea, linked to understandings of just why Israel had courted divine anger through apostasy.[24] Whether or not the commandments in Deuteronomy and Exodus are deliberately anticipating such an analysis, we find it expressed as part of the Deuteronomistic assessment in the early chapters of Judges.[25] Judges 2 notes the failure to

[22] Possibly to be translated as a simile, not identifying the peoples, but the abominations with the nations listed; cf. T. C. Eskenazi and E. P. Judd, 'Marriage to a Stranger in Ezra 9–10', in Eskenazi and Richards, *Second Temple Studies*, vol. 2, 266–85, especially 268.

[23] It is widely recognized that Ezra 9–10 reflects the work of more than one hand; cf. most recently, Y. Dor, 'The Composition of the Episode of the Foreign Women in Ezra IX–X', *VT* 53 (2003), 26–47, who argues for a series of stages. I think that there is coherence between the sources in this respect, however.

[24] These ideas, and their links with Proverbs 1–9, are explored in more detail in Nancy Nam Hoon Tan, 'The "Foreignness" of the Foreign Woman in Proverbs 1–9: A Study of the Origin and Development of a Biblical Motif', Ph.D. thesis (University of Durham, 2004).

[25] Note that the idea is also found in other historiographical material; cf. Num. 25, with its account of the infamous sin at Peor. J. J. Quesada, 'Body Piercing: The Issue of Priestly Control over Acceptable Family Structure in the Book of Numbers', *Biblical Interpretation* 10 (2002), 24–35, suggests that this passage served to validate the post-exilic rejection of foreign wives and the priestly role in defining the purity of the

destroy the peoples, their continued presence as a snare (2: 1–3), and the apostasy of Israel, which leads to the cycle of punishment and rescue that characterizes the historiography of the book. God ultimately leaves some nations undestroyed himself, to test Israel's behaviour (2: 20–3), and to provide continued practice in warfare (3: 1–4). So it is that the Israelites are living amongst the Canaanites, Hittites, Amorites, Perizzites, Hivites, and Jebusites, and, according to 3: 6, 'took their daughters for themselves as wives, gave their own daughters to their sons, and served their gods'.[26]

Nehemiah refers obliquely to the conquest commandments, but directly to the fact that Solomon was corrupted by intermarriage: although he was the greatest of kings, loved by God, 'foreign women caused even him to sin' (Neh. 13: 26). The reference, of course, is to 1 Kgs. 11: 1–6, which begins:

And King Solomon loved many women, the daughter of Pharaoh, Moabites, Ammonites, Edomites, Sidonians, and Hittites, from the nations about which YHWH had said to the Israelites 'You must not go with them or they go with you:[27] surely they will turn your hearts aside after their gods.' It was to these that Solomon clung for love . . . and his wives turned aside his heart. And it was in Solomon's old age that his wives turned his heart aside after other gods . . . (1 Kgs. 11: 1–4)

The passage goes on to specify the foreign gods he followed, and to contrast Solomon's infidelity with the fidelity of David, but it

community. The issue has been put in a much broader context by Camp, *Wise, Strange,* who ties the motif together with the post-exilic vying for power and legitimacy of the different priestly groups, and the formation of identity in that period.

26 Camp, *Wise, Strange,* 23, doubts that intermarriage could have been an issue before the post-exilic period, and accordingly dates all the relevant materials late, including the texts in Deuteronomy and Exodus. The question is reasonable, but her solution a little drastic. My own suspicion is that the issue arose (as a historical analysis rather than a social policy) within an earlier bid to establish 'Israelite' identity after the fall of the Northern Kingdom, perhaps in the context of claims to its territory. See S. Weeks, 'Biblical Literature and the Emergence of Ancient Jewish Nationalism', *Biblical Interpretation* 10 (2002), 144–57, especially 156. Without denying Camp's broader historical hypothesis (although that poses many challenges), I think the themes she explores originate earlier, and that Proverbs 1–9 is less closely connected to the concerns of priestly groups.

27 'Go with/into' here probably has a sexual reference; in the coy Latin of *HALOT,* 'coire cum femina'.

deliberately refers back to the commandments against intermarriage. Later, the Deuteronomistic Historian also associates the corruption of Ahab with his marriage to a foreign wife, who leads him into apostasy: 'and it was a matter of little consequence for him to go in the sins of Jeroboam ben-Nebat beside the fact that he took as [his] wife Jezebel, the daughter of Ethbaal, king of the Sidonians, and went and served Baal, and bowed down to him' (1 Kgs. 16: 31); in the summary of his reign, it is noted that he committed apostasy like the Amorites whom YHWH had expelled, having been seduced into it by Jezebel (1 Kgs. 21: 25).[28]

It would be too much to say that these different references constitute a major theme in Deuteronomistic thought, but they are a distinctive element within the broader concern with apostasy. In the analysis of 2 Kgs. 17: 7–23, it is principally the fact that they followed the ways of the previous inhabitants of the land, including their worship of other gods, that leads to the destruction of the Northern Kingdom. According to the predictions of Deuteronomy and Exodus, and also according to certain accounts in Judges and Kings, intermarriage is one way, and perhaps the main way, in which such undesirable assimilation to the religious beliefs of these peoples can occur. Whatever the extent of this motif in earlier literature, and whatever the actual socio-political background, the idea of such seduction into apostasy is offered by the principal biblical sources as the key justification for the proposed ban on intermarriage in the community of the Return. The term 'foreign woman' is not only given prominence by that controversy, therefore, but it is also

---

[28] The verb used is סות, the same as used in Deut 13: 7 (ET, 6) of family members seducing one into apostasy. On the presentation of Jezebel, see Tan, 'Foreignness', 58–62. It is interesting to note that his marriage to Ahab's daughter is, in turn, linked by 2 Chron. 21: 6 to the sins of the Judahite King Jehoram. J. B. Burns, 'Solomon's Egyptian Horses and Exotic Wives', *Forum* 7 (1991), 29–44, notes also the account of Athaliah in 2 Kgs. 8, and claims that the texts about her and Jezebel 'provide an effective paradigm of the royal foreign wife who imports and spreads the cult of her god with the compliance of her husband' (41). It is possible that the emphasis on Jezebel in the texts of Kings is a product, at least in part, of later editing, and the same may be true of the material about Solomon's wives; cf. Camp, *Wise, Strange*, 23, 173–80. Burns, however, sees the Jezebel material as the basis for the spread of opposition to all foreign women.

given very specific associations with the corruption, or seduction, of Jewish men into apostasy from YHWH.[29]

In a way that other identifications do not, this association supplies a reason for the arch-seductress of Proverbs 1–9 to be called a 'foreign woman', and for the strong emphasis on her persuasiveness: foreign women, after all, can corrupt and destroy even a Solomon. It would be wrong, however, to start asking whether the woman is supposed to be a lapsed Israelite, a foreign resident, or one of the 'people of the land': there is little in Proverbs 1–9 to suggest that it is simply trying to wade into a debate on intermarriage.[30] Rather, it seems likely that the author is using the 'foreignness' of the woman primarily in a poetic way, exploiting the connotations of the term, not setting out an exclusivist agenda.

E. The Foreign Woman in Context

How, then, should we read the foreign woman in the context of Proverbs 1–9 and its imagery? Proverbs 2: 12 promises protection from the man who speaks 'perversity', a concept associated in Proverbs more widely with the mischievous sowing of discord (cf. 16: 28, 30). This man apparently typifies those who leave upright paths to follow their own crooked and devious ways,[31] and the structure of the poem sets him in parallel with the strange, foreign woman. This would be an odd juxtaposition, and a dramatic shift from the general to the specific, were the reference merely to a particular class of woman within, or on the fringes of the community, but she too is a type: for the original readers, her name conjures up associations with the seduction of Jews into apostasy, and the

---

[29] That the concern with foreign women persists into later literature is clear from Tobit 4: 12; see T. Hieke, 'Endogamy in the Book of Tobit, Genesis, and Ezra-Nehemiah', in G. Xeravits and J. Zsengellér (eds), *The Book of Tobit: Text, Tradition, Theology. Papers of the First International Conference on the Deuterocanonical Books, Pápa, Hungary, 20–21 May, 2004* (SJSJ 98; Leiden: Brill, 2005), 103–20.

[30] And just as little, I think, to suggest that it is confronting a situation of actual mass apostasy, *contra* Blenkinsopp, 'Social Context'.

[31] The term נלוז is also used in Prov. 14: 2 to contrast with one who walks in uprightness; interestingly, it is also associated in Is. 30: 10–11 with those who have decided to 'turn off the way, turn aside from the path', and who seek 'smooth' sayings.

association is reinforced by the further reference to smooth speech as her principal characteristic. What follows is difficult, but probably best taken to function at two levels. The similarities to the language in Mal. 2: 14–15 suggest that the terminology in 2: 17 is superficially that of divorce—an issue with close connections to the foreign wives controversy.[32] The words can also be construed in terms of apostasy, however, not only because breach of covenant is involved, but also, perhaps, because a metaphorical contrast between Israel's separation from YHWH and the happiness of their youthful marriage is an established figure in biblical literature.[33] In any case, this woman offers a direct route to the underworld, and those who go to her are irrevocably doomed.

When the foreign woman reappears in chapter 5, after the significance of instruction and the path imagery has been established, the dangerous power of her speech and the deadly nature of her path are reiterated, although it is suggested (5: 6) that she is unaware of her own wandering from the path of life. Here, and in 6: 20–35, which starts again by emphasizing her seductiveness, we run into the problem discussed earlier: in explaining the admonitions to stay clear of her, one passage focuses upon the alienation of one's authority and labour, the other upon the inevitable consequences of adultery. It is probable that we should take these as different scenarios: marriage to the foreign woman if she is single, perhaps after divorce from one's original wife, and adultery with her if she is not: what the woman seems to represent, after all, does not involve her having a fixed or specific marital status, merely the capacity to corrupt and ruin.[34] It is tempting to speculate, of course, that these

[32] The Jews, of course, are supposed to divorce their foreign wives, which would leave those women necessarily as divorcees, albeit not by their own choice. The condemnation of divorce in Malachi is actually set beside that work's condemnation of intermarriage (2: 10–12), which talks of priests profaning the sanctuary through marriage 'to the daughter of a foreign god'. We need not posit any direct link between Proverbs 1–9 and Malachi to infer that the intermarriage controversy may have been part of a broader debate about the status of particular marriages and the legitimacy of divorces.

[33] Famously, Is. 54: 5–7; Jer. 2: 2; Hos. 2: 17 (ET, 15). See also, perhaps, Joel 1: 8, and the more complicated imagery of Ezek. 16.

[34] Cook, 'אשה זרה', 465–8, observes that LXX understands the woman in these chapters as foreign wisdom, reflected separately in warnings against unmarried women in chapter 5, and married in chapter 6.

scenarios have a significance of their own that goes deeper than making sample charges against her.[35] Adultery, after all, is the classic biblical figure for apostasy, and a case could be made for viewing 6: 20–35 in these terms.[36] It is much harder, however, to make any similar case for chapter 5.

Just as chapter 2 promised protection, so we find in chapters 5 and 6 a strong emphasis upon the need to be protected by instruction from the woman, and from the consequences of association with her: this theme appears within the parental appeals (5: 1–2 and especially 6: 20–3), in the speech of the ruined man (5: 12–14), and in the reflections of 5: 21–3. Alongside the woman's persuasiveness, this is the issue given most prominence here, and that emphasis obviously affirms the suggestions made by Aletti that we examined earlier: that the woman presents a danger against which the uninstructed have no protection. Further, though, the association of the needed instruction with the Law seems to be made specific in 6: 22, which is surely a deliberate reminiscence of Deut. 6: 7: the broader message is that learning and internalizing the Law enables one to recognize and resist attempts to lure one aside from the way of life approved by God.

The block of material dealing with the foreign woman reaches its climax in chapter 7, where she is yet again introduced as a figure from whose persuasive talents one requires protection. The parental appeal begins by echoing in 7: 1–2a the words of 2: 1 and 4: 4b, then includes, among some new material in 7: 2b–3, the reference to writing on the heart from 3: 3: it is the last appeal, and harks back to some of

---

[35] Newsom, 'Woman', 155, points out that 'When symbolic thinking is carried forward by means of concrete objects or persons, statements and actions pertaining to these concrete entities can never be merely pragmatic on the one hand or simply metaphorical on the other.'

[36] A rather different significance in 6: 20–35 is suggested by R. E. Murphy, 'Wisdom and Eros in Proverbs 1–9', *CBQ* 50 (1988), 600–3, who suggests that 'the emphasis on proper sexual conduct has in fact a double meaning: sexual fidelity is also a symbol of one's attachment to Lady Wisdom' (603); cf. also his *The Tree of Life: An Exploration of Biblical Wisdom Literature* 2nd edn (Grand Rapids, MI: Eerdmans, 1996), 17–18. His strongest statement on the matter goes much further: the author has framed Wisdom 'against the background of Israel's sad history by the sexual emphasis, and by the contrast between Lady Wisdom and Dame Folly. The issue is now life and death, fidelity to the Lord or infidelity'; see 'The Personification of Wisdom', in Day *et al.*, *Wisdom in Ancient Israel*, 222–33, especially 226.

the others. Verses 4–5 identify the keeping and internalizing of the father's words with the acceptance of Wisdom as a sister or cousin, which is what offers protection against the woman. This introduces the opposition between the woman and personified Wisdom that will dominate chapters 7–9, but it also suggests a mechanism for the protection promised: the relationship with Wisdom pre-empts the invitations of the woman, and, one might say, fills the space she is seeking to occupy. A proper internalization of the Law brings one to a condition beyond the risk of corruption, expressed in terms of accepting wisdom.

The story starts with the father describing how an uninstructed youth wanders carelessly, turning aside into the dangerous, darkening road that leads to the woman's house. As we saw earlier, he is already in trouble before encountering her, but perhaps not inescapably so. She, meanwhile, has dressed for effect, but doesn't wait for callers, lurking instead in the streets for a victim, at 'every corner' where she can make someone turn aside. This adds a new dimension to the description: she is not always a static danger, a trap to be avoided by staying away from her door (5: 8, cf. 9: 14), or at least out of range of her eyes (6: 25), but can, rather, be a predator, actively seeking prey. She accordingly seizes and kisses the youth, actively seeking to lure him to her home, the way to Sheol (2: 18; 7: 27; 9: 18). The temptation to turn aside is an active, moving danger, which cannot be evaded simply by knowing and avoiding its address.

In the speech that follows, the woman justifies her desire for celebration in religious terms, paints an attractive picture of her perfumed bedroom, and promises that the man of the house will not return unexpectedly. The essential message is alluring, a promise of sex that is illicit but safe, and the details may be no more than ornamentation. It is possible that some are meant to imply some religious affiliation, but not necessary to presume that they do so.[37] In any event, it is this speech—her own 'teaching' (7: 21)—that

---

[37] Camp has made the attractive suggestion that in 7: 14 the woman is in the situation of being about to make, or having just made sacrifices that require ritual cleanliness until the food has been consumed, on that day or the day after. Sex at this time would incur the penalty of being 'cut off' from the people, and Camp notes that this is also the penalty in Exod. 30: 33 for making an oil similar to the anointing holy oil, which contained two of the spices found on her bed. The former suggestion is

persuades the youth to follow her, like an animal heading to its death. It also provokes a further warning from the father, in 7: 24–7, warning against turning aside into her ways, affirming the connection between her house and Sheol, but adding the new information that she has already claimed countless victims.[38] This last detail offers confirmation of her figurative, typical nature, but also reinforces another key point in this chapter: the woman is not merely a catalyst for destruction, or even just complicit in men's self-destruction, but actually bears responsibility for their deaths. She is more a Jezebel than a Helen.[39]

This denial of male culpability or responsibility must necessarily be discomforting for a modern reader, but whatever social and sexual attitudes it may betray, it is intended to make a point that lies outside the sphere of male–female relationships. Turning aside requires assent, but even this is an uninformed assent, given by those who

more persuasive than the latter, although I am not sure that the penalty is the key point. Being rather vague about the timing of her sacrificial feast, which might already have been consumed, the woman issues an invitation that makes her sound pious, but which may conceal an invitation to break the Law. C. V. Camp, 'What's So Strange about the Strange Woman?', in D. Jobling, P. L. Day, G. T. Sheppard (eds), *The Bible and the Politics of Exegesis: Essays in Honor of Norman K. Gottwald on his Sixty-fifth Birthday* (Cleveland, OH: Pilgrim Press, 1991), 17–32, especially 21–2; *Wise, Strange*, 45–7.

[38] Newsom, 'Woman', sees the house as symbolic of the womb (149), and argues that the presentation here exposes 'the monstrous, mythic dimension of the strange woman. She is not just a woman who has seduced a simple-minded young man. She is a predator who has slain multitudes. Indeed, her vagina is the gate of Sheol. Her womb, death itself' (156). I think the house represents something less precise than a womb, but it does seem clear that the woman becomes archetype rather than type in the father's warning.

[39] I think Camp goes too far, however, in suggesting that the woman is a 'quasi-human, quasi-mythical incarnation of evil', or that the language of death 'is transformed in Proverbs to articulate a force—defined here as female—that begins to split the religious cosmos into a dualistic moral system'; 'What's so Strange', 30–1; *Wise, Strange*, 66. If the poetry has any such mythical significance, it is hardly to be understood through anachronistic conceptualizations of good and evil, and Camp goes on, essentially, to lift the character out of the text altogether. We might compare, however, the view of Philip Nel in his very different study, *The Structure and Ethos of the Wisdom Admonitions in Proverbs* (BZAW 158; Berlin and New York: de Gruyter, 1982), 120, that 'the *zārâ* has become symbolized evil... The loose-living Israelite woman represents a manifestation of the subtle and seductive method by which evil lures one into its power... Thus, the wisdom literature represents evil as the reality opposed to wisdom.'

lack the ability to recognize their danger. Humans are portrayed in Proverbs 1–9 as malleable creatures, capable of being shaped for good or bad, but dependent on outside influence to set them on their course: to resist the bad, they must first embrace the good. The presentation of the foreign woman, drawing as it does on existing notions of corruption into apostasy by such women, illustrates the downfall of men through reference to associated potential fates—the alienation of what is one's own, or the penalty for adultery—but it also stands for all the ruinous fates that can await humans who unwittingly choose the bad. In chapter 7, indeed, the narrative finishes without telling us what actually happens to the youth. Is he lost to his community? Caught by an angry husband? Choked on cinnamon? We are offered no answer, because the details of what follows are irrelevant: to accept her invitation is enough to seal one's fate.

F. The Foreign Woman and the Other 'Bad' Characters

Before leaving the subject of the foreign woman, it is worth mentioning briefly the other characters who appear on her side. First there are the sinners, who only appear directly in the first section of the work, 1: 8–19. Their role, both as counterparts to Wisdom and as destroyers of the unwary, is subsequently displaced by that of the woman. So despite the prominence accorded them by their position at the beginning of Proverbs 1–9, they seem to represent a false start or cul-de-sac, and the term used to describe them, חטאים, has no apparent resonance or associations beyond the obvious.

In fact, their presence is probably to be explained by the fact that the presentation of these characters does differ in some important respects from that of the foreign woman: what they offer is more tempting, but they offer it less temptingly. Although they entice or deceive, the verb used for their doing so (פתה) is not used of the woman, and we are offered no details about smooth lips or persuasive speech. The sinners do, however, offer something much better than sex, promising not only to play the role of Sheol, rather than be its victim, but also to attain the sort of wealth that Wisdom is later to promise in chapter 8 (1: 13, cf. 8: 18, 21). Where the emphasis with the foreign woman is on her own power to seduce, the emphasis here is on the tempting prospect of security and wealth without work, things that the woman could not promise. For the first opponents to Wisdom, then, the book introduces characters who are more general, and who can put a stronger case for sinning than can the foreign woman, whose associations are, in this respect, a limiting factor.[40]

In the light of this, it is particularly interesting to note that in the closing scenario of the work, we also find a bad character who is, nominally at least, distinct from the foreign woman. We have already examined the evidence for connecting Folly, or 'the woman of follies', in 9: 13–18 with the foreign woman, but it is also important to note the differences. For a start, this character is presented more directly as a counterpart to Wisdom—apparently a personification rather than a type. Further, no mention is made of her persuasiveness, which was the key attribute of the foreign woman, and her invitation in 9: 17 is a strange one, seeming to stress that the pleasure of her meal derives from its very wrongness. Perhaps the most telling difference, however, lies in the contrast between Wisdom's busy preparations, in 9: 1–2, and the woman's stolen food. This picks up nothing in the material about the foreign woman, whose vices do not explicitly include laziness or theft. It does hark back, however, to the sinners of chapter 1, who also offer, through theft, a deadly shortcut to the rewards promised by Wisdom.

We might say, then, that Proverbs 1–9 provides a frame, or at least bookends, for the central material in which the foreign woman acts as Wisdom's counterpart. Chapters 1 and 9 use bad characters who are linked to the foreign woman, and who play a similar role, but who put across a rather different point. While the material on the foreign woman emphasizes above all the perils of her plausibility and seductiveness, the first and last chapters address, more generally, the problem that sin and folly promise much the same as Wisdom, and without the work.

---

[40] Christl Maier looks at it in a slightly different way: 'While the male "outsider" transgresses conventional behaviour in economic matters, the female "outsider" transgresses the sexual mores that are an important criterion for boundaries and social organizations'; 'Conflicting Attractions: Parental Wisdom and the "Strange Woman" in Proverbs 1–9', in Brenner, *Feminist Companion*, 92–108, especially 104.

2. STRAYING FROM THE PATH

We observed much earlier that, in addition to its employment of characters like the foreign woman, Proverbs 1–9 lays considerable emphasis on a set of images related to ways and paths. Particular metaphorical ways are described, especially in chapter 4, but there is also a concern with ideas of walking straight ahead or turning aside, and these are integrated, to some extent, with the portrayals of characters, and the settings of their speeches. We rejected the suggestion that this is underpinned by a simple, bipolar notion of a 'good path' and a 'bad path', seeing instead a more complicated image of paths as the directions taken by individuals.

A. Paths in Foreign Instructions

If it is difficult to find many close analogies to the foreign woman in other instructions, the same cannot be said of the path imagery.[41] Because ways and paths often have a metaphorical significance in Egyptian, there are various Egyptian instructions that use the terms, and sometimes the resemblance to ideas in Proverbs 1–9 is quite striking: a passage of instruction on Papyrus Chester Beatty IV, for instance, has the writer claim to be teaching about the *wзt n ꜥnḫ*, the 'way of life', and to be setting his hearer upon a path without trouble.[42] Among other things, this path offers protection, is a good and joyous light, and is shade without heat; to follow the

---

[41] On the 'way of life' motif in Egypt, see especially B. Couroyer, 'Le Chemin de vie en Egypte et en Israël', *RB* 56 (1949), 412–32, and the fuller study by D. Devauchelle, 'Le Chemin de vie dans l'Egypte ancienne', in R. Lebrun (ed.), *Sagesses de l'Orient ancien et chrétien: la voie de vie et la conduite spirituelle chez les peuples et dans les littératures de l'Orient Chrétien. Conférences IROC 1991–1992* (Uer de Théologie et de Sciences Religieuses Institut Catholique de Paris. Sciences Théologiques & Religieuses 2; Paris: Beauchesne, 1993), 91–122. See also Zehnder, *Wegmetaphorik*, 208–92.

[42] *Verso* col. 6 ll. 4 ff. Devauchelle, 'Le Chemin de vie', 101, notes similar claims in an inscription from Amarna and a royal decree by Horemheb. The prologue to the instruction of Amennakhte also refers to 'sayings for the way of life'; Posener has suggested that this prologue (the only part extant, if there was ever more) should be associated with Pap. Chester Beatty IV; cf. G. Posener, 'L'Exorde de l'instruction éducative d'Amennakhte (Recherches littéraires, v)', *RdE* 10 (1955), 61–72.

teaching will bring personal recognition and, ultimately, access to the afterlife. In the Demotic Papyrus Insinger, moreover, although the term *myt*, 'path', is often simply equivalent to 'teaching', there seems also to be some reference to a personal way that is the way of the god, or along which the individual may be guided by the god.[43]

Although path imagery is quite widespread in Egyptian literature, such specific references are relatively uncommon in the Egyptian instructions, and are confined to quite late texts. Furthermore, other references to paths, even in the New Kingdom, sometimes employ the imagery in a rather different way. The *Instruction of Amenemope*, for example, uses the term *mit n ꜥnḫ*, 'path of life', in connection with the commutation of debt: one will find it a 'path of life' to reduce the debt of a poor man.[44] Here the phrase seems to connote little more than a source of personal happiness, and the path is identified with the consequences of a single action. In the introduction to that same work, guidance on 'paths of life' is listed among the purposes of the instruction, and again associated with specific actions leading to general well-being.[45]

It would be quite possible, then, to speculate that Egyptian instructions might have provided inspiration for the path imagery in Proverbs 1–9, even if the closest parallels are in texts that the Proverbs author is unlikely to have known, and even if there is no overall consistency in the Egyptian usage. While it is also conceivable, moreover, that instructions from elsewhere might have played some part, the evidence is very slender: no similar concept is prominent in the Mesopotamian works,[46] although there is a single, somewhat dubious reference in the Aramaic *Ahiqar*.[47] It is very doubtful, however, that we need to resort to foreign texts at all, when there is a more obvious source far closer to home: path imagery is so very common in other Hebrew literature that it seems impossible to believe that our writer could have overlooked it or avoided its influence.

---

[43] The references are noted in Devauchelle, 'Le Chemin de vie', 111.

[44] Col. XVI, ll. 5–10.

[45] Col. I l. 7.

[46] On its use in Mesopotamian literature more generally, see Zehnder, *Wegmetaphorik*, 182–93.

[47] See Zehnder, *Wegmetaphorik*, 206–7.

B. Path Imagery in Hebrew Literature

Although the Hebrew דרך, 'way', is often used literally to describe a road or route, it is also used by most of the biblical writers to refer to human behaviour, either in terms of specific actions, or, more commonly, in terms of a general pattern of behaviour. Many texts stress, correspondingly, that individuals will be judged according to their ways. By extension, perhaps, this sometimes leads to a use of 'ways' to connote a person's circumstances, so that their ways may be said to prosper or be brought to ruin. It also, though, enables a generalization of the concept, so that a single way, or pattern of behaviour, can be said to characterize whole groups, and it is possible to 'walk in the way' of others by imitating what they do.

This image is most famously a common characteristic in the historical works of both the Deuteronomistic historian and the Chronicler, who often classify (and judge) kings according to which earlier king they have imitated: Josiah, for instance, is praised because he 'walked wholly in the way of his ancestor David, and he did not turn aside to the right or left' (2 Kgs. 22: 2; cf. 2 Chron. 34: 2). Implicit in such language is the idea that there are good and bad ways to be followed: although each individual's way is simply a generalization of their own behaviour, it may be aligned with exemplary, or almost abstract ways. The associated vocabulary involves 'walking', 'following', and other terms that suggest that the metaphorical character of the 'way' continued to be recognized, above and beyond its reduction to a common idiom.

Given such usage, it is not surprising that the idea of a path or way came to have very specific religious and moral connotations in some Hebrew literature. Probably from the notion of good and bad ways, either of which might be imitated, there arises the image of a single path approved by YHWH, which is influential on Deuteronomy's expression of proper behaviour: 'You must take care to act as YHWH your God has commanded you, and must not turn aside to the right or the left. It is wholly in the way which YHWH your God has commanded that you must walk, so that you may survive, prosper and live long in the land which you shall own' (Deut. 5: 32–3).[48] This

---

[48] See also, for example, Deut. 8: 6; 11: 22; 19: 9; 26: 17; 28: 9; 30: 16.

way is explicitly identified with the conditions of the covenant—in other words, with the Law. To turn off this path is to break the conditions of the covenant, but apostasy, more specifically, can be expressed in terms of turning aside to follow other gods (e.g. Deut. 11: 28), while the crime of the false visionary in Deuteronomy 13 is to push the people off the proper path (Deut. 13: 6 [ET, 5]). Deuteronomy's use of the metaphor, then, has key elements of the more explicit imagery that we find in Proverbs 1–9: a path that leads to survival and prosperity, from which one must not turn aside, and deviations from that path to follow others.[49] It is especially striking to note that Deuteronomy's warning against the foreign women of the land is expressed using this language in Deut. 7: 4.

It is hardly surprising that the Deuteronomic association between 'way' and 'law' persists into the Deuteronomistic history, which furnishes many examples,[50] but it is interesting to find a similar concept in other works that were less directly inspired by Deuteronomy. When Job, for instance, declares that he has followed in God's footsteps, and kept God's way without turning aside, he is referring explicitly to the divine commandments (Job 23: 10–12), and it is the wicked who reject God's ways in Job 21: 14 and 34: 27. The idea is also important in the Isaianic corpus,[51] and here it may have played a role in the development of an eschatological concept: Is. 30: 21 promises supernatural guidance along the proper way, while 35: 8 promises a 'holy way', which is probably to be linked to the level paths of 40: 3 and elsewhere. Among the other prophetic books, Jeremiah, Micah, Zechariah, and Malachi all associate the way of Yahweh with the Law,[52] and the idea is common in Hebrew psalmody.[53] Indeed, so familiar does the concept seem to have become in the post-exilic period, that Is. 30: 11, 21; Job 31: 7; and Mal. 2: 8 all use 'the way', without further qualification, to mean the

---

[49] It seems clear in passages such as 17: 20 and 28: 14, incidentally, that the path imagery, and the identification of the path with the divine commandments, is present in Deuteronomy even where there is no explicit mention of the path itself.

[50] See Josh. 22: 5; Judg. 2: 22; 1 Kgs. 2: 3; 3: 14; 8: 58; 11: 33, 38; 2 Kgs. 21: 22. The concept also appears in the Chronicler's work: cf. 2 Chron. 6: 16, 27.

[51] See, for example, Is. 2: 3 (cf. Mic. 4: 2); 30: 11; 42: 24.

[52] See Jer. 2: 17; 5: 4–5; 7: 23; Mic. 4: 2; Zech. 3: 7; Mal. 2: 8.

[53] See, e.g. Ps. 18: 22–3 (ET, 21–2); 119: 1, 14, 33. Note also 2 Sam. 22: 22–3.

Law.[54] This absolute usage is also found occasionally in the Qumran texts, which, like much other post-biblical Jewish literature, regularly associate the divine way with the Law.[55] In a similar fashion, terms for 'way' or 'path' may themselves disappear in favour of expressions that assume knowledge of the theme; Lev. 26: 3, for instance, speaks simply of 'walking in my statutes'.[56]

It seems clear, then, that the idea of a divine way was well-known in Jewish literature of the exilic and post-exilic periods, and that this way was strongly identified with the Law, as the route that one should follow. This route ensures divine protection, and the prosperity of one's own journey. Correspondingly, though, one might ignore or 'turn aside' from the way, becoming unfaithful to Yahweh and disobedient to the Law.[57] This may be punishable in itself: Elihu, for instance, declares that God will strike down the wicked for their wickedness 'because they turned aside from following him and ignored all of his ways' (Job 34: 26–7). The penalty may more simply be, however, in the character of the other ways in which one then walks: such ways no longer enjoy divine guidance and illumination, but may be dark, treacherous, and crooked.[58]

C. Teaching and the Way

I suggested in the last chapter that the terminology used of teaching and instruction would have had strong associations with the Law for

---

[54] In fact, Gunnar Östborn, *TŌRĀ in the Old Testament: A Semantic Study* (Lund: Ohlssons, 1945), argues that 'there are grounds for regarding "showing the way" as a connotation originally inherent in תורה' (169), rather than an evolved sense.

[55] Path imagery at Qumran, of course, develops in a variety of other ways, especially within the sectarian literature; see, e.g. R. C. Van Leeuwen, 'Scribal Wisdom and a Biblical Proverb at Qumran', *DSD* 4 (1997), 255–64.

[56] Cf. Exod. 16: 4; Lev. 18: 3–4; 20: 23; Deut. 13: 4; 2 Chron. 6: 16; 34: 31; Neh. 5: 9; Ps. 78: 10; 89: 31 (ET, 30); 119: 1; Jer. 32: 23; 44: 23; Ezek. 11: 20; 20: 13, 16, 18, 19, 21; 36: 27.

[57] For turning aside as disobedience to the Law, see, e.g. 2 Sam. 22: 23; 2 Kgs. 18: 6; Ps. 119: 102; Dan. 9: 5; Mal. 3: 7. Perhaps because fidelity to Yahweh is strongly associated with obedience to the covenant law in Deuteronomic thought, the 'turning aside' of the people in Deuteronomy, and some other passages, is used of apostasy in particular; cf., for instance, Deut. 9: 16; 11: 16.

[58] See 1 Sam. 2: 9; Job 5: 14 (perhaps recalling Deut. 28: 29); 12: 25; 18: 5–11; 24: 13–17; Ps. 125: 5; Prov. 21: 8; Qoh. 2: 14; Is. 59: 8–10; Jer. 23: 12.

Jewish readers of Proverbs 1–9, and it is surely the case that the same would have been true of the work's path imagery. Indeed, the right way—that is to say, the way approved by God—is itself depicted in various biblical passages as something to be taught,[59] and so is a proper subject for instruction. When the father, in 4: 10–19, claims to have taught a way free of obstacles, and urges his son to keep hold of the teaching, so as to avoid the dark and treacherous path of the wicked, all of this is strongly evocative of language and ideas used frequently in Jewish literature to describe learning and keeping the Law.

We also noted, in the last chapter, that Prov. 3: 11–12 draws on a Deuteronomic idea of God as father and teacher. This is an idea found frequently in connection with the image of 'the way', and Ps. 25: 8–10, for instance, has God instructing, teaching and leading in his way. Since, indeed, it is more often than not God who is asked for, or who offers such teaching, we may reasonably ask whether that is, perhaps, what Proverbs 1–9 itself has in mind. A simple identification of the father with God, however, seems highly unlikely. Not only do we have to reckon with references to teaching by the mother and by the father's father, but we also find the father looking out of his window on to the town in 7: 6: it would require some very fancy footwork to explain all that in divine terms. That said, the introduction of the mother and of the father's father, like the switch to the voice of Wisdom in the appeal of 8: 32, do show that Proverbs 1–9 envisages instruction as something more than just the teaching by a father. Accordingly, 3: 11–12 is probably to be taken in the context of an understanding that instruction has more than a single source or author. This poses no obstacle to association with the Law, which is to be taught to individuals variously by parents or by God (and can additionally be taught to the people *en masse*).

D. Conclusions on 'the Way'

The path imagery in Proverbs 1–9 has points of contact with motifs to be found in Egyptian instructions, but there is a striking and

---

[59] See Exod. 18: 20; 1 Sam. 12: 23; 1 Kgs. 8: 36 (= 2 Chron. 6: 27); Pss. 25: 8–9, 12; 27: 11; 32: 8; 86: 11; 119: 33; 143: 8; Is. 48: 17. The language, incidentally, is picked up in the New Testament gospels: see Matt. 22: 16; Mk. 12: 14; Lk. 20: 21; cf. also Acts 18: 25.

detailed resemblance also to imagery found across much of the biblical literature, which is hardly likely to have been ignored by a contemporary Jewish readership. That biblical imagery embraces the concept of a way set by God, from which one must not deviate, and it is strongly associated with ideas of the Law. In later texts, at least, the Law can be referred to as 'the way', while the basic path imagery becomes so familiar that subsidiary ideas of walking or turning aside can be used by themselves of obedience and disobedience. The way approved by God can also be taught, and the idea of instruction on the subject in Proverbs 1–9 is quite compatible with common biblical usage.

3. GENERAL CONCLUSIONS

Our examination of the foreign woman and the path imagery in this chapter has done nothing to contradict the conclusions about wisdom and instruction that I presented in the last. Rather, it has tended to confirm that the sources of the images and allusions in Proverbs 1–9 are to be sought primarily in Jewish tradition, rather than external sources. As an archetype for the corruption of the unwary, the foreign woman can trace her roots back to a biblical motif concerning the seduction of Israelites into apostasy, which had itself been given a new prominence in the post-exilic debate about intermarriage. The path imagery, while less specific and similar in some respects to certain Egyptian expressions, accords closely with a well-established biblical language used of individual behaviour and of the Law.

The interrelationship of these elements in Proverbs 1–9 is not without its problems, and the personification of wisdom involves some particular difficulties. Put together, though, they present a fairly coherent message. Wisdom is an attribute that permits one to understand the divine will, and to discern right from wrong, thus enabling prosperity and long life through divine favour; its validity comes from its association with God, and it is a divine gift. This attribute is attained through the internalization—that is, the binding to oneself and writing on one's heart—of instruction. That necessary instruction is not named or detailed exhaustively in the work, but the terminology used of it is much the same as that associated with the Jewish Law, a connection that is unlikely to have escaped a contemporary Jewish audience, and the epitome in Prov. 3 is compatible with such an understanding.

Those who have not received instruction are vulnerable to the allure of immediate gratification, or of easier paths to prosperity, since they do not recognize the dangers posed by them. This allure is typified, above all, in the figure of the foreign woman, who evokes in her person motifs of apostasy and corruption, and who persuades and seduces, but inevitably destroys. Protection against her, or others like her, is a primary function of instruction, and an implicit contrast between her and personified Wisdom transmutes eventually into a more explicit contest between Wisdom and Folly, each seeking to attract the simple to their table. Wisdom and instruction, then, are not mere duties, or even just enhancements to one's well-being, but necessities in a dangerous world.

6

The Significance of Proverbs 1–9

1. DATE AND PLACE OF COMPOSITION

Since it is clearly known to Ben Sira, whose own work was probably composed in the early second century BCE, Proverbs 1–9 cannot have been composed later than that date. It is difficult to set a *terminus ad quem* earlier than this; I think it probable that we may, at least, regard Proverbs 1–9 as earlier than the book of Job, but the problems of dating Job itself make this a less useful observation than it may sound.[1] As regards the *terminus a quo*, I do not believe there to be any persuasive grounds for taking the composition to be genuinely Solomonic, although that view is still defended in some quarters. If the post-exilic debate about foreign wives did help to shape its portrayal of the foreign woman, then Proverbs 1–9 is unlikely to have been composed earlier than that issue became a concern,[2]

---

[1] I base that suggestion not on any presupposition that sceptical literature must necessarily be later—which would be unsustainable given the Near Eastern antecedents of both works—but on the probability that Job 15: 7–9 and 40: 19 are referring to Prov. 8: 25 and 8: 22 respectively, the former sarcastically. I think it is also likely that the poem in Job 28 is a response to the ideas about wisdom in Prov. 1–9, although that is not demonstrable. Robert, 'Les Attaches,' 1935, 511, thinks that Job 5: 17 alludes to Prov. 3: 11–12.

[2] Beyond the obvious fact that it can be no earlier than the late sixth century BCE, the date of that debate is, arguably, a question in itself. I am inclined to share the serious reservations of some scholars about the historicity of much that is depicted in the books of Nehemiah and, especially, Ezra; Lester Grabbe is surely right to demand that 'we should cease to write the history of Judah in the first part of the Persian period by lightly paraphrasing the book of Ezra'. See L. Grabbe, 'Reconstructing History from the Book of Ezra', in P. R. Davies (ed.), *Second Temple Studies*, vol. 1: *Persian Period* (JSOTS 117; Sheffield: Sheffield Academic Press, 1991), 98–106, especially 105; also his *Ezra-Nehemiah* (London and New York: Routledge, 1998). It seems probable that intermarriage was a concern in the post-exilic period, but the

although, conceivably, the motif might have been derived directly from Deuteronomy or the Deuteronomistic History. Even if we accept a date after the Return, however, that still leaves a period of some three centuries, from roughly 500–200 BCE, in which the work could be placed.[3] Our relative ignorance about the development of Jewish thought in this period, combined with the lack of historical references in the text, make it difficult to be more precise, and while there is some scope for the investigation of links with other texts at the level of vocabulary and incidental detail, individual cases are of limited value.[4] Consequently, attempts to narrow the range have tended to rest on supposed polemic features, or concerns with a specific situation. It seems far from obvious, however, that Proverbs 1–9 has any such concerns, and it is the very root of our problem, perhaps, that the author has succeeded all too well in making his message timeless.[5] It is no easier to be sure of the place of

nature of the sources makes it difficult to pin down a date, or to disentangle the real circumstances not just from attempts to link them to the past, but from efforts to link Ezra with Nehemiah and to associate later interests with them both.

[3] A similar range, 'between the beginning of the sixth century BCE and the end of the third century BCE—most likely sometime in the Persian period', is suggested by Yoder, *Wisdom*, 38, on the basis of a detailed linguistic and orthographic study. The orthographic part of this is problematic, being based on the highly optimistic assumption that 'MT Proverbs 1–9 and 31: 10–31 accurately reflect the texts' original orthography' (35); it is also a shame that the two sections of Proverbs are considered together, it being by no means certain that they were composed around the same time, whatever their relationship in the editorial scheme (cf. Camp, *Wisdom and the Feminine*, 186–91). Nevertheless, the linguistic evidence adduced is suggestive.

[4] We might note, for example, that 8: 27 shares with Is. 40: 22 the notion of dry land separated from water as a חוג, but that does us little good if we cannot determine when the idea arose or was supplanted. Any such approach requires a substantial accumulation of evidence, which nobody has yet provided, and which may simply be unavailable. Baumann, *Weisheitsgestalt*, 271–2, assembles a small number of parallels with Third Isaiah, conceding that they support no more than composition in the same general period, but even that is pushing the evidence further than it can really go. Robert, 'Les Attaches', lists many more or less convincing links with Deuteronomy, Jeremiah, and Isaiah, which he takes to indicate Proverbs 1–9's dependence on them (cf. 1935, 503); rather less persuasively, although very ingeniously, he argues that the *lack* of any apparent connections between Proverbs 1–9 and Zechariah 9–14, despite the fact that they presuppose the same milieu and problems, must mean that they were composed at around the same time, in the early 5th century BCE (1935, 517).

[5] On Maier's arguments for a particular social background in the late Achaemenid period (*Die 'Fremde Frau'*, 262–9), see Fox, *Proverbs 1–9*, 48. However, Fox's own

composition, although it is true that a town or city environment seems to be envisaged. The issue of 'foreignness', moreover, might be taken to suggest that this is a Palestinian, not a diaspora work.

2. THE CONTEXT OF PROVERBS 1–9

Given the problems of dating, it is easier in some respects to deal with the relationship between Proverbs 1–9 and those texts that are clearly later, than to try to establish its immediate background. More precisely, it is interesting to ask how close the work stands to those later texts that were seemingly aware of it. Given the quantity of such material now available, a general study of its influence would be a book in itself, but some important points arise even from a brief survey of the ways in which subsequent Jewish literature has picked up and understood key points of the imagery on which we have focused.

A. Ben Sira

Best known of the later compositions that draw on Proverbs 1–9 is the Wisdom of Ben Sira, and there are so many points of contact between the works that it is impossible to do justice to them all.[6] It is striking, though, that Ben Sira essentially cherry-picks the imagery of Proverbs 1–9, so that the bad characters, most notably the foreign woman, have disappeared (although there is an echo of her, perhaps, in the sayings of Sir. 9: 1–9 or 23: 22–6),[7] but we still find reference to the language of paths, and extensive use of personified Wisdom.[8]

---

attempt to date the work to the Hellenistic period (see especially 49, 199), rests on the very slender supposition that the term עדה ('congregation', cf. 5: 14) had fallen out of use, and was revived in a later period by both Ben Sira and Proverbs 1–9, alongside a perception that Prov. 8 must reflect a time when Judaism was under pressure to match foreign ideas.

[6] Some examples of parallels with Proverbs more generally are given on 43–4 of P. W. Skehan and A. A. Di Lella, *The Wisdom of Ben Sira* (AB 39; New York: Doubleday, 1987).

[7] See J. Marböck, *Weisheit im Wandel: Untersuchungen zur Weisheitstheologie bei Ben Sira*, 2nd ed. (BZAW 272; Berlin and New York: de Gruyter, 1999), 42 n. 3.

[8] On the presentation of wisdom in the book generally, cf. A. A. Di Lella, 'The Meaning of Wisdom in Ben Sira', in Perdue *et al.*, *In Search of Wisdom*, 133–48; Marböck, *Weisheit*.

Wisdom appears, indeed, at the very beginning of the work, which starts by declaring that 'All wisdom comes from the Lord, and is with him for ever' (1: 1). That claim is followed in 1: 2–10 by further assertions based loosely on Prov. 8, culminating in a statement that wisdom has been poured out upon creation by God, and supplied to those who love him. Wisdom is then associated strongly with fear of the Lord in 1: 11–20 (21, in the longer GII version), and 1: 20 picks up the image of wisdom as a tree used in Prov. 3: 18.[9] The material that follows in 1: 22–30 is less obviously coherent, but includes the explicit statement that wisdom will be provided by God to those who 'keep the commandments' (1: 26; cf. later 15: 1).

The personification in chapter 1 is erratic, betraying, perhaps, a consciousness of its poetic nature, but is carried through more consistently when Wisdom reappears in 4: 11–19. Drawing partly on Prov. 8: 32–6, this describes how Wisdom benefits her sons, loving those who love her, just as they are loved by God in turn. In 1: 16–19, however, we find ideas that are not familiar from Proverbs: if one obtains wisdom, one's descendants will continue to possess her; she will, at first, test and torment her followers, until she is confident in them; she will forsake any who goes astray. The idea of torment appears also in 6: 23–31, where the ornaments she offers (perhaps another reference to Proverbs 1–9) start out as fetters and restraints. In 14: 20–15: 8, however, we return to more recognizable derivatives from Proverbs 1–9, albeit with some interesting twists: 14: 22 suggests lying in wait like a hunter on Wisdom's paths, an apparent reversal of the imagery used by Proverbs, while 15: 2 associates her with the wife of one's youth, perhaps an interpretation of Prov. 5: 18–19 as a symbolic reference to Wisdom.

The climax of Ben Sira's presentation of wisdom comes in Sir. 24, a carefully structured speech by Wisdom herself.[10] She tells of how she emerged from God's mouth and covered the earth like a mist, gaining

---

[9] See also Sir. 24: 13–17. In Sir. 1: 20, the image is of a tree whose roots are fear of the Lord and whose branches are long life; since the preceding verses suggest that fear of the Lord is a product of wisdom, as in Proverbs 1–9, the imagery reflects the effects of wisdom, not its basis.

[10] The structure is discussed in P. W. Skehan, 'Structures in Poems on Wisdom: Proverbs 8 and Sirach 24', *CBQ* 41 (1979), 365–79, who takes it to be an adaptation of the structure in Prov. 8.

a foothold in every nation, before she was ordered to Israel. There she dwelt in Jerusalem, among the chosen people, ministering to God in the Temple and flourishing like a tree. Scented like spice and offering plentiful fruit, she now invites those who desire her to eat of that fruit, promising that none who accept her help will sin. In verses 23–9, the account switches to the third person, apparently interpreting what has preceded. 'All these things', it claims, 'are the book of the covenant of the highest God, the law which Moses commanded us, an inheritance for the congregations of Jacob' (24: 23). Like a river, it fills men with wisdom and understanding, and makes instruction shine out as a light. Wisdom will never be perfectly known: her thought is more abundant than the ocean, but also as unfathomable. When Wisdom herself resumes the speaking voice, in verse 30, she picks up this imagery: she started out intending no more than a water channel for her garden, but the channel became a river, and the river a sea. She now promises to make instruction shine out, to pour teaching out like prophecy, and to leave it for future generations.

After this, Wisdom disappears from sight until the autobiographical poem in Sir. 51: 13–22. Most of this is preserved in Hebrew in the Qumran text 11Q5 (see below), where it is an alphabetic acrostic poem with romantic, perhaps erotic overtones.[11] This appendix or addition to the book makes some use of motifs from Proverbs 1–9: having known her from his youth, and found much instruction by bending his ear to it, the speaker has walked a straight path, and has remained devoted to her. The tone is rather different, however, from the book's earlier material about Wisdom.

Overall, the portrayal of Wisdom in the book is broadly consistent with that found in Proverbs 1–9,[12] although it bears the marks of Ben Sira's own concerns and emphases. One significant interpretative question, however, concerns the relationship seen here between Wisdom and the Law. Di Lella reflects a common view when he states

---

[11] T. Muraoka, 'Sir. 51, 13–30: An Erotic Hymn to Wisdom?', *JSJ* 10 (1979), 166–78, gives a more measured account of the eroticism than does Sanders' edition.

[12] Cf. J. J. Collins, *Jewish Wisdom in the Hellenistic Age* (Edinburgh: T&T Clark, 1998), 54: 'this understanding of wisdom is firmly rooted in the tradition represented by Proverbs, and this tradition provides the primary intellectual context for Sirach's teaching'.

simply that 24: 23 'identifies Wisdom with the Law',[13] but we should be clear that this is, at most, identification 'with' and not identification 'as'.[14] Elsewhere, 6: 37 sees Wisdom as a reward for meditation on the Law, and 15: 1 as something gained by holding to it, while 19: 20 asserts that in all wisdom is a ποίησις ('handiwork', 'outworking') of the Law.[15] The view of Ben Sira seems to be that one achieves wisdom through internalization of the Law, as in Proverbs 1–9, but that Law is also, in some way, a product of wisdom. In any case, there seems to be no radical difference in this respect between the concepts of wisdom as associated explicitly with Law, in Ben Sira, and as associated with instruction, in Proverbs 1–9. Otherwise, of course, Ben Sira does seek to historicize wisdom much more, cementing it within a framework of national election and viewing it as something to be passed down the generations. He also views it as a discipline, much more than does Proverbs 1–9: Wisdom in Ben Sira tests and chastises. These changes are both, however, linked to broader concerns in the work, and there is nothing to suggest that they stem from a different interpretation of Proverbs 1–9.[16]

Such broader concerns also explain the absence of the foreign woman. Ben Sira is, in some important respects, an internationalist; he promotes Israel, but not at the cost of denigrating other peoples. It is noteworthy that, in 47: 19, he even changes the traditional, biblical understanding of Solomon's downfall: the wives are no

---

[13] Skehan and Di Lella, *Ben Sira*, 336.

[14] It hardly seems likely that ταῦτα πάντα could refer to Wisdom; in the lines that follow, moreover, the function of the Law is to fill humans with wisdom, not to *be* wisdom. The verse probably refers to the preceding description, in verses 19–22: Wisdom's sweet inheritance (v. 20) is the 'inheritance for the congregations of Jacob' (v. 23, citing Deut. 33: 4), and the idea is probably picked up again in v. 33, with its reference to Wisdom's teaching, left for future generations. The other texts listed as 'explicit evidence' for identification in E. J. Schnabel, *Law and Wisdom from Ben Sira to Paul: A Tradition Historical Enquiry into the Relation of Law, Wisdom and Ethics* (WUNT 2nd series 16; Tübingen: Mohr-Siebeck, 1985), 69–73, similarly show no more than close association, while some of the 'implicit' evidence (73–7) surely, in fact, distinguishes wisdom from Law. All becomes clear from the discussion of terminology (90–1), where Schnabel apparently feels that only a pedant would hold 'identification' to mean 'identification': he uses it as a synonym for 'correlation'.

[15] For similar usage, see e.g. Ps. 18: 2 LXX (=MT 19: 2).

[16] McKinlay, *Gendering*, chapter 6, notes also that the effect of Ben Sira's overall presentation is to subsume feminine Wisdom within the model provided by the male ancestors.

longer foreign, and the problem is a sort of sexual subjugation, not apostasy.[17] More generally, though, Ben Sira has no interest in incorporating from Proverbs 1–9 the issues of temptation and seduction into sin. Humans do have a choice, but it is presented in 15: 11–20 as a choice without coercion: Ben Sira is anxious to emphasize human free will, where Proverbs 1–9 presents humans as vulnerable and malleable.

In short, then, Ben Sira clearly uses Proverbs 1–9 selectively, to suit his own thematic and generic perspectives, but where he does adopt such motifs as personified wisdom, he shows a perception that he is dealing with a literary, poetic personification, and seems to understand the material in a way similar to that which we have outlined.

B. Texts from Qumran

Personified Wisdom features also in several works discovered at Qumran,[18] most famously in 4Q185 (4QSapiental Work),[19] which uses brief parental appeals to introduce its sections,[20] probably in imitation of Proverbs 1–9. In ii: 1–2, 4 this text exhorts seeking out a way to life, and speaks of paths to be avoided or trodden (the latter apparently associated with paths laid down for Jacob and Isaac). Much of the second column, however, concerns something that has been given to Israel by God; the reference in ii: 11 to God killing those

---

[17] Camp, *Wise, Strange*, 63 n. 27 takes this rather differently, as demonstrating 'the conflation of sexual and national "strangeness"'.

[18] For a recent survey of the texts particularly relevant to personified Wisdom and the wicked woman, which concludes, *inter alia*, that none of those texts are likely to be sectarian, see B. G. Wright III, 'Wisdom and Women at Qumran', *DSD* 11 (2004), 240–61; cf. A. S. van der Woude, 'Wisdom at Qumran', in Day *et al.*, *Wisdom in Ancient Israel*, 244–56; Schnabel, *Law and Wisdom*, 166–226. Note Harrington's caveats about the difficulties of determining where wisdom is actually personified in some of these texts, D. J. Harrington, 'Ten Reasons Why the Qumran Wisdom Texts are Important', *DSD* 4 (1997), 245–54, especially 252.

[19] Published in J. M. Allegro, *Qumrân Cave 4. I (4Q158–4Q186)* (DJD 5; Oxford: Clarendon Press, 1968), 85–7. See also J. Strugnell, 'Notes en marge du volume V des "Discoveries in the Judaean Desert of Jordan"', *RevQ* 7 (1970), 163–276, especially 269–73; F. G. Martínez and E. J. C. Tigchelaar (eds), *The Dead Sea Scrolls Study Edition*, paperback edition (Leiden: Brill and Grand Rapids, MI: Eerdmans, 2000), vol. 1, 378–81; D. J. Harrington, *Wisdom Texts from Qumran* (The Literature of the Dead Sea Scrolls; London and New York: Routledge, 1996), 35–9.

[20] See Harrington, *Wisdom Texts*, 37.

who hate his wisdom suggests that this gift is personified Wisdom, and this is confirmed by the language that follows: she must be sought, found, and held; with her is long life, health, and happiness. The text goes on to make clear that she was given to a man's ancestors, will be inherited by him, and will be passed on to his children, so that the connections with nation and law are fairly explicit, and reminiscent of the ideas in Ben Sira.

Two of the texts on 11Q5 (11QPsalms[a]) refer to personified Wisdom.[21] One, which was already known in Syriac (xviii. 1–16: 'Psalm 154'), claims that wisdom has been given to humans in order to make known God's glory, greatness, and power. Her voice is heard from the gates of the righteous, her song from the assembly of the pious, and she is the topic of conversation at their gatherings, where they meditate on the Law. The second corresponds to Sirach 51: 13–19, part of the first-person description of a quest for Wisdom.

In 4Q525 (4QBeatitudes) fragment 2 col. ii, a series of macarisms relates the happiness of those who cling to Wisdom's statutes rather than the paths of iniquity, who rejoice in her rather than bragging[22] in those paths, and who seek her with pure hands, not deceitfully.[23] The last in the series is much longer, recounting the happiness of the man who attains Wisdom, walks according to God's Law, and remains constant to her. He always meditates on her, is apparently protected thereby from walking in the ways of iniquity, and is elevated by her. Interestingly, this material is followed by a parental appeal, and another is found on fragment 14, suggesting that appeals may also have been used to structure this work. The reader is subsequently, in fragment 5,[24] warned not to abandon their inheritance to 'the children of the foreigner', advice that is linked to keeping Wisdom's ways and walking in her statutes.[25]

---

[21] J. A. Sanders, *The Psalms Scrolls of Qumrân Cave 11 (11QPs ᵃ)* (DJD 4; Oxford: Clarendon Press, 1965); Martínez & Tigchelaar, *Dead Sea Scrolls*, vol. 2, 1172–9; Harrington, *Wisdom Texts*, 26–30.

[22] יביעו, literally 'pour out', but cf. Ps. 94: 4; Prov. 15: 28.

[23] E. Puech, *Qumrân Grotte 4. XVIII. Textes Hébreux (4Q521–4Q528, 4Q576–4Q579)* (DJD 25; Oxford: Clarendon Press, 1998), 115–78; Martínez and Tigchelaar, *Dead Sea Scrolls*, vol. 2, 1052–9; Harrington, *Wisdom Texts*, 66–70.

[24] Fragment 4 in works earlier than Puech's edition.

[25] There are many other references in this text that suggest a direct knowledge of Proverbs 1–9, not least its opening (Frag. 1: 2–3), which imitates Prov. 1: 4–6.

If this last reference is a reminiscence of Proverbs 5, then the foreign woman may not have become wholly divorced from personified Wisdom. However, when we do find a clear reference to her at Qumran, in 4Q184 (4QWiles of the Wicked Woman), she appears by herself—although this may just be because we only have one portion from what may have been a rather longer work.[26] The fragmentary state of the text also robs us of a name for the figure, so we cannot know whether she was actually called 'foreign' here.[27] That we are dealing with a characterization derived from Proverbs 1–9 seems beyond doubt, however, and the text shows a clear understanding of the woman's role in that work: she is a trap, 'the beginning of all the ways of iniquity' (1: 8) whose paths lead astray to iniquity, and a deadly seducer whose house is no more than a front for Sheol. In this text, she lies in ambush not for the uninstructed, but for the righteous and upright. She seeks to separate them from the Law, and 'to turn aside their steps from the ways of righteousness' (1: 16). This change of target reflects a shift in ideas also, since righteousness is evidently no longer its own protection, but the figure from Proverbs has clearly been interpreted accurately, as a corrupter, not a mere prostitute or adulteress.[28]

It would be possible to discuss many other possible links between Proverbs 1–9 and materials found at Qumran, especially with respect to the language of ways and paths, but it is generally difficult to establish the nature and closeness of such broader connections. From the explicit personifications of wisdom, the portrayal of the wicked woman and, indeed, the use of parental appeals, it is clear not only

---

[26] J. M. Allegro, 'The Wiles of the Wicked Woman, a Sapiental Work from Qumran's Fourth Cave', *PEQ* 96 (1964), 53–5; Allegro, *Qumrân Cave 4*, 82–5; Strugnell, 'Notes', 263–8; Martínez and Tigchelaar, *Dead Sea Scrolls*, vol. 1, 376–7; Harrington, *Wisdom Texts*, 31–5.

[27] The common name for her, 'Lady Folly', is based on Prov. 9; it has no particular justification in this text, although she is said, in the first line, to speak folly.

[28] R. D. Moore, 'Personification of the Seduction of Evil: "The Wiles of the Wicked Woman"', *RevQ* 10 (1981), 505–19, argues a detailed defence of the text being a 'generalized reflection on the character of evil', against early attempts to see a polemic against a specific group, symbolized by the woman. We need hardly identify her, incidentally, with later presentations of demonic figures, as does S. W. Crawford, 'Lady Wisdom and Dame Folly at Qumran', *DSD* 5 (1998), 355–66, especially 361. See also J. M. Baumgarten, 'On the Nature of the Seductress in 4Q184', *RevQ* 15 (1991), 133–43.

that Proverbs 1–9 was influential upon some of the texts found here, but that they understood certain key elements in much the way that we have taken to be their original meaning. As in Ben Sira, the associations of wisdom with the Law are made more explicit than in Proverbs, and no clear trace remains of the antithetical presentations of Wisdom and the woman.[29] Once again, then, later writers have selected and developed key elements from Proverbs 1–9, but in doing so have shown themselves to understand the intended significance of those elements.

C. Wisdom of Solomon

The very extensive materials in Wisdom of Solomon defy brief summary, but the influence of Proverbs 1–9 is discernible at various points, especially in its portrayal of wisdom.[30] So, for instance, 6: 12–20 presents not only a personified figure, but one who goes about seeking those worthy of her, appearing to them in their paths (indeed, they do not even have to wait at her gates, as in Prov. 8: 34— she comes to theirs). In the same passage, she is associated with true desire for instruction, and heeding her laws brings imperishability and closeness to God (cf. also 7: 14). Wisdom, we are told later in 9: 9, is with God, having been present at the creation, so that she understands what pleases him, and what is right according to his commandments. If these and other descriptions reflect clear dependence on and understanding of Proverbs 1–9, however, there is much in the book that seems very different.

Wisdom of Solomon does not go down the same path as Ben Sira, building on the association of wisdom with the Law,[31] but presents wisdom (in 7: 22–8: 1) as a vapour, or exhalation of God, a reflection of what he does, a single entity that can, nevertheless, influence many

---

[29] This may, of course, be just an accident of preservation in the manuscripts. Occasional phrases in the more fragmentary sections of 4Q525 suggest that a figure like the foreign woman might originally have appeared there; cf. especially frag. 16.

[30] See D. Winston, 'Wisdom in the Wisdom of Solomon', in Perdue *et al.*, *In Search of Wisdom*, 149–64; Skehan, *Studies*, 172–91.

[31] Cf. Collins, *Jewish Wisdom*, 196; Schnabel, *Law and Wisdom*, 129–34, especially 134.

things and be in many souls. Furthermore, the protection that wisdom offers, by teaching humans how to please God (cf. 9: 18),[32] is exemplified, especially in chapters 10 and 11, by (strangely an- onymized) examples drawn from the biblical accounts of history. The effect of all this is to draw wisdom firmly into the realm of divine action: it is a way in which God saves humans from himself by showing them what he requires. This is not so very different from the ideas in Proverbs 1–9, but a very different feel is given, not only by the historical references, but also by the emphasis upon wisdom as something that emanates from the divine.

More generally, Wisdom of Solomon takes over elements of the path imagery, including descriptive details (e.g. 5: 6–7; 17: 1), but none of the foreign woman material; indeed, the whole theme of seduction and choice seems to be absent. This may be explained in large part by the substitution of a world view in which the wicked, belonging to the side of the devil (2: 24) and in a relationship with death (1: 16), are motivated by a false perception that human exist- ence is transient and without meaning. They do not try to convert the righteous, so much as to attack and torment them. God, on the other hand, works to save and correct the unrighteous, even the ancient peoples of the land, whose wickedness is congenital (12: 3–11). There is little space here for the simpler and starker scheme of Proverbs 1–9.

Wisdom of Solomon, then, works to integrate important motifs from Proverbs 1–9 into its own, very different perception of the world, which has been influenced not only by changing Jewish beliefs, but, in all probability, by Hellenistic philosophical ideas. In doing so, it draws wisdom not further into the realm of Law and nation, like Ben Sira, but into a more universalist picture of a God who works to save humans. Despite these differences, its handling of material from Proverbs 1–9 seems to reflect a clear understanding of that work's concept of wisdom, as something that saves individuals through imparting knowledge of the divine will.

---

[32] On the links between this function of wisdom and Philo's Logos, see Collins, *Jewish Wisdom*, 201–2, and on Philo himself and Proverbs, J. Laporte, 'Philo in the Tradition of Biblical Wisdom Literature', in R. L. Wilken (ed.), *Aspects of Wisdom in Judaism and Early Christianity* (University of Notre Dame Center for the Study of Judaism and Christianity in Antiquity 1; Notre Dame, IN: University of Notre Dame Press, 1975), 103–41.

D. 1 Baruch

Where Ben Sira and the texts from Qumran avoided absolute identification of wisdom with the Law, and Wisdom of Solomon took the personification in a rather different direction, 1 Baruch uses an understanding of wisdom as Law to underpin its analysis of Israel's relationship with God. In a lengthy section about wisdom (3: 9–4: 4), Israel's exile is explained as the result of abandoning the 'fountain of wisdom', and wisdom is portrayed as unknown to foreign peoples, or even to the ancient giants. Found by God, she has been given to Israel, and has subsequently dwelt among humans (3: 37, the only point at which wisdom is explicitly personified). At the beginning of chapter 4, wisdom is then openly identified as the Law, the book of the commandments of God, and Israel is urged to walk towards her light, rather than give its glory to another and its profits to a foreign nation. 'Happy are we, Israel,' the section concludes, 'because the things which please God are known to us' (4: 4).[33]

In important respects, this is all very different from Proverbs 1–9, and in the accounts of wisdom's inaccessibility, Job 28 has clearly influenced 1 Baruch at least as much. However, there are interesting links, not least in the possible reminiscence of Prov. 5: 9 in Bar. 4: 3, which interprets the alienation of self and property in terms of the exile; and in the closing 4: 4, which reflects an understanding of wisdom's function, if not its nature, close to that of Proverbs 1–9.

E. Proverbs 1–9 and the Later Materials

This has been a brief survey, and not a comprehensive one,[34] but it should be clear that Proverbs 1–9 exerted a strong influence on some

---

[33] Collins, *Jewish Wisdom*, 55, rightly says this assertion leaves no doubt 'that the identification of wisdom and the law is understood in an ethnocentric, particularist sense'. cf. Schnabel, *Law and Wisdom*, 95–9.

[34] Although it is probably late, mention might also be made of the short poem in Enoch 42, where Wisdom can find no home among humans, and has to return to live among the angels, while a personified Iniquity goes out and, without meaning to, ends up living among humans, 'like rain in a desert'. See M. Ebner, 'Wo findet die Weisheit ihren Ort. Weisheitskonzepte in Konkurrenz', in M. Fassnacht, A. Leinhäupl-Wilke, S. Lücking (eds), *Die Weisheit—Ursprünge und Rezeption:*

subsequent literature, most visibly through its characterization of wisdom. Where later works took up its themes, moreover, they generally did so in a way that accords closely with our understanding of their original meaning. So, the foreign woman reappears as a seductress, Wisdom (more or less closely associated with the Law) as a guide to God's will, and the path imagery as a basic figure for human behaviour. There are differences, to be sure, and no text tries to reproduce the whole scheme of imagery and thought from Proverbs 1–9, but there is also a certain consistency visible. When such a variety of texts pick up the figure of Wisdom and associate her with the Law, it is manifestly simpler to deduce that they all understood this association to be implied in their common source, than to propose that they influenced each other or independently succumbed to some outside influence. Conversely, if the foreign woman of Proverbs 1–9 is simply, say, an adulteress, then why has 4Q184 taken her to be an almost elemental force of corruption?

These texts are the nearest things we shall ever possess to the reactions of those who first read Proverbs 1–9, and they point strongly to significant elements of that work having been understood in the terms outlined in this book, at least by about the second century BCE.[35] Understandably enough, these various compositions adapt their source to reflect their own various viewpoints, but it is interesting to note that they all more or less dispense with the antithesis and problem of choice, which seem crucial to Proverbs 1–9 itself. It would be wrong simply to generalize from this, and suggest that Proverbs 1–9 therefore represents some specific stage of Judaism, during which the temptation of alternatives to the Law loomed larger—not least because we can never really know how far any single text is typical of its time. All the same, it is curious that the opposition between Wisdom and the foreign woman, or Folly, which

Festscrift für Karl Löning zum 65. Geburtstag (Neutestamentliche Abhandlungen n.s. 44; Münster: Aschendorff, 2003), 79–103. It is difficult to know whether the Wisdom/Iniquity pairing here reflects a knowledge or understanding of the antithesis in Proverbs 1–9. Schnabel, *Law and Wisdom*, 100–12, looks at issues of wisdom in Enoch as a whole.

[35] The complicated questions surrounding the LXX translation preclude a proper study here, but note that Cook, *Septuagint*, defends the view that the LXX too understands material in Proverbs 1–9 to be rooted in ideas of Law; see especially 328–31.

seems so obviously significant in Proverbs 1–9, finds so little resonance in the later works.

There is no block of texts or single voice in the later period that might provide a fixed point for comparison. It does seem apparent, though, that many of the key ideas of Proverbs 1–9 have been subsumed with little radical change to them, and that there is a basic continuity in that direction. Looking backwards, there are many key ideas in some of the later texts that are absent from Proverbs 1–9, sometimes reflecting more general changes in understanding. Because attention has so often been drawn to it in the past, one of these—the interest in history that characterizes Ben Sira's work, in particular—deserves special comment.

3. THE PLACE OF HISTORY

It would not be quite true to say that Proverbs 1–9 shows no interest in national history: the foreign woman imagery, as we have seen, probably draws on an aspect of Deuteronomistic historical analysis, and if that does, furthermore, embody any specific contemporary concerns about exogamy, then it also betrays a more general interest in national identity. In such matters as its use of the divine name, moreover, Proverbs 1–9 shows no obvious intention to be international or universal in scope. Nevertheless, it would be hard to maintain that an understanding of the past is an explicit or direct interest of the work. This cannot be called simply a generic trait—not least because some instructions do discuss history (*Merikare* is the most obvious example)—and the past is, in a rather different sense, key to the testimonial aspect of the genre. We might better describe it as a consequence of the subject matter: Proverbs 1–9 is interested in talking about individuals and their decisions, rather than about the people as a whole. This is also true of much of Ben Sira's content, where the historical elements stand rather distinct. It is not true, however, of the Deuteronomic tradition, in which the actions of individuals are closely linked to the fate of Israel, and this would seem to raise questions about how far the association of wisdom and law in Proverbs 1–9 can really be said to draw on that tradition. It is the lack of interest in history before Ben Sira, after all, that has traditionally been seen as one of the distinctive, almost definitional aspects of wisdom literature.[36]

A proper discussion of such issues would take us far beyond the scope of this study, but it must certainly be considered true that none of the wisdom literature appeals to the notions of covenant or history that characterize Deuteronomy, or explicitly considers the fate of individuals to be bound up with that of the nation. Consequently, while Prov 2: 21–2, for instance, shares the Deuteronomic interest in remaining in the land (cf. also Prov. 10: 30), it does not envisage that the actions of the wicked might lead to the upright being cut off from it also.[37] We might say that Deuteronomy and Proverbs are distinguished primarily in this respect by notions of corporate and individual responsibility. If these actually represent distinct traditions, rather than being different facets of the same one, as seems more likely, we have no way of determining which was historically normative. For all that much of the biblical tradition tends to privilege the corporate, it seems difficult to believe that, in the daily conduct of religion, individual piety and prayer were not motivated to some degree by individual expectations of reward or punishment,[38] and

[36] By which is meant, of course, a lack of interest in specific national history, rather than in such events as the creation. Attempts, like that of Schmid, *Wesen und Geschichte*, to see the texts as 'historical', inasmuch as they are influenced by historical circumstances, are addressing a different issue.

[37] Fox, *Proverbs 1–9*, 123–4, picks up this issue, and draws from it the conclusion that the 'land' in these verses must, therefore, be not Israel, but the earth. While his point is important, I think the example illustrates, rather, the extent to which covenantal language and motifs become detached from their original, collective context in the post-exilic development of a more individualistic piety, which yet seeks its roots in the Torah.

[38] Part of the problem of assessing this issue is the fact that, where the biblical texts do emphasize individual responsibility, this may serve as a criterion for scholars to see wisdom influence or composition, as so often in the Psalms. Conversely, of course, psalms that present themselves as individual speeches are often taken to be corporate. Presuppositions about the underlying views have so penetrated and entangled discussions of date and origin that it is almost impossible to address the question without involvement in dozens of separate discussions and debates. L. Boström, *God of the Sages*, 193–6, touches on the broader issues, and discusses the key studies of personal piety by Albertz and Vorländer; see also 213–35.

the later mainstream emphasis on individual responsibility is being proclaimed as early as Ezekiel 18.[39] In any case, the primary interest of wisdom literature is in the ability of the individual to achieve a desirable existence, and there is little scope within this for covenantal ideas that make that possibility contingent on the behaviour of the whole nation.[40]

The Law is represented as something corporate within the broader historical analyses, but it always has an individual aspect. Obedience to the Law is, of course, the criterion for individual reward in Ezekiel 18, and this is clearly the basic understanding of much material in the Psalms and later literature. Job apparently avoids it by adopting a pre-Mosaic setting, and Qoheleth seems to ignore it,[41] but Proverbs 1–9 and, later, Ben Sira clearly see no problem in taking on that individual aspect without incorporating the associated historical concepts of national reward and punishment. In doing so, they are following the example of much other Jewish literature, and there is no good reason to believe that they are breaking some unwritten rule of wisdom literature.

---

[39] So Murphy, 'Religious Dimensions', 450, notes with respect to the assumption that 'Yahwistic theology of covenantal salvation is incompatible with wisdom's emphasis on creation and personal well-being', that 'it is hard to see how the average Israelite...would have made the academic distinction that is implied by this view. Wisdom and salvation are not incompatible in human experience; prosperity and adversity are personal as well as communal.'

[40] Jon Levenson's study of Psalm 119, 'The Sources of Torah: Psalm 119 and the Modes of Revelation in Second Temple Judaism', in P. D. Miller, P. D. Hanson, S. D. McBride (eds), *Ancient Israelite Religion: Essays in Honor of Frank Moore Cross* (Philadelphia: Fortress Press, 1987), 559–74, is important in this context. He argues (564) that 'it is an error to derive all concern for law and commandments from covenant theology', pointing out that, for all the clear Deuteronomic influences on the psalm, its ideas about Torah lack key elements of the Deuteronomic framework.

[41] This is not the place to discuss the unwillingness of the 'sceptical' writers to engage with the claims of the Torah, but I would venture to suggest that in Job's case it reflects a desire to avoid clouding the more basic issues that the book sets out to discuss; Qoheleth's whole world view, on the other hand, would seem to exclude revelation of the divine will (but how seriously we are expected to take that world view may be another matter).

4. PROVERBS 1–9 AND THE PLACE OF WISDOM LITERATURE

Ben Sira is often taken to represent something wholly new—a coalescence of historical and legal traditions with wisdom ideas—which marks, in some sense, the integration of a rather separate entity into mainstream Jewish writing. Even on quite a conservative reading, however, it would be hard to avoid noticing that much of what Ben Sira makes explicit is already present in Proverbs 1–9. Let us set aside, for a moment, the conclusions reached earlier about the resonance of particular terminology, and ignore such indications as the religious content of chapter 3, with its reference to Deuteronomy. We are still left with a work that repeatedly exhorts obedience to a teaching through which compliance with the divine will may be achieved, and personal security thereby assured. No alternative identification of that teaching is offered, and, for all the attempts to isolate 'wisdom circles' from other strands of Jewish thought,[42] it strains credulity to believe that a contemporary Jewish reader would not have made some link with the Law. Proverbs 1–9 lacks Ben Sira's interest in history, and the works differ in other significant respects, but Ben Sira does not mark a radical re-interpretation of the basic world view and ideas expressed in Proverbs 1–9. This is no less true of the texts from Qumran.

Since it is difficult to date Proverbs 1–9 relative to other materials in Proverbs, the nature of its relationship with earlier wisdom literature is more opaque, as, indeed, is the underlying ideology of that literature. It is relatively straightforward to say that Prov. 31: 1–9, for instance, has no interest in the Law, but much harder to ascertain what assumptions form the basis for, say, the righteous–wicked contrasts that dominate the start of 10: 1–22: 16.[43] It does seem

---

[42] It is interesting to note that the Qumran materials are themselves starting to undermine this tendency, if only for the later period. J. J. Collins, 'Wisdom Reconsidered, in Light of the Scrolls', *DSD* 4 (1997), 265–81, although adopting a functional approach to defining wisdom in terms of instruction, rightly notes that 'wisdom has its own developmental history. It is not a collection of timeless truths ... we should view with suspicion any attempt to associate wisdom with one particular point of view or to use it in antithesis to other viewpoints in Judaism' (281).

[43] See especially Scott, 'Wise and Foolish, Righteous and Wicked'.

apparent, at least, that no other material in Proverbs seeks actively to draw out and identify the nature of wisdom and instruction in the same way. From that point of view, if we are going to scrawl any thick black lines at all across the development of Jewish wisdom literature, then one probably ought to lie between Proverbs 1–9 and other parts of Proverbs, rather than between Proverbs 1–9 and the later texts.[44]

A more fruitful approach, however, which does greater justice to the nature of Proverbs 1–9, involves taking account of its place both in wisdom thought and in biblical literature more generally. It is notoriously difficult to define 'wisdom literature', but any description sufficient to embrace all three biblical wisdom books would need to include a recognition that some wisdom texts are interested not only in imparting knowledge of how to live, but in examining the basis and credentials of such knowledge. In the context of ideas about a transcendent deity, indeed, questions about the very possibility of that knowledge can become crucial, as in Job, Qoheleth, or from a different setting, Papyrus Insinger.

The central problem of recognizing true or false speech, high-lighted by Aletti, is essentially an epistemological problem of this sort,[45] and Proverbs 1–9 responds to it with the idea that, through instruction, one can attain a state of discernment that enables one to make proper decisions in the certainty that they correspond to the will of God. It deals, therefore, with a type of problem that lies at the heart of other post-exilic wisdom literature, and if Proverbs 1–9 does not respond in the same way as either Job or Qoheleth, the three works are at least all playing in the same ballpark. At the same time, however, Proverbs 1–9 employs forms and modes of speech typical of other sections of Proverbs, and one might say, therefore, that it lies at the heart of biblical wisdom literature, sharing important features in common with all of the material normally categorized in that way.

[44] The place of conventional Jewish piety elsewhere in Proverbs is too big an issue to discuss here, but there are other points in the book (e.g. 28: 4, 7, 9) where we should probably understand there to be an explicit interest in the Law.

[45] cf. Newsom, 'Woman', 149: 'In giving discourse a privileged position and in representing the world as a place of conflicting discourses, Proverbs 1–9 appears to acknowledge the socially constructed nature of reality and the problematic status of truth. Such reflections were part of the broader wisdom tradition...'

The fact that Proverbs 1–9 can be so central to wisdom literature, and yet draw so strongly on other Jewish traditions, makes it significant for our understanding of the position that wisdom literature occupied in Judaism. I have argued elsewhere that the historical evidence is very weak for this literature having been composed in circles that were professionally and ideologically distinct.[46] The literary evidence for this has long been problematic, at least since it became evident that claims for 'wisdom influence' were threatening either to draw much of the canon into the ambit of wisdom, or to render the term itself all but meaningless.[47] None of that is to say that we should deny the existence of people who called themselves 'wise', or even that we should cease to speak of 'wisdom literature' (although the term needs careful handling). It does suggest, however, that we should avoid setting up artificial barriers around the wisdom books and their authors, cutting them off from the broader currents of contemporary Jewish religion and thought.

Just as the Egyptian instructions embody the ideas and outlooks of their own periods, so Proverbs 1–9, an instruction itself, confronts the problems of temptation and discernment with ideas that draw on the existing Jewish ideas and literature with which the author and his readers would have been familiar. What evidence we possess suggests that much of Judaism in the Persian and early Hellenistic periods was strongly influenced by concern with the Deuteronomic Law, more or less closely linked to an acceptance of the Deuteronomistic analysis of history. Jewish literature already had an interest in the internalization of the Law, and Deuteronomy itself affirmed associations between the Law on the one hand, and both wisdom and parental instruction on the other. For the rest, Isaiah connects wisdom to the knowledge and fear of YHWH (11: 2; 33: 6), and Jeremiah sets divine wisdom in the context of creation (10: 12; 51: 15). We need not assume that the writer of Proverbs 1–9 knew, or was intentionally alluding to all these texts, but they show that many key components of his world view, and of his solution, were already current in Jewish thought.[48]

---

[46] *EIW*, especially chapter 5.

[47] See especially J. Crenshaw, 'Method in Determining Wisdom Influence upon "Historical" Literature', *JBL* 88 (1969), 129–42.

[48] Problems of dating make it very difficult to use evidence from the Psalms in this context, but we might note, anyway, a convergence of wisdom and Law in some

When he makes use of them, there is no good reason to regard this as a confluence of separate traditions: Proverbs 1–9 is a Jewish instruction, and so it naturally draws on Jewish ideas.

5. PROVERBS 1–9 AND THE FOREIGN INSTRUCTIONS

The fact that Proverbs 1–9 is an instruction, then, does not mean that it should be read in isolation from other early Jewish literature. Equally, it does not imply that it should be treated as pedestrian didacticism. As we have seen, it is in fact a very ambitious work of poetry, which employs extended imagery and allusion to convey a deeper understanding of its message. It relies upon its readers to recognize key terms and motifs—as they surely would have done more readily than we can—but only to that extent is it wilfully obscure: it is not an extended riddle or an allegory. If the style is rich and intricate, however, the basic message is essentially a simple one: internalization of the Law is a prerequisite for an understanding of God's will, and for protection against the temptations of sin.

There is no reason why such a message should not be conveyed in the form of an instruction, but it is interesting to wonder why the author should have chosen this genre. We can only speculate about motives, but the Jewish associations of 'instruction' with the Law may have been a starting point, and if the author was aware of such things as the Egyptian 'way of life' imagery, or of the admonitions in foreign instructions against the dangers of certain women, then these may have furnished further points of contact, as may, on the Jewish side, the idea of God as father. Without knowing how much the

psalms (most notably 1, 19B, 37), which owes no obvious debt to Proverbs 1–9 or to Ben Sira, but which shows at least the ease with which it was possible to bring the two together. Levenson, 'Sources', emphasizes the idea of 'non-Pentateuchal tôrâ', or 'non-scriptural authority', as something distinct from the mere supplementation of the written sources in early Judaism, and it seems likely that we should understand the attitudes to Law in Proverbs 1–9, and perhaps also Ben Sira, in terms of this broader conception.

author knew about other instructions, it is impossible to tell what might be deliberate reinterpretation, and what is simple coincidence.

What we can say, standing on rather firmer ground, is that the foreign instructions offer, at most, a very shallow basis for understanding Proverbs 1–9. Where they traditionally present a single, testimonial speech, Proverbs 1–9 has a process of parental education and multiple voices; where they tend to offer specific advice, Proverbs 1–9 presumes that the specifics are known; where they sometimes offer passing advice against types of woman, Proverbs 1–9 devotes half its length to developing a sophisticated, figurative contrast between two women. If we rely on the foreign instructions to explain this work, all we do is trivialize most of it into bombastic exhortations to heed parental advice, with an abnormal and prurient interest in illicit sex. It is the Jewish roots of this work, not its resemblances to Egyptian texts, that provide a key to understanding what it is trying to say.

This is not the place to discuss the matter at length, but it is tempting to point out that much the same is true of most other early Jewish wisdom literature. We should not neglect the influence of *Amenemope*, or ignore the foreign materials altogether, but it is important to keep the parallels in perspective. Carole Fontaine puts the matter interestingly when she speaks of the way that the Jewish wisdom writers 'were comparative thinkers: because of their association "vertically" through time with "tradition" and "horizontally" (across cultures during the same time period) with wisdom contacts in other cultures, they did not perform their intellectual activities in a theological, ethical, literary or practical vacuum'.[49] It may certainly be the case, as she goes on to say, that 'the sages worked with the connections and similarities of their teachings to those of their neighbours',[50] but the problem is where one places the emphasis in this. While it is not difficult to find thematic or verbal parallels and points of contact, it is much harder to find cases where the biblical texts have clearly sought to absorb or reconcile specifically foreign

---

[49] C. Fontaine, 'The Social Roles of Women in the World of Wisdom', in Brenner, *Feminist Companion*, 24–49, especially 26–7.

[50] Ibid., 27.

ideas with those of Judaism. These are not really the 'ecumenists' Fontaine wants them to be.[51]

None of that means that the work's presentation of its content as instruction is insignificant; it implies merely that we should not equate 'instructional' with 'foreign'. On the positive side, we have seen that its self-presentation as instruction does offer some insights into the poetic character of the text, into its fictional father–son setting, and perhaps into its attribution. Generic considerations also have an important contribution to make to discussions of unity. Since it is unlikely that the work adopts an instructional setting wholly fortuitously or coincidentally, then it would be wrong to avoid considering the implications.

6. THE PURPOSE AND SETTING OF PROVERBS 1–9

One area in which its genre has rarely been neglected is the discussion of the work's *Sitz im Leben*. We saw, much earlier, that assumptions about the 'textbook' character of foreign instructions are, at best, profoundly misleading. Whether any or all of those works were written specifically for pedagogical use—a matter that is itself debatable—the fact that instructions were used for education and enculturation does not mean that they should be read as little more than morally elevating exercises in writing, or 'guidebooks for success'. If we are to take such usage as determinative for the nature of Proverbs 1–9, and insist, on that basis, that it was designed for teaching (a notion as difficult to disprove as to prove) then we should, at least, allow that its character may be as sophisticated as that of its foreign counterparts. I do, however, have considerable reservations about the idea that the appropriation of generic conventions must necessarily involve the appropriation of their *Sitz im Leben*. In short, it is questionable whether foreign instructions were designed for school use, but their use in schools would not in any case prove

---

[51] I have addressed these more general issues in the first chapter of *EIW*; see especially 16–19, and also 157–8.

that Proverbs 1–9 must have been written with that function in mind.[52]

Other arguments for an educational function tend to draw on the self-presentation of the work itself, either taking the father–son setting literally—as an indication of education within the family unit—or seeing it as a cipher for a teacher–pupil relationship. It is doubtful, however, that anything very useful can be said on the basis of this setting: it is an entirely conventional, generic feature, and any reality reflected within it dates from the point at which the convention was established. Common though it is, this argument from the setting only really has any strength if one is willing to disregard the connection with the instruction genre, and take the father–son setting there as coincidental. Much the same may be said of the admonitory, didactic tone of the material and of the parental appeals, since these stem from that setting and from the work's genre.

Ultimately, questions about the *Sitz im Leben* and function of Proverbs 1–9 are broadly implicated in more general questions about the nature of post-exilic Jewish literature. It may be, as David Carr argues, that we should take much of the existing biblical literature to have been used for education and enculturation, although I am more inclined to see a forum for professional writers whose work was sponsored and performed for entertainment and moral elevation. In any case, I doubt that it is helpful to assign very specific functions and locations within a context about which we know so little.

Correspondingly, all we can say about the purpose of Proverbs 1–9 is limited to what we can deduce from its content and its presentation of that content. At the most obvious level it presents a case for the learning and internalizing of 'instruction', which I have taken to imply the Law, however that was understood in this period. Within this, it evokes a range of biblical texts and motifs, but not with such focus that we can really take it to be a deliberate interpretation, or Midrash, on any one of them. It probably exploits, furthermore, a major post-exilic concern with intermarriage, but not in such a way that it actually seems to be engaging in that debate directly. Presentational issues

---

[52] On the vexed question of whether any schools actually existed, see the extensive discussion in Crenshaw, *Education,* and my own review of the evidence in *EIW,* 132–56.

aside, if the message is innovative, this is probably in terms of the way it relates wisdom to instruction, and delineates the problems of temptation. So far as we can say anything about the intended audience, it seems likely that they would have been expected to recognize both the genre and the biblical references, and also that they would have been expected to appreciate the belletristic, poetic style. The writer, then, is offering a relatively simple message, dressed up in a very complicated presentation, probably for quite a sophisticated and well-read audience, but any attempt to place his work historically must necessarily be speculative.

Annotated Translation

PRIMARY MATERIAL

Introductory Passage (1: 1–7)

1: 1   The sayings of Solomon, son of David, king of Israel.

1: 2   For knowing wisdom and instruction, for understanding words of understanding;

1: 3   For gaining instruction in insight, righteousness, justice, and equity;

1: 4   For giving shrewdness to the ignorant, knowledge and resourcefulness to the young

1: 5   —Let the wise man hear and increase in learning, and the intelligent gain guidance—

1: 6   For understanding a saying and an allusion, the words of the wise and their figures.

1: 7   Fear of Yahweh is the start of knowledge: it is wisdom and instruction that fools despise.

Section 1: Speeches by the Sinners and by Wisdom (1: 8–33)

1: 8   Heed, my son, your father's instruction, and do not forsake your mother's teaching,

1: 9   For they are a lovely wreath for your head, and pendants for your neck.

1: 10   My son, if sinners tempt you, don't succumb,

1: 11   If they say, 'Come with us—let's lie in wait for blood, lurk in ambush, unprovoked, for the innocent;

1: 12   Like Sheol, let us swallow them alive and whole, like those who descend to the Pit:

1: 13	We'll find all sorts of precious object, and fill our homes with plunder.
1: 14	Throw in your lot with us—there will be one purse for us all.'
1: 15	My son, do not walk on the way with them—hold your foot back from their path.
1: 16	For their feet run to evil, and hurry to the shedding of blood.
1: 17	For futile as it is to cast a net where any bird can see it,
1: 18	These men lie in wait for their own blood, and lurk in ambush for their own lives:
1: 19	Such are the ways of all who plunder for plunder: it takes away its owner's life.
1: 20	Wisdom cries out in the street, raises her voice in the thoroughfares,
1: 21	Cries out on top of the walls; at the gateways in the city, she says what she has to say:
1: 22	'How much longer will you ignorant love ignorance,—and mockers delight in their mockery—and will fools hate knowledge?
1: 23	Turn to my teaching and I shall pour my spirit out to you, explain my words to you.
1: 24	It is because I called and you rejected—I put out my hand and no one paid attention,
1: 25	but you ignored all my advice and would not take my teaching—
1: 26	That I too shall laugh—at your distress, mock when your dread comes,
1: 27	When your dread comes like a storm—and your downfall will arrive like a tempest—when pain and anguish come upon you.
1: 28	Only then will they call on me: and I shall not answer. They will seek me, but they will not find me.
1: 29	As they hated knowledge, and chose not fear of Yahweh,
1: 30	Would not take my advice, and spurned all my teaching,
1: 31	So shall they eat of the fruit of their way, and be replete with their plans.
1: 32	For it is the turning away by the ignorant that will kill them, and the complacency of fools that will destroy them,

1: 33   But whoever listens to me will dwell safely, and be secure from dread of evil.'

Section 2: Statement of Ideas (2: 1–22)

2: 1   My son, if you accept my words, and treasure up my commandments with you,

2: 2   so as to bend your ear to wisdom, and turn your heart to understanding

2: 3   —yes, if you call out for insight, and cry for understanding,

2: 4   if you seek it like silver, and hunt for it like hidden treasure,

2: 5   Then will you understand the fear of Yahweh and find knowledge of God.

2: 6   For it is Yahweh who gives wisdom: from his mouth are knowledge and understanding.

2: 7   He saves up prudence for the upright, a shield for those who walk in integrity,

2: 8   To guard the paths of justice, and preserve the way of his godly.

2: 9   Then will you understand rightness and justice and equity—every good path.

2: 10   For wisdom will enter your heart, and knowledge be pleasant to your soul;

2: 11   Resourcefulness will stand guard over you, understanding will watch you:

2: 12   To deliver you from the way of evil, from a man who speaks perversity,

2: 13   Those who abandon straight paths to walk on ways of darkness,

2: 14   Those who take joy in doing evil—they delight in the perversity of evil—

2: 15   Whose paths are twisted, and are crooked in their routes.

2: 16   To deliver you from a strange woman, from a foreign woman who has polished her words,

2: 17   She who abandons the companion of her youth, and has forgotten the covenant of her God.

2: 18   For her house reaches down to death, and her paths to the shades:

2: 19   None who go to her returns, and they never reach the paths of life.

2: 20   So you will walk on the way of the good, and keep to the paths of the righteous,

2: 21   For the upright will inhabit the land, and those with integrity stay in it;

2: 22   But the wicked will be cut off from the land, and the treacherous torn away from it.

Section 3: Precepts for Behaviour towards God (3: 1–10)

3: 1   My son, do not forget my teaching, and let your heart keep my commandments,

3: 2   For more length of days, and years of life, and peace will be yours.

3: 3   Let loyalty and faithfulness never leave you: tie them round your neck, write them on the tablet of your heart,

3: 4   and find favour and appreciation in divine and human sight.

3: 5   Trust in Yahweh with all of your heart, and do not rely on your own insight:

3: 6   Know him in all your ways, and he will make your paths straight.

3: 7   Do not be wise in your own eyes: fear Yahweh and turn away from evil.

3: 8   It will be healing to your flesh, and a tonic to your bones.

3: 9   Honour Yahweh out of your wealth, and out of the first-fruits of all your produce,

3: 10   Then your storerooms will be filled with plenty of food, and your vats burst with new wine.

Section 4: Wisdom (3: 11–20)

3: 11   Do not reject, my son, the instruction of Yahweh, and do not abhor his teaching:

3: 12   For it is whom he loves that Yahweh teaches, like a father the son with whom he is pleased.

3: 13   Happy is the human who finds wisdom, and the human who gets discernment,

3: 14   For her profit is better than the profit on silver, and her yield better than gold's;

3: 15   She is worth more than corals, and there is nothing you desire that compares with her.

3: 16   Length of days is in her right hand: in her left, wealth and honour.

3: 17   Her ways are pleasant ways, and all her paths are peace.

3: 18   She is a tree of life to those who grasp her, and those who hold her are blessed.

3: 19   Yahweh, using wisdom, founded the earth; he set up the heavens using discernment.

3: 20   By his knowledge the depths broke out, and the clouds drop the dew.

Section 5: Precepts for Behaviour towards Humans (3: 21–35)

3: 21   My son, guard prudence and resourcefulness, do not let them slip from your sight,

3: 22   And they will be life for your throat, and adornment for your neck.

3: 23   Then you will walk in safety on your way, and your foot will not stumble;

3: 24   If you lie down you won't be anxious, and when you have lain down, your sleep will be sweet.

3: 25   Do not fear sudden dread, or the ruin of the wicked when it comes,

3: 26   For Yahweh will be your confidence, and will keep your foot from being caught.

3: 27   Do not withhold good from those due it, when it is in your power to act.

3: 28   Do not say to your neighbour, 'Go and come back, and I'll give it tomorrow,' when you have it with you.

3: 29   Do not plot evil against your neighbour, when he lives beside you trustingly.

3: 30   Do not pick a quarrel with someone for no reason, if they have done you no harm.

3: 31   Do not envy the man of violence, and do not choose any of his ways,

3: 32   For the crooked man is an abomination to Yahweh, while his confidence is with the upright.

3: 33   The curse of Yahweh is on the house of the wicked, while he blesses the home of the righteous.

| 3: 34 | To mockers he is mocking, while to the humble he shows favour. |
| 3: 35 | Wise men get honour, but rebellious fools, disgrace. |

Section 6: The Father's own Instruction (4: 1–9)

4: 1	Heed, O sons, a father's instruction, and pay attention, so you'll know understanding.
4: 2	For it is good teaching I give you: do not abandon my instruction.
4: 3	For I was a son to my father, vulnerable, and an only child before my mother,
4: 4	and he directed me and said to me: 'Let your heart grasp my words, keep my commandments and live.
4: 5	Get Wisdom, get understanding—do not forget, and do not turn aside from the words of my mouth—
4: 6	Do not forsake her, and she will preserve you; love her, and she will guard you.
4: 7	The start of wisdom: *get* wisdom, and, whatever you get, get understanding.
4: 8	Exalt her and she will raise you up: she will honour you for embracing her,
4: 9	Will put a lovely wreath on your head, and deliver to you a beautiful crown.'

Section 7: The Way of Wisdom (4: 10–19)

4: 10	Listen, my son, and accept my words, that you may have many years of life.
4: 11	I have pointed you on the way of wisdom, I have set you on your way in straight paths.
4: 12	When you walk, your pace will not be cramped, and if you run you will not stumble.
4: 13	Hold on to instruction—do not let go, keep her, for she is your life.
4: 14	Do not set foot on the path of the wicked, and do not follow the way of the evil:
4: 15	Leave it alone, do not go along it: turn off it and pass on.
4: 16	For they cannot sleep if they've done no wrong, and their slumber is stolen if they've made no one stumble.

4: 17   For they eat the bread of wickedness, and drink the wine of violence.

4: 18   And the path of the righteous is like a bright light, growing ever brighter till the fullness of the day:

4: 19   The way of the wicked is like darkness: they don't know what they're tripping over.

Section 8: Keeping to the Path (4: 20–7)

4: 20   My son, pay attention to my words, bend your ear to the things I say:

4: 21   Do not let them slip out of your sight, guard them within your heart,

4: 22   For they are life to those who find them, healing to all the flesh of each.

4: 23   Above all else you keep safe, look after your heart, for from it come the sources of life.

4: 24   Keep away from you any crookedness of mouth, and put twisting of lips far away from you.

4: 25   Let your eyes look to the front, and your eyeballs be straight before you:

4: 26   Watch carefully the course of your feet, and all your ways will be established,

4: 27   Turn neither to the right nor to the left: keep your foot away from evil.

Section 9: The Foreign Woman (5: 1–23)

5: 1   My son, pay attention to my wisdom, turn your ear to my understanding,

5: 2   That you may keep resourcefulness, and that your lips may guard knowledge.

5: 3   For the lips of a strange woman drip honey, and her palate is slicker than oil,

5: 4   But her end is bitter as wormwood, sharp as a double-edged sword.

5: 5   Her feet are going down to death, her steps will grasp Sheol,

5: 6   So that she pays no attention to the path of life: she does not know that her courses stray.

5: 7   And now, O sons, listen to me, and do not depart from the words of my mouth:

5: 8   Keep your way far from her, and do not approach the door of her house,

5: 9   Lest you cede your authority to others, and your years to one who is cruel,

5: 10   Lest strangers take their fill of your strength, and your toils be in the house of someone foreign,

5: 11   And you groan in the future, when your body and flesh are spent,

5: 12   And you say:
        'How I hated instruction, and my heart despised teaching,

5: 13   And I did not listen to the voice of my teacher, or turn my ear to my instructor.

5: 14   I was quickly in complete ruin, in the very midst of the congregation and assembly.'

5: 15   Drink water from your well, and flowing waters from inside your cistern:

5: 16   Outside, your springs will overflow, water-channels in the street.

5: 17   Let them be for you, you alone, and let none be for strangers with you.

5: 18   Let your fount be blessed, and take pleasure from the wife of your youth

5: 19   —a lovely hind, a charming mountain doe: her love will intoxicate you constantly, and you will always be giddy with her loving.

5: 20   So why make yourself giddy, my son, with a strange woman, and why clasp at the bosom of a foreign woman?

5: 21   For the ways of a man are in the sight of Yahweh, and he watches over all his paths.

5: 22   His own crimes trap the wicked man, and he is caught in the cords of his sin:

5: 23   He will die for lack of instruction, and in his great folly go astray.

[6: 1–19, see Secondary Material, p. 225]

Section 10: Avoiding the Foreign Woman (6: 20–35)

6: 20   Guard, my son, your father's commandments, and do not forsake the teaching of your mother.

6: 21   Bind them always on your heart, tie them round your neck.

6: 22   She will guide you in your walking, guard you in your resting, and talk with you when you awake.

6: 23   For commandment is a lamp and teaching a light, while what is learned from instruction is a way to life,

6: 24   To keep you from the woman of evil, from the smoothness of the foreign woman's tongue.

6: 25   Do not desire her beauty in your heart, nor let her capture you with her eyelids,

6: 26   For a prostitute's catch is a piece of bread, but a married woman hunts a precious soul.

6: 27   Can a man snatch up fire in his breast, and his clothes not be burned?

6: 28   Will a man walk on embers, and his feet not be scorched?

6: 29   Such is he who goes with the wife of his neighbour: none who touches her will be exempt.

6: 30   A thief is not despised if he steals to fill his belly when hungry,

6: 31   but if he is caught he will pay sevenfold, give all he has in his home.

6: 32   One who commits adultery with a woman lacks sense: whoever does it destroys his soul.

6: 33   It is beating and disgrace that he will encounter—and his shame will never be wiped out.

6: 34   For jealousy is a man's rage, and he will have no mercy in the day of retribution,

6: 35   He'll be bought off by no compensation, and will never yield, however big you make your bribe.

Section 11: The Foreign Woman and Wisdom (7: 1–8: 36)

7: 1   My son, keep my words, and treasure up my commandments with you.

7: 2   Keep my commandments and live, and (keep) my teaching as the pupil of your eye;

7: 3	Bind them on your fingers, write them on the tablet of your heart.
7: 4	Say to Wisdom, 'You are my sister', and call understanding 'cousin',
7: 5	To keep you from the strange woman, from the foreign woman who has polished her words.
7: 6	For at the window of my house, I have looked down through my lattice,
7: 7	And seen among the ignorant, made out among the youths, a young man lacking sense,
7: 8	Passing along the street by a corner. And he sets foot on the road to her house,
7: 9	Into the twilight, into the evening of the day, into the eye of night and darkness.
7: 10	And look, a woman to meet him—a whore's dress, but close of heart.
7: 11	She is exuberant and rebellious, her feet don't stay at home:
7: 12	Now in the street, now in the thoroughfares, and by every corner she lies in wait.
7: 13	And she grabs him and kisses him, sets her face, and says to him,
7: 14	'Owing sacrifices, I paid my vows today,
7: 15	So I have come out to meet you, to seek your face, and I have found you.
7: 16	I have draped my couch with coverings, embroideries of Egyptian linen,
7: 17	I have sprinkled my bed with myrrh, aloes, and cinnamon.
7: 18	Come, let us be intoxicated with love till morning, pleasure ourselves with loving.
7: 19	There's no man at home: he has set off on a journey from afar;
7: 20	He took a purse of money in his hand, and will come home at full moon's day.'
7: 21	She turns him aside with much persuasion, with the smoothness of her lips drives him.
7: 22	And suddenly he's going after her—like a steer going to slaughter, like a mountain-goat skipping into a snare

7: 23 —until an arrow pierces its liver—, like a bird rushing into a trap: and he does not realize that it's costing his life.

7: 24 And now listen to me, sons, and pay attention to the words of my mouth.

7: 25 Do not let your heart turn aside to her ways, stray not into her paths,

7: 26 For many are the victims she's brought down, and countless are those killed by her:

7: 27 The ways to Sheol are her house, going down to the halls of death.

8: 1 Does Wisdom not call, and understanding give voice?

8: 2 At the top of the slopes on a road, among paths she takes her stand,

8: 3 By the side of the gates at the mouth of the town, at the entrance of the portals she cries out:

8: 4 'It is to you, men, that I am calling, and my cry is to sons of man.

8: 5 Learn prudence, you who are ignorant, and learn intelligence, you fools.

8: 6 Listen, for *I* shall speak straightforwardness, and the utterance of *my* lips will be uprightness,

8: 7 For it is truth that *my* palate will utter, and wickedness is an abomination to *my* lips.

8: 8 In righteousness are all the words of *my* mouth: not one among them is bent or twisted.

8: 9 All of them are straight to one who understands, and right for those who find knowledge.

8: 10 Take my instruction, not silver, and knowledge rather than fine gold,

8: 11 For wisdom is better than corals, and no desires compare with it.

8: 12 I, Wisdom, have established prudence, and it is knowledge and resourcefulness that I shall offer.

8: 13 Fear of Yahweh is hatred of evil: it is pride, arrogance, and an evil way, and a mouth of perversions that I hate.

8: 14 Counsel and good sense are mine: I am understanding, I have strength.

8: 15 It is by me that kings reign, and rulers decree what is right;

8: 16 It is by me that princes rule—nobles, all the governors of the earth.

8: 17 I love those who love me, and those who seek me out will find me:

8: 18 Wealth and honour are with me—extraordinary wealth, and righteousness.

8: 19 My fruit is better than gold or fine gold, and my yield than choice silver.

8: 20 It is on the path of righteousness that I walk, amidst the roads of justice,

8: 21 Endowing with wealth those who love me—and I shall fill their treasuries.

8: 22 Yahweh got me as the start of his way, the beginning of his deeds of old.

8: 23 Since long ago have I been formed, since the first beginnings of the world.

8: 24 It was when there were no depths that I was born, when there were no springs abundant in water,

8: 25 In the time before mountains were planted, before hills was I born;

8: 26 When he had yet to make land and ground, or the first of the world's soil,

8: 27 When he set up the heavens, I was there, when he cut out a disc on the face of the deep,

8: 28 When he fixed clouds above, when he strengthened the springs of the deep,

8: 29 When he set for the sea its limit—and the waters will not transgress his word—when he dug the foundations of the earth.

8: 30 And I have remained at his side faithfully, and I remain delightedly, day after day, celebrating before him all of the time,

8: 31 celebrating in the earthly world, and my delight is with the sons of man.

8: 32 And now, sons, listen to me, and follow the steps of my ways:

8: 33   Hear instruction, and be wise, and do not neglect it.

8: 34   Happy is the man who heeds me, by watching at my gates day by day, guarding the posts of my doors.

8: 35   For he who finds me finds life, and gains favour from Yahweh,

8: 36   But he who misses me harms his very self: all who hate me love death.'

Concluding cameo: Wisdom and the woman (9: 1–6, 10 f., 13–18)

9: 1   Wisdom has built her house, she has set up her seven pillars,

9: 2   She has prepared her meat, mixed her wine, even set her table.

9: 3   She has sent out her maids to issue her invitation, on the slopes of the town's banks:

9: 4   'Who is ignorant? Let him turn this way!' To anyone who lacks sense, she says:

9: 5   'Come, eat of my bread, and drink of wine which I have mixed.

9: 6   Forsake the ignorant and live, and advance on the way of understanding.

9: 10   Fear of Yahweh is the beginning of wisdom, and understanding is knowledge of the holy.

9: 11   For by me will your days be multiplied, and the years of your life be increased.'

9: 13   Folly delights in ignorance, and she knows nothing.

9: 14   She sits at the doorway of her house, on the throne of the town's slopes,

9: 15   To issue her invitation to those who pass by on the road, going straight on their way:

9: 16   'Who is ignorant? Let him turn this way!' And to anyone who lacks sense, she says:

9: 17   'Stolen waters are sweet, and the bread of secrecy pleasing.'

9: 18   And he does not know that shades are present, that those she has called are in the depths of Sheol.

Notes

1: 3	*insight*: although a preposition might be expected in the Hebrew for 'instruction *in* insight', MT is to be preferred to the Syriac's linking of the two with 'and'. The Hiphil of שׂכל seems to have two related senses: 'be insightful' and 'be successful'.
1: 4	*ignorant*: the Hebrew implies lack of knowledge, rather than mental incapacity.[1]

shrewdness: outside Proverbs 1–9, ערמה is found only in Exod. 21: 4 and Josh. 9: 4. There may be some connotation of foresight or preparedness.

resourcefulness: the term מזמה seems to imply the ability to make plans: it is often used to mean the plans or purposes themselves.

1: 5   This verse is either parenthetical or a secondary gloss: it breaks the pattern of verses 2–4 and 6, all of which are purpose clauses with 3 words in each stich, and its sense is close to that of 9: 9, which is most probably secondary. *learning*: לקח expresses what is known or taught, but also the ability to put one's teachings or ideas across.

1: 6   *allusion*: מליצה appears elsewhere only in Hab. 2: 6, where it refers to a polemical poem, whose target is described figuratively. Although it is usually associated with the verb ליץ, ('scorn'), מליץ is used of interpreters and mediators, e.g. in Gen. 42: 23. Here, and in Hab. 2, therefore, the word may refer to something in need of interpretation or understanding, rather than to taunting. *figures*: חידה is found alongside מליצה in Hab. 2: 6, and the term is clearly not confined to describing formal puzzles; in Ps. 78: 2, it is hard even to see anything enigmatic about the material that follows. It is possible that the terms here point forward to the symbolic character of the material to come.

---

[1] So Richardson's translation, 'simpleton', (cf. RSV 'simple') is quite inappropriate, as McKane notes; see H. N. Richardson, 'Some Notes on *lyṣ* and its Derivatives', *VT* 5 (1955), 163–79, especially 172.

1: 7   *start*: on ראשית, see pp. 117–18, above. In the second stich, the verb may be taken to agree either with the fools or with wisdom and instruction, making it hard to determine which is subject and which object. It is tempting to suppose that this ambiguity is deliberate, implying that the despite is mutual, and this suspicion is strengthened by the exceptional absence of ל after בוז (contrast 6: 30), which removes any explicit indication of the object.

1: 11   *blood...innocent*: דם נקי, ('innocent blood'), is a common expression in Deuteronomy, the Deuteronomistic History, and Jeremiah, with a few uses elsewhere.[2] Here the cliché has been split apart, with the two words standing in parallel. To spill the blood of those who do not deserve death seems to be almost a 'classic' sin in Deuteronomic thought, and it incurs blood-guilt for Israel (cf. Deut. 19: 10). The idea is emphasized by חנם, (literally 'without cause'): cf. 1 Kgs. 2: 31.

1: 12   While all the dead go to Sheol, to be swallowed alive is particularly dreadful: the supplicant of Ps. 55: 15 apparently wishes such a fate upon his enemies, and it is what happens to Korah and his household in Num. 16: 31–3.[3] The expression יורדי בור, ('those who descend to the pit'), however, is a common way of describing the dead.[4] It is possible that the sinners' victims are 'like those who descend to the pit', but the parallelism suggests that the reference is to the sinners themselves: they are comparing their attacks to seizing by the underworld and the dead.

1: 13   *all...object*: כל־הון יקר appears in Prov. 24: 4, where knowledge fills a room with wealth; this is part of the saying that begins 'By wisdom a house is built', and some connection with Proverbs 1–9 seems likely.

1: 16   Identical to the first half of Is. 59: 7, except that it lacks the description of the blood as 'innocent' (but cf. v. 11);

---

[2] See Deut. 19: 10; 27: 25; 1 Sam. 19: 5; 2 Kgs. 21: 16; 24: 4; Ps. 94: 21; 106: 38; Prov. 6: 17; Is. 59: 7; Jer. 7: 6; 22: 3; 26: 15. Cf. Deut. 19: 13; 2 Kgs. 24: 4; Jer. 19: 4; 22: 17.

[3] Camp, *Wise, Strange*, chapter 5, sees an interplay, and wordplays, between Lev. 10, Num. 16, and Num. 25, linked to ideas of strangeness and the strange woman.

[4] Cf. Ps. 28: 1; 88: 5; 143: 7; Is. 38: 18; Ezek. 26: 20; 31: 14, 16; 32: 25, 29, 30.

note that the Isaiah passage goes on to use the path
imagery that plays such a prominent role in Proverbs
1–9. The verse is absent in key Septuagint manuscripts,
but this is by no means conclusive evidence of secondary
insertion.

1: 17   *cast*: the meaning and derivation of מזרה are disputed,[5]
but the general sense of the verse seems clear: birds will
not be caught in a net which they have seen being prepared or thrown,[6] but the sinners have either ignored or
not foreseen the self-destructive consequences of their
actions.[7]

bird: the term is a poetic one, literally 'lord of wing'.
A similar expression is found in Qoh. 10: 20.

1: 19   *ways*: it is not necessary to emend ארחות to אחרית,
('end'), as BHS proposes.

1: 20   *Wisdom*: the form here is plural, although the subsequent
verbs and pronominal suffix revert to the singular after
the first verb. The same 'plural' form with a singular
meaning recurs in 9: 1 and is elsewhere used in Ps. 49: 4
[ET, 3]; Prov. 14: 1; 24: 7. It probably appeared in the
original text of 8: 1. A similar form may be used for 'folly'
in 9: 13. The author elsewhere uses the normal singular
form for wisdom/Wisdom, and this abnormal form,

---

[5] It is most often taken to be a Pual participle from זרה, ('winnow, scatter'); cf.
BDB. Following rabbinic commentators, but also drawing dubious parallels with
Arabic usage, Winton Thomas understood the reference to be to seed 'strewn' on a
net as bait; cf. D. W. Thomas, 'Textual and Philological Notes on some Passages in the
Book of Proverbs', SVT 3 (1955), 280–92, especially 281–2. G. R. Driver, on the other
hand, takes it to be either a Hophal participle from זור, ('press, squeeze'), or the Qal
passive participle of a verb from the root מזר: in either case, he takes the reference to
be to 'drawing tight' the net; cf. G. R. Driver, 'Problems in the Hebrew Text of
Proverbs', *Biblica* 32 (1951), 173–97, especially 173.

[6] If מזרה is indeed to be derived from זרה, then the reference may be either to a baited
trap that is spread out for a bird to walk on, or to a throwing-net used by a stalker: both
ideas suit the context and the verb's basic sense of scattering by throwing in the air.

[7] McKane, following Winton Thomas: even though they can see the trap coming,
birds are too greedy to resist the bait, and the robbers are likewise carried away by
their appetite. This relies on the doubtful idea that 1: 17 refers to the spreading of
bait, but also stretches the sense of חנם much further than seems justifiable. That term
may have some implication of futility (e.g. Mal. 1: 10), but does not elsewhere refer to
the failure of an anticipated outcome.

whether it be an archaic, a foreign or an intensive form, is apparently used to highlight the personification of Wisdom when she makes her speeches.[8]

1: 21   *walls*: while המיות may be a participial form from המה, and mean something like 'noisy places' (so Fox: 'bustling crossroads'), there are good grounds for emending ה to ח, and associating the term with the Phoenician חמית, ('walls'), and Moabite חמת, ('wall', as LXX).

1: 22   The verbs here are very confused: a second-person plural imperfect, a third-person plural perfect, and a third-person plural imperfect. There are no secure grounds for emendation, and it seems best to regard the second stich as a parenthetical interjection. Just possibly, we are supposed to imagine Wisdom pointing to different groups.

how much longer?: questions introduced by עד מתי are a feature of Jeremiah's style in particular,[9] but they do occur elsewhere, especially in the Psalms,[10] so this is not a sufficient basis for characterizing the speech as 'prophetic'.

ignorance: as a noun, פתי is only found here.

mockers: it has been suggested that ליץ has to do with being talkative, but this is at odds with the usage.[11] The term seems rather to refer to those who are not merely uninstructed, but who actively repudiate instruction (e.g. 3: 34). English 'sceptic' comes close to the sense, but implies too intellectual a basis for the dissent.

1: 23   I have not translated הנה, which is usually taken to be an exclamatory 'behold!' Some commentators, though, take it to be a conditional particle like the Aramaic הן ('if'),

---

[8] On the form, see especially Fox, *Proverbs 1–9*, 96–7.

[9] See Jer. 4: 14, 21; 12: 4; 13: 27; 23: 26; 31: 22; 47: 5.

[10] Exod. 10: 3, 7; Num. 14: 27; 1 Sam 1: 14; 16: 1; 1 Kgs. 18: 21; Neh. 2: 6; Ps. 6: 3; 74: 10; 80: 4; 82: 2; 90: 13; 94: 3; Pro 6: 9; Is. 6: 11; Dan. 8: 13; 12: 6; Hos. 8: 5; Hab. 2: 6; Zech. 1: 12.

[11] The suggestion is made in Richardson, 'Some Notes', but rejected by most commentators. McKane declares that he finds it attractive because economy of speech is valued in Egyptian instructions, but, wisely, sticks to the translation 'scoffers'.

which has been misplaced from the beginning of the
verse.[12] It seems unnecessary to emend the text and
invent a new Hebrew particle, when the sentence can
quite readily be taken as conditional without any word
for 'if'.[13] If we do not take it that way, it is just possible
that the sentences in vv. 22 and 23 should be divided
differently, to read 'How much longer will you ... keep
returning to my teaching? Behold ...'

teaching: תוכחת is often found in parallel with מוסר
('instruction'), with a similar sense; it is also used,
though, to describe argument and reasoning, as in Job
13: 6, and there may be some element of that in this verse:
Wisdom is demanding that her case be heard.

1: 27   *storm*: the Kethib, שאוה, may be read as from שאה
('crash'); cf. שאיה in Is. 24: 12. The Qere, שואה, has the
more general sense 'devastation' or 'ruin', as in 3: 25, but
it seems to indicate a storm in Ezek. 38: 9, and the
parallelism may suggest that more specific sense here.[14]
The extended temporal construction is similar to that
used in 8: 25–9.

1: 28   the verse is reminiscent of Hos. 2: 7 and 5: 6 (cf. also Jer.
7: 27), and the vocabulary used is regularly associated
with calling upon or seeking Yahweh. On the change to
the third person, see Baumann, *Weisheitsgestalt*, 193–4.

2: 7   *prudence*: תושיה is also found in 3: 21 (written defect-
ively), but elsewhere only in Job and Isaiah. Job 5: 12
suggests that it can be something done with the hands,
but Is. 28: 12 places it in parallel with counsel. It probably
has a basic meaning close to that of חכמה, but here and in
3: 21 may indicate something more like a sense of self-
preservation.

2: 8   *godly*: the term חסיד is used to describe the pious and
faithful, principally in the Psalms. The Qere suggests a
plural here, and is supported by the versions. Yahweh's
'godly ones' are explicitly identified with the people of

---

[12] See Driver, 'Problems', 174.   [13] Cf. GK §159b.

[14] Driver, 'Problems', 174, and McKane want to derive the Qere from a hypothetical שואה = ('evil day'), citing a presumed Arabic cognate.

Israel, or perhaps some ideal, 'true' Israel, in Ps. 50: 5; 85: 9 (ET, 8); and 148: 14, and the expression comes close to being a technical term even before its later use to describe Jews of a particular party.

2: 9   *rightness, justice, equity*: these three concepts are also found together in 1: 3, which would seem to count against Driver's proposed emendation of ומישרים to ומשמר.

2: 10   *soul*: נפש refers to the living 'self', with its desires and appetites, but can also refer to the throat and palate (which McKane would understand here).

2: 12   *perversity*: תהפכות is used widely in Proverbs, often in connection with speech, but only once outside the book, in Deut. 32: 20, where the 'generation of perversity' is a reference to Israel's apostasy. Related terms suggest implications of reversal, transformation, and distortion, and the reference here is probably to speech that misstates and distorts, with subversive consequences.

2: 13   *those who*: there is no obvious explanation for the sudden switch to plural forms in vv. 13–15, unless the writer is trying to make clear that he is defining the individuals who may be identified with the figure of v. 12.

    straight: see 4: 11, below.

2: 15   *in their routes*: taking נלוזים, ('crooked'), and the suffix pronoun on מיגלות, ('routes') to agree with the 'paths' of the first stich. This requires that מיגלות refer to the course of the paths, rather than to actual tracks, but that sense is attested elsewhere (cf. 4: 26). The usual rendering, which takes נלוזים to refer to the individuals of 2: 13–14, makes the prepositional ב on מיגלות redundant, and places intolerable strain on the relative construction.

2: 16   *strange... foreign*: the meaning of these terms is discussed above in chapter 3. Fox, taking the woman to be an adulteress, picks up a much older suggestion by Humbert, and argues that נכרי, although 'probably marked for foreignness in a way that *zar* is not... can by extension be used of locals or indigenous people who are alien to the relationship in question—exactly like *zar*—especially when in parallelism with the latter. There may be a note of intensity or hyperbole in this use.' For instances outside Proverbs 1–9 of נכרי meaning something other than literally 'foreign', he cites Gen. 31: 15; Job 19: 15; Ps. 69: 9 (ET, 8); Prov. 27: 13 (which he seems to have merged accidentally with a discussion of 27: 2); Qoh. 6: 2; Jer. 2: 21. In Jer. 2: 21, it is not the case that the reference is to the vine 'not being the vintner's own': the point is that the vine has not come true from the pure seed with which it was sown, a matter of genetics, if not ethnicity. In the other cases, the issue is, indeed, essentially one of metaphorical or hyperbolic usage, rather than simple ethnicity. Gen. 31: 15; Job 19: 15; Ps. 69: 9 (ET, 8), are all passages that emphasize the complete rejection by family: the speaker is not just rejected as kin, not just treated as a stranger, but absolutely excluded, like a foreigner. In Prov. 27: 2 there is probably a similar step up from 'strangeness': 'Let a stranger praise you, and not your mouth; [better still] a foreigner, and not your lips'; cf. 27: 13, and Qoh. 6: 2, where the idea is, again, 'someone *completely* different'. Is. 28: 21, rather differently, uses זר and נכרי with reference not to a person, but to the wholly new and unexpected nature of coming divine action; the implication is essentially the same, though: 'foreignness' as a figure for 'complete difference', rather as we might say in English that something is 'utterly foreign' to someone's nature. Complete otherness does not mean 'alien to the relationship in question', as Fox would like, and the very fact that נכרי can be used hyperbolically would tend to exclude such a looser sense. Better, though hardly compelling, evidence for 'another man's wife' would be furnished by Fox's last example, were it actually the case that נכריה 'is parallel to "a neighbour's wife" in Prov 6: 24' without an emendation to the text.[15] Many of the same objections

---

[15] See Fox, *Proverbs 1–9*, 139–40; P. Humbert, 'La Femme étrangère du livre des Proverbes', *RES* 4 (1937), 49–64; 'Les Adjectifs "zâr" et "nokrî" et la "femme étrangère" des Proverbes Bibliques', in *Mélanges syriens offerts à monsieur René Dussaud,*

raised against Fox and Humbert apply also to the
evidence presented by L. A. Snijders[16] to support his
contention that the woman is not foreign but a social
outsider, severed from normal behavioural constraints.
This is picked up by McKane in *Proverbs*, 285; he allows,
however, some element of foreignness, and talks of 'the
popular estimate which is formed of a foreign woman in
any community. She is strange and nonconformist in
many respects, and to the men she is fascinating, alluring
and mysterious... [she] then becomes a type or paradigm of any woman who spurns the conventions of the
society in which she lives, and is regarded generally as
defiant and wanton.' This has been an influential viewpoint, but it does sound a lot more like St Andrews in the
1960s than Palestine in the first millennium BCE, where
many ethnic groups certainly coexisted in almost every
period, and especially after the Exile.[17]

2: 17   *companion of her youth*: see p. 86.

covenant of her God: the reference is probably just to a
marriage covenant, divinely witnessed or ratified,[18] but
the specification ברית אלהיה has given rise to much
speculation about the woman's religious affiliations. It
is true that the word אלהיה need not necessarily refer to
YHWH (cf. Ruth 1: 15; Is. 21: 9; Jer. 46: 25), and the
phrase therefore implies no particular affiliation. That is
unlikely to be the prime reason why it is used, however:
the divine name cannot take a suffix, and with ברית יהוה,
the sentence would be a simple statement of apostasy.
The writer may indeed wish to imply that through his
imagery, but he is not trying to (or, perhaps, is trying not
to) say it outright.

---

*secrétaire perpétuel de l'Académie des Inscriptions et Belles-Lettres par ses amis et ses
élèves* (Paris: Librairie Orientaliste Paul Geuthner, 1939), vol. 1, 259–66.

[16] 'The Meaning of זר in the Old Testament', *OTS* 10 (1954), 1–154, especially 88–104.

[17] cf. Maier, *Die fremde Frau*, 65, 254. A detailed depiction of the bustling
cosmopolitanism of the Persian period is given in Yoder, *Wisdom*, 39–48.

[18] So, e.g. Fox, *Proverbs 1–9*, 120–1.

2: 18   *reaches down*: if שׁחה is from שׁוח, ('sink down'), then it cannot agree in gender with בית, ('house'), and it is commonly suggested that it should instead be derived from שׁחה, ('bow down'), the Qal stem of which is only otherwise attested in Is. 51: 23, where it is used of lying flat on the ground. LXX read this as a form of שׁוה, ('set', 'place'). BHS proposes נתיבתה, ('her path') for ביתה, ('her house'). If the precise reading is elusive, and the RSV's 'sink down' a little too evocative of an elevator, the general sense, at least, seems clear.

2: 21   *for*: כי might have emphatic rather than explanatory force here, but otherwise explains not her behaviour, but the need for deliverance from her.

3: 2   *more ... will be yours*: literally, 'they will increase for you'. Since 'teaching' and 'commandments' are feminine nouns, they are unlikely to be the subject of the masculine verb, and this should be taken as an impersonal construction with passive sense.

3: 3   *tie them*: Plöger, Fox take the teachings of v. 1 to be the antecedents, which would match other passages (6: 21; 7: 3), but that would leave v. 3a stranded, as a parenthetical interjection or gloss, and it is hard to interpret that stich in either role. It seems marginally better to take this as a deliberate variation on the motif.

     tablet: see p. 105, above.

3: 4   *appreciation*: שׂכל־טוב is difficult to translate. In 2 Sam. 18: 30 שׂכל is used of military success, but more generally it seems to mean 'insight' or 'interpretation' (cf. Neh. 8: 8). In 2 Chron. 30: 22, שׂכל־טוב is what the Levites sing to God, but in Psalm 111: 10, it is set in parallel with wisdom, as something possessed by those who practise 'fear of YHWH'; 1 Sam. 25: 3 contrasts the beauty and טובת שׂכל of Abigail with the churlishness of her husband. No single translation is really satisfactory, but what seems to be implied is a quality of perceptible intelligence, and perhaps piety, which wins admiration; so שׂכל־טוב in Prov. 13: 15 is said to win favour (cf. 14: 35) in contrast to the way of the wicked.

3: 5　　*with all your heart*: to behave in some way towards Yahweh 'with all one's heart' is a characteristically Deuteronomic formulation. So, in Deuteronomy: Deut. 4: 29; 6: 5; 10: 12; 11: 13; 13: 3; 26: 16; 30: 2, 6, 10. In the Deuteronomistic History: Josh. 22: 5; 1 Sam. 7: 3; 12: 20, 24; 1 Kgs. 2: 4. The expression is also found in Jer. 29: 13; Joel 2: 12; Zeph. 3: 14.

3: 7　　*wise in your own eyes*: found a few times in Proverbs, and once in Isaiah, this expression apparently refers to conceit about one's own abilities; cf. Prov. 12: 15; 26: 5, 12; 28: 11; Is. 5: 21.

3: 8　　*healing*: רפאות is only found here, but probably means much the same as רפאה, ('remedy', 'medicine').

　　　　flesh: שר only otherwise in Ezek. 16: 4, where it apparently refers to the umbilical cord, but the שרר of Song 7: 3 is often taken to be the same word, albeit more probably with the sense 'vagina'.[19] Emendation to שאר or בשר is commonly suggested: both mean 'flesh', which provides a good parallel to the 'bones' of the second stich. Aramaic cognates meaning 'strength' or 'health', however, lead some commentators to propose that emendation is unnecessary, and McKane points to the apparent meaning 'health' for שר in the Hebrew of Sir. 30: 16.[20] Something more tangible than 'health' or 'strength' seems to be required by the context, and I would therefore either emend to בשר, or else take שר in a sense close to that of שריר, which probably means 'muscle' in Job 40: 16.

　　　　tonic: שקוי is literally 'drink', cf. Ps. 102: 10 (ET, 9); Hos. 2: 7. Possibly a liquid medicine (so Driver, 'Problems', 175; Whybray), but the idea is probably similar to that in Job 21: 24: there the prosperous, fortunate man is one who dies with fat in his body and whose bone-marrow has been 'watered' (ישקה). Hence the emphasis upon the

---

[19] See, e.g. E. Ullendorf, 'The Bawdy Bible', *BSOAS* 42 (1979), 425–56, especially 448.

[20] Driver, 'Problems', 175, attempts to show that 'strength' is a natural semantic development from 'cord', but it seems far from self-evident that 'cord', in any general sense, is a meaning of שר.

dryness of dead bones in Ezek. 37: 2, while in Ezek. 37: 11 and Prov. 17: 22, the dryness of bones reflects depression or a sorry state. There seems to have been some idea that good health depended upon providing liquid for one's bones.

3: 10   *storerooms*: אסם is found only otherwise in Deut. 28: 8, where Yahweh will bless the people's storerooms in return for their obedience.

plenty: LXX 'plenty of grain' is often taken to be a conflation of two readings: the present שבע and an original שבר, ('grain'). That seems unnecessary: שבע always means 'a plenitude of food' (cf. Gen. 41: 29, 30, 31, 34, 47, 53; Qoh. 5: 1) without any need for specification, and is an adequate parallel to the 'new wine', or 'must', of the second stich.

3: 11–12   The appeal has strong links with the theme and vocabulary of Deut. 8: 5 and Job 5: 17, and only in the Job passage is there any obvious stress upon the disciplinary aspect of instruction. Some commentators (cf. BHS) read ויכאיב or some similar causative form of כאב, ('be in pain'), in place of כאב, ('as a father'). This can hardly be justified on the basis of LXX, which has probably just tried to take כאב as a verb. In Job 5: 18, יכאיב does appear, but that verse has no specific connections with Prov. 3: 11–12. Nothing in the context suggests that these verses are to do with accepting punishment from Yahweh.

3: 14–15   *gold...corals*: see on 8: 10–11, below.

3: 18   *tree of life*: see p. 109.

blessed: the Pual of אשר is found also in Is. 9: 15 ('be led') and Ps. 41: 3 (ET, 2; 'be protected'?) The two participles in the second stich do not agree in number, and מאשר should perhaps be emended to a plural.

3: 20   The change of tense between the two stichs reflects a difference between the two events: the eruption of the depths is past and complete, the dropping of the dew something that continues to happen.

3: 21   In MT, the clause beginning 'do not let them slip...' precedes 'guard prudence...', but there is no obvious antecedent for the suffix pronoun 'them', and I have followed the usual practice of reversing the clauses. Fox believes that a couplet has been lost, which is very possible.

3: 22　　*throat*: there may be a play on the meanings of נפש here: 'throat' makes a good parallel to 'neck' in the second stich, but life is given to a 'soul', or 'self'.

3: 24　　*lie down*: תשב, ('you sit down'), is sometimes read for תשכב in the first stich (cf. LXX). This is attractive, but unnecessary (it also implies a level of paranoia beyond normal night-time anxiety: how often does sitting down induce fear?).

3: 27　　*those due it*: there is some question about whether בעליו, ('its owners'), can mean 'those to whom it is owed', but the idea that something properly belongs to someone who is owed it seems reasonable enough.

3: 31　　*choose*: Prov. 24: 19 is closely associated with Ps. 37: 1, and this saying is reminiscent of both. It is not so close, though, that we should follow BHS's command (which cites the LXX misleadingly) to emend תבחר, ('choose') to the תתחר, ('fret at') found in those passages.

3: 32　　*abomination to Yahweh*: the expression is used in a variety of contexts, only by Proverbs and Deuteronomy; McKane's distinction between a monolatric demand in Deuteronomy and perception of moral flaw in Proverbs is false (compare, e.g., Deut. 25: 16; Prov. 11: 1).

3: 34　　*to mockers*: the general sense is clear, but the first two words of the Hebrew, אם ללצים, (literally 'if to mockers'), present some difficulties. BHS suggests עם לצים, on the model of Ps. 18: 26, and this may be the best solution.[21]

3: 35　　*rebellious*: מרים seems to be a singular participle, from the Hiphil stem of רום, ('be high'), while the apparent

---

[21] Driver ('Problems', 176) and McKane take אם as concessive, which is a possibility, but this does require understanding the Waw conjunctive of the second stich to mean 'yet', or omitting it altogether. Both scholars also retain the ל prefixed to לצים: Driver as an accusative particle taken from Aramaic, and McKane, more realistically, as a prepositional 'with respect to'. Neither suggestion is very convincing.

subject, 'fools', is plural. Parallelism with the first stich, moreover, would lead us to expect a verb of acquisition, not elevation. Fox, on the basis of 14: 29, thinks that acquisition may be an extended sense of the verb; this is attractive, but tenuous. I take the verb of the first stich to be understood in the second, so that מרים, is a participle or adjective describing the fools. If so, it may be a Hiphil participle—ממרים, from מרה,—with the usual meaning 'rebellious', from which the initial מ has been lost (squeezed between two others). This is only one of many unsatisfactory possibilities, but it fits the context well.

4: 3 *for*: or 'when'.

only child: the meaning of the term יחיד is clear (cf. Jer. 6: 26; Amos 8: 10; Zech. 12: 10), but its implication here is not. Some manuscripts read לבני for לפני, but the latter is to be preferred.

4: 4–7 Unless the order of stichs is reversed, the second part of verse 5 must be taken as an interjection, and the syntax of 4: 7 is awkward. The problems are not so serious, though, as to demand emendation, and the LXX confusion here does not point to a different Hebrew *Vorlage*.

4: 11 The tense is suggested by v. 12: the promise to the son is not conditional here.

straight: ישר can indicate literal straightness or moral uprightness: both senses are in play here.

4: 13 *her*: מוסר is masculine, and if the feminine pronouns here are not to be corrected,[22] then we must assume that instruction has been personified as a woman, perhaps on the model of Wisdom. That would accord with the very physical החזק, ('hold'), at the beginning of the verse.

4: 16 *stumble*: the Kethib is from the Qal stem, so it would be the wicked themselves who stumble; the Qere, though, is from the causative, Hiphil stem.

---

[22] The suffix pronoun might be repointed as an unusual defective spelling of the masculine, and one manuscript does have הוא for היא (Whybray); these are very slight grounds for correction, though.

4: 18   The conjunction at the beginning of the verse, and the break in continuity, are both strong grounds for reversing the order of 4: 18 and 19; the present text, though, is by no means impossible.

bright light: perhaps specifically the light of dawn (Fox). *growing ever brighter*: ה(ו)לך, followed by ו + adjective/participle indicates continual development; e.g. 1 Sam. 17: 41; 2 Sam. 3: 1.

4: 22   *to them ... each*: retaining the plural participle in the first stich, and the singular pronoun in the second.

4: 23   *look after your heart*: surely not to do with careful speech (Fox), but with preserving one's integrity, which is what keeps one alive.

sources: תוצאות is normally used of the extremities of a territory, although in Ps. 68: 21 (ET, 20) it may describe 'escape' from death. The sense here is probably closer to that of מוצא, a 'source' or 'going out'.

4: 24   *twisting*: לזות occurs only here. The verb לוז is used variously to describe being crooked or slipping away (as in v. 21), and parallelism suggests that the former is more likely to be the connotation of the noun here.

4: 25   *eyeballs*: cf. Ugaritic ʿpʿp.

4: 26   *watch carefully*: the sense of פלס is unclear, although the verb appears a number of times, usually taking roads or paths as its object.[23] Some commentators take it to mean 'make straight', or 'level', while others prefer 'pay attention', or 'scrutinize'. Neither solution is entirely satisfactory.

5: 2   *lips*: it is not necessary to make the son the object of this sentence through extensive emendation (cf. BHS); it is interesting, though, that the son should become a protector of the qualities that protect him. A similar expression is found in Mal. 2: 7.

5: 3   Many commentators insert a warning against the foreign woman before this verse, taking the motive clause here to

---

[23] The verb occurs elsewhere in connection with a road or roads in Ps. 78: 50; Prov. 5: 6, 21; Is. 26: 7. The only other occurrence is in Ps. 58: 3 (ET, 2).

be inappropriate for the admonition that precedes it. Two minor stylistic issues tell against this: the presence of זרה in the text already, which would surely be repeating any inserted admonition, and the catchword linking through 'lips'. More importantly, emendation is unnecessary: as in 2: 16, protection from the power of the woman's speech is itself an adequate motive for receiving instruction.

drip honey: this expression evokes the seductiveness both of the woman's speech and of her person: when a similar metaphor is used in Song 4: 11, the reference is probably to kissing.

5: 4   *end*: the word is ambiguous, and many commentators take it to mean the outcome inflicted on the woman's victims. Its use in 5: 11, and the expression of the woman's ignorance in 5: 6, however, suggest that it is her own fate that is being described here as bitter and painful, in direct contrast to her words. The son is being warned against being dragged down with her.

double-edged: the emendation of פיות to the reduplicated form פיפיות (cf. Is. 41: 15; Ps. 149: 6) enjoys some manuscript support, but is hardly necessary: cf. Judg. 3: 16. The edges of swords are, literally, 'mouths' in Hebrew, and so there is a play on the imagery of the previous verse which cannot be rendered in English.

5: 5   *going down to Death . . . grasp*: the verse echoes the ideas of 2: 18 (cf. also 7: 27, 9: 18). The first verb lacks a following preposition or subsequent *he locale*, which possibly reflects a late idiom (cf. Ezek. 32: 27; Ps. 55: 15 [ET, 16]; Job 7: 9; 17: 16). The second verb presents a suspiciously odd picture of steps 'clutching' a path. We might either emend the verb to a singular form and take Sheol as the subject (which would suit the word-order well) or point the verb as Niphal and insert a ב before Sheol. Either course would yield an image similar to that of 5: 22, where the same verb is used, but both would require changes to the consonantal text, and it seems simpler to accept the imagery as it stands.

5: 6   *so that she does not*: פֶּן ('lest') is unlikely to be an error for
            a simple negative, and the second stich is apparently
            parallel with the first, so it seems likely that both are
            consequent on the previous verse. Further, it is possible
            that the verbs should be read as 2 m.s. instead of 3 f.s.,
            suiting the LXX assertion that the woman deliberately
            impedes the son: 'so that you do not watch the way of
            life, her tracks stagger (and) you do not know'. I think,
            however, that if the author intended a change of person,
            he would have signalled it. In any case, the vocabulary
            matches that of 4: 26, and suggests a failure to obey the
            advice given there.

            does not know: there is no conjunction before the verb,
            and the preceding clause is probably to be taken as its
            object; the first stich seems to have a similar word-order.

5: 7   *sons*: although the verbs are singular, there is no need to
            emend to 'son': plural forms are found in the other
            resumptive appeals at 7: 24 and 8: 32.

5: 9   *authority*: הוד is usually the majestic appearance of a king
            or of God as king. In Num. 27: 20, however, it is used in
            the context of Moses investing Joshua with some of his
            own authority, and a similar sense is probable here.

            others... cruel: although it sounds like the preceding
            אחרים and rhymes with נכרי at the end of the next
            verse, אכזרי has a sense quite different from the other
            terms used here: it indicates not foreignness but cruelty,
            and, as a substantive, it may be used of ruthless divine
            punishment (e.g. Is. 13: 9). However, that would make
            little sense here, and the association may be with the
            ruthlessness of foreign enemies depicted in e.g., Jer.
            6: 22–3; 50: 42. It is conceivable that, from such usage,
            the term has actually acquired some secondary connota-
            tion of foreignness. In any case, the singular should be
            retained: the reference is probably to the same individual
            who is נכרי in v. 10.

5: 10   *strangers... foreign*: the two adjectives commonly used of
            the woman are here split apart, but associate the refer-
            ence with her.

strength... toil: although כח means 'wealth' in Job 6: 22, עצב never does (cf. Gen. 3: 16, Prov. 10: 22; 14: 23; 15: 1; Ps. 127: 2), and Prov. 10: 22 would be nonsensical if the word had this sense. The reference here, then, is not to the payment of compensation after an act of adultery, but to labouring for the benefit of others. Meinhold usefully compares Hos. 7: 9, and McKane Sir. 26: 19 (which may itself draw on Proverbs 1–9).

5: 11   *groan*: used of a lion's growling elsewhere, but of human complaint also in Ezek. 24: 23.

in the future: cf. Prov. 19: 20. Literally 'your' future.

flesh: cf. Ps. 73: 26.

5: 12–13   *instruction... teaching*: the failure is expressed using the language of the appeals. 'Hating instruction' is used in Ps. 50: 17 of the wicked, who ignore God and keep company with thieves and adulterers.

teacher... instructor: I repoint the nouns as singular (cf. LXX): the reference is clearly back to the father, and 'turn my ear' picks up the vocabulary of this section's initial appeal.

5: 14   *quickly*: as Fox. כמעט more often means 'almost', but there is no indication that the son has retrieved his situation, and it is doubtful the writer believes that he could (cf. 2: 19). For the meaning 'in a little time', see Song 3: 4 and especially Ezek. 16: 47.

congregation and assembly: whatever historical institutions, if any, might have been described using these terms, in combination they probably refer simply and generally to the assembled people of Israel. The son is not making public confession to some council, but declaring that his ruin, caused by alienation from his own community, took place in the very heart of that community.

5: 15–17   The water imagery in these verses has been interpreted in many ways, most memorably as a reference to distribution of the son's semen. I take the central distinction here to be between water that is confined inside and water that runs freely: wells and cisterns are enclosed, private sources, in contrast to the springs and streams of water that are inevitably dissipated outside the household. The 'inside' here is probably not an existing marriage, but the Jewish community within which the son is to marry: he is to drink from a source which is enclosed, and involves no distribution of resources to strangers.

from inside: מתוך picks up בתוך in the last verse, indicating the link between this metaphorical cistern and the community it represents. It is contrasted with חוצה in the next verse.

springs... channels: these are public sources of water, which cannot be confined to a private dwelling. The פלג may be a fabricated drain or canal (cf. Job 38: 25), and is depicted as a source of refreshment in Is. 32: 2; in Prov. 21: 1 it is something that may be redirected. We might think in terms of an irrigation channel, or perhaps, in this context, a gutter.

overflow: for this sense of the verb, cf. Zech. 1: 17, although the common implication of 'scattering' may still be present.

let them be: the subject of the verb is the waters.

5: 18   *fount*: מקור picks up the preceding imagery, but is not a part of that metaphor. Having described the ruin to be caused by involvement with the foreign woman, the writer now proposes a happier alternative. The fountain is not the wife, but the source of the man's prosperity (cf. Hos. 13: 15; Jer. 51: 36), which will be blessed by his proper behaviour.

5: 19   *hind... doe*: this language is probably borrowed from love poetry.

love: repointing דדיה with some versional support (cf. BHS), and in line with 7: 18, where this vocabulary is echoed.

giddy: שגה, here and in the next verse, can be used of alcoholic intoxication (cf. Is. 28: 7; Prov. 20: 1), which is apparently the underlying metaphor here, as the writer extends his drinking imagery. Its basic sense, though, is of going astray, or, by extension, of committing a sin without being aware of it (e.g., Job 6: 24; Lev. 4: 13).

This is the meaning picked up in verse 23, creating a wordplay that is impossible to reproduce in English.

6: 21   *bind*: קשר is used in Deut. 6: 8 and 11: 18 of binding commandments to one's hand.

6: 22   *walking ... lying down ... awake*: cf. Deut. 6: 7; 11: 19.

she: the subject of the three feminine singular verbs here is the תורה of the initial appeal, unless the writer is looking forward to the three concepts described in the next verse.

6: 23   *lamp ... light*: the word of God is described, using the same terms, in Ps. 119: 105. More generally, God is to send out a light that guides in Ps. 43: 3, and Jacob is to walk in God's light in Is. 2: 5. As Whybray observes, 'light' in many texts was regularly interpreted as a metaphor for the divine law by later Jewish commentators.

what is learned: emending תוכחות to תוכחת with some textual support (cf. BHS). Proverbs 1–9 usually prefers the singular form (cf. 1: 23; 3: 11; 5: 12).

6: 24   *woman of evil*: this may be an explicit identification of the woman, or else (perhaps more probably) an error for the expected זרה. Some commentators repoint to read 'the wife of a neighbour', which would be plausible in this context (cf. v. 29), and was probably how the LXX read it; this, however, presents a less satisfactory parallel to 'foreign'.[24]

smoothness: חלקות is used also in Ps. 12: 3–4 and Is. 30: 10 to indicate speech that is agreeable but false (cf. the similar forms in Dan. 11: 21, 32, 34); the related adjective has already been used in 5: 3 of the woman's palate.

tongue: repointing to the construct.

6: 25   *beauty ... eyelids*: the bizarre image may have been inspired by the assonance between יפיה ('her beauty') and עפעפיה ('her eyelids', or 'eyeballs').

6: 26   *for ... hunts*: notoriously obscure, although there is general agreement that this contrasts the aims of the married

---

[24] The Greek expression clearly means 'the wife of another man' when it is used elsewhere, in Sir. 9: 9; 41: 21.

woman with those of a prostitute. The abnormal length suggests that the text may be corrupt. Unless we accept the suggestion of Driver that בעד can mean 'price' or 'fee', which has little evidence to support it, it seems best to delete the ב as an error (inspired by the common preposition בעד). BDB proposes 'prey' for עד as a noun, but the usage elsewhere in Gen. 49: 27 and Is. 33: 23 suggests that it means not 'what is sought' but 'what has been caught'. I therefore read the verse literally as: 'a catch [consisting] of a piece of bread is the prostitute's catch'.

precious soul: it seems unlikely that נפש יקרה here means nothing more than a wealthy or important man:[25] the married woman is surely not just in search of further financial support. It is hard to ignore Ezekiel 13: 17–23, which attests to a magical practice in which women apparently 'hunt souls' (the vocabulary is the same as that used here), using amulets or bands that apparently give them power of life or death over the wearer. Such a practice may have informed the imagery: the woman seeks such power. יקר ('precious') is used in 1: 13 of the spoils sought by the robbers; ironically, the noun used in Esth. 1: 20 of the honour owed by wives to their husbands is closely related to this adjective.

6: 27   *snatch up . . . breast*: the verb is used of picking up burning coals in Is. 30: 14. The reference is apparently to using a fold of clothing to carry loose objects.

6: 30   *is not despised*: the verb is impersonal, rather than strictly passive: 'they do not despise'. It could be translated as a question: 'Do they not despise?', but this seems the less natural reading. The point is that a thief is punished even when his desperation might evoke some sympathy; the adulterer does not have this excuse, and his punishment is thus all the more certain.

6: 31   *sevenfold*: Exod. 21: 37–22: 6 [ET, 22: 7] suggests that this exaction is more harsh than the biblical law demands.

---

[25] Winton Thomas, 'Notes', 283–4.

Penalties for theft are not prescribed systematically or comprehensively in the biblical sources, however, and this may be either a customary penalty or, more likely, a general way of saying 'many times over' (cf. Gen. 4: 15, 24; Ps. 79: 12).

6: 32   *destroys his soul*: note the reference back to v. 26; my loose translation 'fill his belly' in v. 30 also reflects a use of נפש.

6: 33   *beating*: the term usually refers to affliction with, or the symptoms of disease. In Deut. 21: 5 (cf. 17: 8), however, it stands in parallel with ריב to indicate a type of case that may be settled by the Levites, and it seems possible that the usage here is technical, implying more than a simple assault. In any case, the cognate verb is used in v. 29 of 'touching' the woman, and so there is probably a deliberate play on words here: the man receives what he has given.

6: 34   *jealousy... day of vengeance*: although קנאה is used to express a husband's jealousy in Num. 5: 14, 30, it is frequently used of divine anger or jealousy (e.g. Deut. 32: 21; Is. 42: 13; Ezek. 5: 13; Zech. 8: 2). The יום נקם ('day of vengeance') also has strong associations with divine action, especially in the Isaianic corpus (cf. Is. 34: 8; 61: 2; 63: 4). The terms קנאה and נקם are linked in Is. 59: 17, while קנאה is associated with the similar יום עברה in Zeph. 1: 18, and it seems highly probable that this terminology would have had strong eschatological connotations in the post-exilic period. The idea of a divine day of anger is found elsewhere in Proverbs (cf. 11: 4). The idea of having no mercy (חמל) is also widely associated with divine action (e.g. Lam. 2: 21; Ezek. 5: 11; Zech. 11: 6).

6: 35   *bought off... compensation*: literally 'he will not lift his face for any compensation'. The expression is used in Deut. 10: 17 to assert God's impartiality. 'Compensation' (כפר) may be paid as an alternative to the death penalty (e.g. Exod. 21: 28–30); a 'bribe' (שחד), on the other hand, is used to pervert or circumvent the legal process (e.g. Prov. 17: 23).

7: 2   *keep*: the verb governs both stichs, although it appears
          only in the first, and is separated from its second object
          by the command to live; stylistically, this is odd.
          commandments... teaching: the same terms are paired as
          in the appeal that began the previous section, and they
          are followed by similar imagery based on Deuteronomy.
          pupil of your eye: Deut. 32: 10; Ps. 17: 8 both use the
          expression for divine protection; in Prov. 7: 9 and 20: 20
          (Kethib), the only other uses, it is associated with black-
          ness. Lit. 'eyes'.

7: 3   *tablet of your heart*: see p. 105, above.

7: 4   *my sister... cousin*: although אחתי ('my sister') is a term
          used to address a lover in Song of Songs (e.g. 5: 1), the
          parallel מדע occurs only in Ruth 2: 1 (Qere) as a reference
          to actual kinship (cf. מדעת in Ruth 3: 2). We should
          probably not, therefore, view this as an explicit invitation
          to take Wisdom as a lover.

7: 5   After the initial verb, this verse is identical to 2: 16. The
          verb has probably been changed to fit verses 1–2, where
          שמר was used in the commands to 'keep' those things
          that are now to 'keep' the son.

7: 6   The LXX, perhaps confused by the lack of an initial verb,
          portrays the woman herself looking out of her window,
          seeking a victim.[26] Independently of this, some scholars
          have suggested that the speaker here is female (the
          mother, or Wisdom), on the basis that we must reckon
          with a familiar literary motif, reflected elsewhere in Judg.
          5: 28; 2 Sam. 6: 16; 2 Kgs. 9: 30.[27] However, looking out
          the window serves a different function in each narrative
          cited, and there is no reason to suppose that a connection
          is supposed to be drawn between the passages, even

[26] On Boström's attempts to see this as the original text, to be read in terms of a
specific Phoenician motif (*Proverbiastudien* 121–2), see C. Maier, *Die 'fremde Frau'*,
198–208.

[27] See, e.g. A. Brenner, 'Some Observations on the Figuration of Woman in
Wisdom Literature', in H. McKay and D. J. A. Clines (eds), *Of Prophets' Visions and
the Wisdom of Sages: Essays in Honour of R. Norman Whybray on his Seventieth
Birthday* (JSOTS 162; Sheffield: JSOT Press, 1993), 192–208, especially 195.

within the context of the Deuteronomistic History. The same objections apply to Robert O'Connell's suggestion that scenes involving women and windows represent a 'type-scene' involving 'not just sexual attraction or its frustrated potential, but also deception and the threat of death'.[28]

7: 7   *lacking sense*: the same expression is used of the adulterer in the last section (6: 23).

7: 8   *a corner*: the MT pointing is apparently an attempt to read the noun with a feminine suffix—'her corner' (cf. GK §91e). While this may make some sense, as the corner at which one turns down the woman's street, it is grammatically improbable, and is not a reading shared by other versions.

    sets foot: the main verb represents a separate action, as the youth turns the corner, which is not simultaneous with the action in the first stich.

7: 9   *eye of night*: the darkness grows deeper with each description, culminating in blackness as dark as the pupil of an eye (cf. on v. 2, above). The growing darkness is a counterpart to the growing light of 4: 18. It is surely no coincidence that the rare אישון appears twice in a few verses here: where the eye was something to cherish before, now it is something deeply menacing.

7: 10   *dress*: The word שית ('dress;') is only found elsewhere in Ps. 73: 6, and its precise meaning is uncertain.

    close of heart: literally 'guarding heart'. The meaning of this expression is uncertain, although it is probably supposed to contrast with the previous description. Perhaps her clothes are revealing, but her heart remains hidden.

7: 11   *exuberant*: the word may refer to the growling of hungry dogs (Ps. 59: 15) or of bears (Is. 59: 11), but also to the playing of stringed instruments (Is. 16: 11), so the reference is not to a particular noise or level of noise. I adopt the common sense of commotion, or 'fizzing' (cf. Zech. 9: 15), rather than the 'loud' of, e.g., RSV.

---

[28] O'Connell, 'Fatal Deception', 237.

rebellious: סרר is used exclusively of Israel's rebellion against God, except in Pss. 66: 7; 68: 7, 19 [ET, 6, 18], where it refers to individuals who resist God. The term apparently has, then, strong religious connotations, to the extent that it is almost a technical term.

7: 12   *lies in wait*: the expression is the same as that used of the sinners in 1: 11, 18.

7: 13   *sets her face*: literally, 'makes her face strong'. The expression occurs also in Qoh. 8: 1 and Prov. 21: 29. In the latter, it implies behaviour that can be contrasted with 'considering one's ways', and so the implication may be of reckless confidence.

7: 14   *sacrifices… vows*: נדר is specifically a vow to a deity (generally YHWH, but once, in Jer. 44: 25, to another god).

7: 15   *your face*: probably just a poetic way of saying 'you'.

7: 16   *embroideries of Egyptian linen*: since the first two words of the stich are both *hapax*, any translation must be uncertain; for the one offered here, cf. *HALOT*. The general sense, though, is suggested by the parallel stich.

7: 18   *intoxicated*: the vocabulary ironically echoes that of 5: 19, where the son was invited to be drunk on the affection of the wife of his youth.

7: 19   *no man*: literally 'there is not the man at home'. The expression is curious: unless we are dealing with an idiom, 'my man'—that is, 'my husband'—would have been more precise. It is just possible, therefore, that the reference is more general, and that 'the man' is the head of the household, whether that be as the woman's husband or as her father: there is no other indication in the story that the woman is married.

     journey from afar: דרך מרחק is unlikely to mean just a 'long journey', and the abnormal uses of מרחק for 'to a distance' in Is. 22: 3; 23: 7 hardly justify ignoring the normal sense of the word. On the most natural reading, the husband is on his way home from a distant starting point.

7: 20   *full moon*: כסא ('full moon') only occurs elsewhere in Ps. 81: 4 [ET, 3], and the meaning is not established beyond doubt. Fontaine, *Smooth Words*, 46, sees in the references to sacrifice and the moon a declaration that the woman is not menstruating. Meinhold takes the full moon reference to be an indication of time (since the current darkness suggests the new moon).

7: 21   *persuasion*: לקח is literally 'teaching', and was used of the parental instruction in 4: 2. In Prov. 16: 21, 23, it implies persuasiveness, but the term is not pejorative.

drives: in Deut. 13: 6, 11, 14 [ET, 5, 10, 13] this verb is used of driving Israel away from God into idolatry (cf. 2 Kgs. 17: 21 Qere; 2 Chron. 21: 11).

7: 22   *suddenly*: פתאם is also used of sudden ruin in 3: 25 and 6: 15.

slaughter: טבח is not a sacrificial term, but refers to the slaughter of animals for food; Is. 53: 7 and Jer. 11: 9 use the similar image of a lamb going to slaughter.

a mountain-goat skipping into a snare: as it stands, this verse seems to mean 'like a bangle to the discipline of a fool', which makes no sense. The text is probably corrupt, and although some commentators, e.g. Plöger, try to retain a reference to the fool, most emend אויל to איל, 'a mountain-goat'. מוסר can be repointed to mean a 'band' or 'fetter', and this could, by extension, suggest a noose, snare or other restraint. As a noun, עכס means an ankle bracelet or bangle (Is. 3: 16), but a verb with the sense 'hop' or 'skip' is attested at Qumran; cf. *HALOT*.

7: 23   *costing his life*: ב of price. The same expression is used in 1 Kgs. 2: 23.

7: 27   *ways*: דרך is apparently feminine here; contrast 4: 26.
halls of death: possibly a mythological reference.

8: 2   *slopes*: Toy suggests that the reference is to raised roads.
on... among: עלי is an unusual poetic form of על, and בית here is usually taken as a late form of בין (attested elsewhere only in Job 8: 17; Ezek. 41: 9).

8: 3   *by the side... at the mouth of*: the sequence of unusual prepositions continues, with two based on body parts. In the next stich, however, 'entrance' unexpectedly lacks a preposition altogether.

town: קרת, used here and in 9: 3, 14, is unusual and probably late.

cries out: the form is plural, as when the same verb is used of Wisdom in 1: 20. There, though, 'Wisdom' itself had a plural form, and we must assume either that the same was originally true of the name here, or that 1: 20 has influenced the text.

8: 4   *men ... sons of man*: the form אישים is found elsewhere only in Ps. 141: 4 and Is. 53: 3; the parallel expression בני אדם is hardly more common (cf. 2 Sam. 7: 14; Ps. 49: 3 [ET, 2]; 62: 10 [ET, 9]).

8: 6   *straightforwardness*: נגידים can hardly have its normal sense of 'princes', but the word is not an adjective, and is unlikely to mean 'princely things'; if it did, we might anyway expect a feminine form. This is probably an unattested or new coinage from the root, perhaps formed by analogy with מישרים in the next stich, which always has a masculine plural form.

8: 7   *palate ... lips*: Wisdom's speech is explicitly contrasted with that of the woman, cf. 5: 3.

8: 8–9   *twisted ... right*: עקש described the paths of the wicked in 2: 15, and so Wisdom is again contrasted with her counterparts, but now using the vocabulary of paths and ways. נכח (in its substantive form) was used in 4: 25 of walking on the path, and ישר appears not only there, but also in 2: 13; 3: 6; 4: 11 as a description of the paths themselves.

8: 10–11   *gold ... corals*: although such declarations of Wisdom's value are not uncommon (e.g. Job 28: 15–19; Prov. 16: 16; 20: 15) the link with the similar comparison in 3: 14–15 is reinforced by the use of these two unusual words. חרוץ, which is rare and always occurs in parallel with כסף, is found again in 8: 19 (see below) and in 16: 16. Otherwise it occurs only in Ps. 68: 14 [ET, 13] and Zech. 9: 3.

no desires compare with it: this is virtually a repetition of 3: 15b.

8: 12–13   At the beginning of 8: 12, I take the verb to be a wrongly pointed Piel (cf. Whybray), since the Qal would surely require a preposition; to take the final character of ערמה as an archaic case-ending seems altogether too desperate. I then take 'Wisdom' to be the object of the verb rather than a reference to the speaker: Wisdom offers wisdom. Finally, I take the מזמות to be the tricks of the bad characters, which Wisdom will expose.

8: 12   *I, Wisdom*: this could be translated as a separate clause: 'I am Wisdom.'

     established... offer: repointing שכנתי as a Piel to mean 'dwell' makes little sense, and would probably require a following preposition. I also emend אמצא to Hiphil אמציא.

8: 13   *pride*: גאה is apparently used as an abstract noun only here, and it is possible that we should instead translate 'the proud man'.

8: 14   *I am*: if it is not a mistake for לי, then אני here echoes the self-introduction in v. 12.

8: 16   *all the governors of the earth*: I accept the usual emendation of צדק to ארץ, which has good versional support and improves the sense.

8: 18   *extraordinary*: עתק is only found here, and its meaning is uncertain. In Is. 23: 18, the similar עתיק might perhaps be understood in terms of the preceding שביה ('plenty'): hence my translation here. A good case could also be made for translating as 'ancient'.

     righteousness: the word is unexpected here, but is probably included because righteousness is seen as the prerequisite for prosperity. Attempts to show that צדקה can mean 'prosperity' seem misguided: even if any convincing instances could be found, it is hardly likely that readers would have ignored the normal sense of the word.

8: 21   *fill their treasuries*: Wisdom promises to accomplish what the robbers had earlier promised falsely in 1: 13 (note also הון in v. 18; cf. 1: 13).

8: 22   *got*: although the sense 'create' is sometimes found for קנה (Gen. 14: 19, 22; Deut. 32: 6; Ps. 139: 13), it nearly always means 'acquire'. Had the writer been aware of the later theological problems caused by this ambiguity, he would doubtless have expressed himself more precisely.

start of his way: Behemoth is described similarly in Job 40: 19, but the expression may have been borrowed from here, and gives no basis for assuming that דרך was a common way of describing the creation. ראשית דרך is most naturally understood as the beginning of a path. It is not certain whether wisdom is acquired *at* or *as* this beginning, but one might expect a preposition for the former. The key assertion is that wisdom and the divine way were already in existence when the world came into being.

8: 23   *formed*: נסך is used of royal installation in Ps. 2: 6 (cf. נסיך, 'prince'), but the form is probably either from a verb, נסך ('pour out', 'spread'), or from סכך, which is used of forming a foetus in Ps. 139: 13, Job 10: 11. The context suggests the last, and what follows, as many commentators have noted, seems to involve an account of Wisdom's birth and growing up.

The temporal construction in the verse is distinctive, with the 'then' clause sandwiched between the 'since' clauses; this pattern is essentially repeated in 24 and in 25–6, and then an extended form is used in 27–9.

8: 24   *born*: the verb may mean 'brought forth' or 'born'. The latter seems more appropriate for a personification, but should not be taken too literally: we need hardly follow Lang, *Wisdom*, 64–5, in looking for a mother or mechanism of birth.

no depths: the writer either does not share the idea of creation depicted in Gen. 1, or else envisages a still earlier stage when the depths of Gen. 1: 1 had not yet come into being.

8: 27   Note the strong alliteration in both stichs: שם / שמים and חוג / בחוקו.

cut out a disc: cf. Job 26: 10, where the disc lies at the boundary of light and darkness. We know too little about the cosmology of the period to establish precisely what is envisaged here. חקק ('cut') can be used of hollowing something out (cf. Is. 22: 16).

8: 28　　　*strengthened*: emending בעזוז to בעזזו (cf. BHS).

8: 29　　　The first two stichs of this verse are not represented in the
　　　　　LXX translation, and the second breaks the pattern of
　　　　　temporal clauses beginning with ב. If original, this sec-
　　　　　ond stich is parenthetical.

　　　　　limit: cf. Jer. 5: 22; Job 38: 10, which both use חק, as here.

　　　　　transgress his word: יעברו־פיו may refer to 'crossing' the
　　　　　divine command, but the expression is a little odd. It is
　　　　　possible that the reference is to the 'measure' of the limit
　　　　　(which is close to some uses of פה with prepositions), or
　　　　　that it is an error for יעברנהו (cf. Jer. 5: 22).

8: 30–31　The last two stichs of verse 30 are clearly structured
　　　　　chiastically with the two stichs of verse 31, as indicated
　　　　　by the pattern of key words: משחקת ... שעשעים ...
　　　　　ושעשעי ... משחקת. The first two stichs, though, are
　　　　　linked by their initial word, ואהיה, and this makes it
　　　　　difficult simply to take the alliterative first stich with
　　　　　the preceding temporal clauses.

　　　　　And I ... faithfully: on my reading of this notorious crux,
　　　　　see S. Weeks, 'The Context and Meaning of Proverbs
　　　　　8. 30a', *JBL* 125 (2006), 433–42. There may be a specific
　　　　　nuance of religious piety.

　　　　　delightedly: I take the use here to be adverbial, but
　　　　　שעשעים might alternatively indicate that Wisdom is an
　　　　　object of delight.

　　　　　celebrating: when this term is used of celebrating before
　　　　　God in 2 Sam. 6: 5, 21, the celebrations involve singing
　　　　　and music; the idea is more one of partying than of
　　　　　childish playing.

8: 31　　　*earthly world*: literally 'the world of his earth'. Cf. Job
　　　　　37: 12.

8: 32　　　*follow*: the text is probably corrupt here. In macarisms,
　　　　　אשרי ('happy') is not an adjective, but a noun in the
　　　　　construct state, and must, therefore, be followed by an
　　　　　expression denoting the possessor of the happiness.[29] If

---

[29] Generally a noun, but a relative clause is sometimes used (Pss 137: 8–9; 146: 5;
cf. the implicit relative in Ps. 65: 5.)

this stich were a macarism, it would be saying, therefore, that the ways themselves are happy, not those who keep them. The initial copula would also be curious, if this were a statement following the initial command. I read אשרי as from אשר ('step' or 'way'), and delete the initial *yodh* from the verb as a dittograph. The literal sense would then be 'and keep the steps of my ways'.[30]

8: 33   *it*: the verb has no explicit object, and a word may have been lost from the end of the stich.

8: 34   *by watching . . . guarding*: these verbs are in the infinitive construct with ל, and cannot be taken as parallel with the main verb.

8: 35   *find*: following the Qere.

8: 36   *his very self*: the contrast with the previous verse suggests that נפשו here means more than just 'himself'.

9: 1   *Wisdom*: for the plural form of the name, see above at 1: 20.
        set up: emending ח to ה, and reading as a Hiphil from נצב, which is used elsewhere of setting up pillars etc. (e.g., Gen. 35: 14; 1 Sam. 15: 12).
        seven pillars: the Hebrew seems clear, but the significance of the act is not.

9: 2   *prepared her meat*: literally 'slaughtered her slaughtering'. For the term טבח, see 7: 22 above.
        slopes: גפי is obscure; I follow *HALOT*.

9: 6   *the ignorant*: פתאים cannot be vocative, since the verb עזב requires an object and there are no other candidates. If the term were an abstract noun, we should expect the feminine, as probably in 9: 13. I take it to indicate the general class of those who are ignorant, which the individual is invited to leave. It is possible, though much less likely, that we should read פתאם, used nominally as in 3: 25 (cf. Job 22: 10), to indicate the coming sudden destruction of the wicked.

9: 10   this verse appears to be a concluding counterpart to 1: 7, and may have been misplaced from the end of the section.

---

[30] MT has probably been influenced by v. 34, but the confusion of the LXX suggests that the misreading may have been very early.

sacred: קדשים most naturally refers to individuals loyal to YHWH (Ps. 16: 3; 34: 9 [ET, 10]; cf. Deut. 33: 3; Dan. 8: 24), or else to heavenly beings (e.g. Ps. 89: 6, 8 [ET, 5, 7]; Job 5: 1). Here, as in 30: 3 and Hos. 12: 1 [ET, 11: 12], it is tempting to take it as a reference to God himself, but a more likely explanation is that the heavenly court is being used as a metonym for the divine realm.

9: 11   *by me*: the first-person suffix here is the sole justification for retaining this verse, while those around it are generally regarded as secondary. It is possible, of course, that בי is itself an error for בה, inspired by the previous כי.

9: 13   *folly*: אשת is probably either an explanatory gloss or a dittograph of the previous word (cf. BHS). The plural form of כסילות, found only here, is apparently intended to match that of חכמות in the first verse.

delights in ignorance: if we take the text as it stands, with המיה indicating that the woman is exuberant, as in 7: 11, then we should read: 'Folly is exuberant, (she is) ignorance.' פתיות, however, cannot be the object when the verb is intransitive, and, since the verb is singular, it would sit uncomfortably as an adjective describing the woman. Several solutions have been proposed. Although פתיות is unique, there is no very good reason to discard it, since it seems a perfectly legitimate coinage, parallel to כסילות. It is simpler to assume that the problem is with the verb, not least because there is no obvious reason to stress the woman's exuberance or restlessness in this context. It is possible that we should emend to היתה, and take the clause as a simple identification, but I prefer to make the more minor change to חמדה. Where Wisdom is skilled and self-sufficient, the woman revels in ignorance, and relies on stolen food.[31]

knows nothing: emendation to כלמה (cf. BHS) is unnecessary. This idiomatic expression is found also in Gen. 39: 8 and 2 Sam. 18: 29 (cf. Whybray).

---

[31] Similar imagery is used in 14: 1 to make a different contrast, between the constructiveness of wisdom and the destructiveness of folly.

9: 14   *throne*: this is a location separate from the woman's house; like Wisdom in 8: 2, she moves around. Just what the term means, though, is uncertain: it is apparently contrasted with the obscure גפי of verse 3.

9: 17   *stolen water... bread of secrecy*: literally, 'waters of thieves, bread of secrets', but גנובים may be formed on the basis of סתרים. The latter is used elsewhere of God's secrets (Deut. 29: 28) or of unknown sins (Ps. 19: 12 [ET, 13]). Compare the 'bread of wickedness and wine of violence' in 4: 17.

9: 18   *he does not know*: the subject is presumably the invitee. There is an echo here of 7: 23.
         shades: cf. 2: 18.

SECONDARY MATERIAL

A Short Collection of Sayings (6: 1–19)

This is regarded as secondary by most commentators. The principal reasons are:

1. It lacks an introductory appeal, but cannot easily be linked with the preceding material.
2. There are only superficial correspondences with the themes and motifs of other materials in Proverbs 1–9, despite that work's tendency toward constant reiteration of its concerns.
3. It seems to interrupt an otherwise consistent focus upon the foreign woman in chapters 5–7.
4. It has affinities with other material that seems to have been inserted secondarily into Proverbs, especially in the second half of chapter 30. More generally, it has much closer links with other material in Proverbs than is typical of chs. 1–9. (Compare 6: 1–5 with 11: 15; 17: 18; 20: 16; 22: 26; 27: 13. Also 6: 6–8 with 30: 25, and 6: 9–11 with the almost identical 24: 33–4. With the distinctive form of 6: 12–15, compare 30: 21–31.)
5. While probably contrived as a short, unified collection, it lacks internal thematic unity, preferring the sort of catchword linking used in the sentence literature.

The material may have been inserted in the present position to pick up the snare imagery of 5: 23. The motive for its insertion is unclear, but it may have been intended to break up a section seen as prurient, by introducing a wider subject matter.

6: 1	My son, if you have given guarantees for your neighbour, struck hands with a stranger,
6: 2	You have been ensnared by the words of your mouth, caught by the words of your mouth.
6: 3	Do this, then, my son, and save yourself, for you have come into your neighbour's grasp: Go, kick and pester your neighbour:
6: 4	Give no sleep to your eyes or slumber to your eyelids,
6: 5	Save yourself, like a gazelle from the hunter, or like a bird from the fowler's hand.
6: 6	Go to the ant, lazybones: watch its ways and be wise.
6: 7	It has no officer, leader, or ruler,
6: 8	It prepares its food in the summer, gathers its provisions at harvest.
6: 9	How long, lazybones, will you lie around? When will you get up from your sleep?
6: 10	A little sleep, a little slumber, a little folding of the hands in rest,
6: 11	Then your impoverishment will catch up like a man strolling along, and your need like a man on his rounds.
6: 12	An evil man is a scoundrel, going around with crooked talk:
6: 13	A wink with his eye, a signal with his foot, a pointing with his fingers.
6: 14	With mischief in mind, he plots evil, stirs up quarrels at every chance.
6: 15	And so his downfall will come suddenly: in a moment he will be broken beyond repair.
6: 16	Six are the things that Yahweh hates, and seven the things that he loathes:
6: 17	Proud eyes, a false tongue, and hands shedding innocent blood,
6: 18	A heart plotting evil schemes, feet hurrying to run to evil,

6: 19   A perjuror telling lies—and one stirring quarrels between
            brothers.

Notes:

6: 1   *for... with*: the prepositions are unclear, but the point
            seems to be that the son has given guarantees to a stran-
            ger on behalf of his neighbour, and will therefore be in
            trouble if his neighbour fails to pay.

6: 2   The sentence may still be governed by the previous con-
            ditional, but is more probably a statement of the position
            into which the son has put himself. The Syriac suggests
            that the repeated expression 'the words of your mouth'
            may be an error in the first stich, and that we should read
            'the word of your lips' (cf. BHS). This would certainly
            give better style.

6: 3   *grasp*: literally 'palm'. Having 'struck palms' to agree the
            deal in v. 1, the son is now ironically in the neighbour's
            palm.

            kick: the verb is obscure. Elsewhere, רפש / רפס is used of
            fouling waters with one's feet (Ezek. 32: 2; 34: 18; cf. Prov.
            25: 26). The only other use of the Hithpael, in Ps. 68: 31
            [ET, 30], is in a very difficult passage, which offers little
            guidance, but does suggest a destructive sense. Appar-
            ently, the son is to do something with his feet. I doubt
            that the other usage permits an extension of this to mean
            'hurry' or 'stir oneself' (cf. LXX), although it is possible
            that he is to 'wear down' the neighbour. I think some-
            thing more direct is intended: he is to kick the neighbour
            into action, literally or metaphorically.

6: 11   *a man strolling along... a man on his rounds*: here and in
            the parallel 24: 34, these terms are notoriously obscure.
            Most translators take the simile to be one of robbers or
            highwaymen intercepting the lazy man, but it is difficult
            to extract this sense. The first word is a Piel participle
            from הלך ('walk'); insofar as the Piel of this verb differs
            in sense from the Qal, it seems normally to indicate a

certain sense of deliberation or stateliness. In 24: 34, the form used is from the Hithpael, which often indicates 'walking about', with no particular place to go. Although the participle of either stem could conceivably have come to attain the special meaning of 'footpad', it is highly improbable that the participles of both stems did so. It is best, therefore, to assume that the reference is to a man walking rather slowly, either aimlessly or with deliberation. The second term seems literally to mean 'man of a shield', but it is difficult to extend this to mean 'an armed man', since words from the root גנן are used exclusively of enclosure or defence: even if it could mean 'soldier', this is hardly the term one would expect for a robber. Albright's attempt to make it mean 'beggar' is based on a misunderstanding of the Ugaritic *mgn*,[32] but the term may be connected with the Hebrew equivalent of that verb, מגן, and I take it to mean something like a 'delivery man', or possibly someone making a presentation. Whatever the precise nuance, the key point is not that the sluggard will be ambushed as he goes on his way, but that he moves so slowly as to be overtaken easily.

6: 12   *scoundrel*: the derivation of בליעל is uncertain, but it is used as a general-purpose pejorative, involving no specific accusation, but some implication of dishonesty (e.g., 1 Sam. 25: 25; 1 Kgs. 21: 13). The normal expression is איש בליעל, but the use of אדם here probably makes no difference to the sense. I take this stich to be a nominal sentence, with הולך in the next stich qualifying the predicate.

crooked talk: literally 'crookedness of mouth'. The term is only otherwise found in 4: 24, but the crookedness here is of a more specific nature.

6: 13   *wink*: winking is also associated with making trouble in 10: 10 and 16: 30.

         signal: many commentators dispute the existence of a verb מלל ('rub') here, and read the participle as from the late verb מלל ('speak'), used metaphorically. The general sense is obvious either way.

6: 14   *mischief*: for this sense of deliberately stirring up trouble through slander, cf. 16: 28.

6: 15   *suddenly... mending*: cf. 29: 1.

6: 16   *things that he loathes*: literally 'the abominations of his soul (נפש)'.

6: 17   *innocent blood*: cf. on 1: 11.

6: 18   *feet... evil*: like 1: 16, this seems to be drawing on Is. 59: 7.

Sayings about Instruction (9: 7–9, 12)

These are less certainly secondary than 6: 1–19, but if original, they have probably been misplaced, since they interrupt and unbalance the cameo. 9: 7–9 stress the consequences of teaching the wise man and the scorner; 9: 12 uses the same opposition to make a separate point, which is more in line with the concerns of Prov. 1–9. If they do belong to the work, they must be taken as an epilogue, perhaps balancing 1: 2–6.

9: 7   He who teaches a scorner gets disgrace for himself, showing a wicked man his defect.

9: 8   Do not correct a scorner lest he hate you; teach a wise man and he will love you.

9: 9   Give to a wise man and he will be even wiser; inform a righteous man and he will grow in learning.

9: 12   If you are wise, you are acting wisely for yourself; if you are a scorner, you will bear the consequences yourself.

Notes:

9: 7   *showing... defect*: I take the second stich to present a second predicate of the teacher: he is humiliated because his teaching uncovers the wicked man's defect. This avoids the need to emend מום, the term used for inherent blemishes, such as those that disqualify potential priests (Lev. 21: 17). Here the meaning is extended, but there is no reason to suppose that it can refer to disgrace rather than imperfection.

9: 8   *teach a wise man:* as in the last verse, יכח does not refer to teaching in a general sense, but to proving a point or correcting an error. With the preposition here, the sense is probably one of showing something new to the wise man. Note the alliteration.

Bibliography of Works Cited

Albright, W. F., 'Some Canaanite-Phoenician sources of Hebrew wisdom', in M. Noth and W. Winton Thomas (eds), *Wisdom in Israel and in the Ancient Near East* (SVT 3; Leiden: Brill, 1955), 1–15.

Aletti, J. N., 'Séduction et parole en Proverbes I–IX', *VT* 27 (1977), 129–44.

Allegro, J. M., 'The Wiles of the Wicked Woman, a Sapiental Work from Qumran's Fourth Cave', *PEQ* 96 (1964), 53–5.

——, *Qumrân Cave 4. I (4Q158–4Q186)* (DJD 5; Oxford: Clarendon Press, 1968), 85–7.

Alster, B., *Proverbs of Ancient Sumer: The World's Earliest Proverb Collections* (Bethesda, MD: CDL Press, 1997).

Arnaud, D., *Recherches au Pays d'Aštata. Emar VI.4 Textes de la Bibliothèque: Transcriptions et traductions* (Synthèse 28; Paris: Éditions Recherche sur les Civilisations, 1987).

Assmann, J., 'Weisheit, Loyalismus und Frömmigkeit', in E. Hornung and O. Keel (eds), *Studien zu altägyptischen Lebenslehren* (OBO 28; Freibourg: Universitätsverlag Freiburg Schweiz, and Göttingen: Vandenhoeck & Ruprecht, 1979), 11–72.

——, 'Schrift, Tod und Identität: Das Grab als Vorschule der Literatur im alten Ägypten', in A. Assmann *et al.* (eds), *Schrift und Gedächtnis: Beitrage zur Archäologie der literarischen Kommunikation* (Munich: W. Fink, 1983), 64–93.

——, 'Weisheit, Schrift und Literatur im alten Ägypten', in A. Assmann (ed.), *Weisheit* (Archäologie der literarischen Kommunikation 3; Munich: W. Fink, 1991), 475–500.

——, *Ägypten: Theologie und Frömmigkeit einer frühen Hochkultur*, 2nd edn (Kohlhammer Urban-Taschenbücher 366; Stuttgart, Berlin, and Cologne: W. Kohlhammer, 1991), part II; ET (of first edition), *The Search for God in Ancient Egypt*, translated by David Lorton (Ithaca: Cornell University Press, 2001).

——, 'Kulturelle und literarische Texte', in A. Loprieno (ed.), *Ancient Egyptian Literature: History and Forms* (Probleme der Ägyptologie 10; Leiden, New York, and Cologne: Brill, 1996), 59–82.

——, 'Cultural and Literary Texts', in G. Moers (ed.), *Definitely: Egyptian Literature*. Proceedings of the Symposium *Ancient Egyptian Literature: History and Forms*, Los Angeles, 24–26 March 1995 (Lingua Aegyptiaca

Studia Monographica 2; Göttingen: Seminar für Ägyptologie und Koptologie, 1999), 1–15.

Baines, J., 'Literacy and Ancient Egyptian Society', *Man* NS 18 (1983), 572–99.

——'Society, Morality, and Religious Practice', in B. E. Schafer (ed.), *Religion in Ancient Egypt: Gods, Myths, and Personal Practice* (London: Routledge, 1991), 123–200.

——, 'Classicism and Modernism in the Literature of the New Kingdom', in A. Loprieno (ed.), *Ancient Egyptian Literature: History and Forms* (Probleme der Ägyptologie 10; Leiden, New York, and Cologne: Brill, 1996), 157–74.

——, 'Contextualising Egyptian Representations of Society and Ethnicity', in J. S. Cooper and G. M. Schwartz (eds), *The Study of the Ancient Near East in the Twenty-First Century: The William Foxwell Albright Centennial Conference* (Winona Lake, IN: Eisenbrauns, 1996), 339–84.

Baumann, G., 'A Figure with Many Facets: The Literary and Theological Functions of Personified Wisdom in Proverbs 1–9', in A. Brenner (ed.), *A Feminist Companion to Wisdom Literature* (The Feminist Companion to the Bible 9; Sheffield: Sheffield Academic Press, 1995), 44–78.

——, *Die Weisheitsgestalt in Proverbien 1–9: Traditionsgeschichtliche und theologische Studien* (FAT 16; Tübingen: Mohr-Siebeck, 1996).

Baumgarten, J. M., 'On the Nature of the Seductress in 4Q184', *RevQ* 15 (1991), 133–43.

Becker, J., *Gottesfurcht im alten Testament* (Analecta Biblica 25; Rome: Pontifical Biblical Institute, 1965).

Bergman, J., 'Gedanken zum Thema "Lehre–Testament–Grab-Name"', in E. Hornung and O. Keel (eds), *Studien zu altägyptischen Lebenslehren* (OBO 28; Freibourg: Universitätsverlag Freiburg Schweiz, and Göttingen: Vandenhoeck & Ruprecht, 1979), 73–104.

Berquist, J. L., *Judaism in Persia's Shadow: A Social and Historical Approach* (Minneapolis: Gortress, 1995).

Bietak, M., *Theben-West (Luqsor): Vorbericht über die ersten vier Grabungskampagnen (1969–1971)* (Österreichische Akademie der Wissenschaften, Philosophisch-historische Klasse 278.4; Vienna: Böhlau, 1972).

Blenkinsopp, J., *Wisdom and Law in the Old Testament: The Ordering of Life in Israel and Early Judaism* (Oxford Bible Series; Oxford: Oxford University Press, 1983).

——, 'The Social Context of the "Outsider Woman" in Proverbs 1–9', *Biblica* 72 (1991), 457–73.

Boström, G., *Proverbiastudien: Die Weisheit und das fremde Weib in Spr. 1–9* (Lunds Universitets Årsskrift, N.F. I.30.3; Lund: Gleerup, 1935).

Boström, L., *The God of the Sages: The Portrayal of God in the Book of Proverbs* (CB OT Series 29; Stockholm: Almqvist & Wiksell International, 1990).

Brenner, A., 'Some Observations on the Figuration of Woman in Wisdom Literature', in H. McKay and D. J. A. Clines (eds), *Of Prophets' Visions and the Wisdom of Sages: Essays in Honour of R. Norman Whybray on his Seventieth Birthday* (JSOTS 162; Sheffield: JSOT Press, 1993), 192–208; reprinted in A. Brenner (ed.), *A Feminist Companion to Wisdom Literature* (The Feminist Companion to the Bible 9; Sheffield: Sheffield Academic Press, 1995), 50–66.

Brunner, H., 'Zitate aus Lebenslehren', in E. Hornung and O. Keel (eds), *Studien zu altägyptischen Lebenslehren* (OBO 28; Freibourg: Universitätsverlag Freiburg Schweiz, and Göttingen: Vandenhoeck & Ruprecht, 1979), 105–71.

——, *Altägyptische Weisheit: Lehren für das Leben* (Darmstadt: Wissenschaftliche Buchgesellschaft, 1988); revised version published as *Die Weisheitsbücher der Ägypter: Lehren für das Leben* (Zurich and Munich: Artemis, 1991).

Buchanan, G. W., 'Midrashim prétannaïtes: à propos de Prov., I–IX', *RB* 72 (1965), 227–39.

Burkard, G., '"Als Gott erschienen spricht er" Die Lehre des Amenemhet als postumes Vermächtnis', in J. Assmann and E. Blumenthal (eds), *Literatur und Politik im pharaonischen und ptolemäischen Ägypten: Vorträge der Tagung zum Gedenken an Georges Posener 5.–10. September 1996 in Leipzig* (Bibliothèque d'Étude 127; Cairo: IFAO, 1999), 153–73.

Burns, J. B., 'Solomon's Egyptian Horses and Exotic Wives', *Forum* 7 (1991), 29–44.

Caminos, R. A., *Late-Egyptian Miscellanies* (Brown Egyptological Studies 1; London: Oxford University Press, 1954).

Camp, C. V., 'The Wise Women of 2 Samuel: A Role Model for Women in Early Israel', *CBQ* 43 (1981), 14–29.

——, *Wisdom and the Feminine in the Book of Proverbs* (Bible and Literature Series 11; Sheffield: Almond, 1985).

——, 'What's So Strange about the Strange Woman?', in D. Jobling, P. L. Day, G. T. Sheppard (eds), *The Bible and the Politics of Exegesis: Essays in Honor of Norman K. Gottwald on his Sixty-fifth Birthday* (Cleveland, OH: Pilgrim Press, 1991), 17–32.

——, 'Woman Wisdom and the Strange Woman: Where is Power to be Found?', in T. K. Beal and D. M. Gunn (eds), *Reading Bibles, Writing Bodies: Identity and the Book* (Biblical Limits; London and New York: Routledge, 1997), 85–112.

——, *Wise, Strange and Holy: The Strange Woman and the Making of the Bible* (JSOTS 320; Gender, Culture, Theory 9; Sheffield: Sheffield Academic Press, 2000).

Carr, D., *Writing on the Tablet of the Heart: Origins of Scripture and Literature* (New York: Oxford University Press, 2005).

Chase, M. E., *The Bible and the Common Reader* (New York: Macmillan, 1944).

Clifford, R. J., *The Wisdom Literature* (Interpreting Biblical Texts; Nashville, TN: Abingdon Press, 1998).

——, *Proverbs: A Commentary* (OTL; Louisville, KY: Westminster / John Knox Press, 1999).

Collins, J. J., 'Wisdom Reconsidered, in Light of the Scrolls', *DSD* 4 (1997), 265–81.

——, *Jewish Wisdom in the Hellenistic Age* (Edinburgh: T&T Clark, 1998).

Conybeare, F. C., Harris, J. R., and Lewis, A. S., *The Story of Ahikar*, 2nd edn (Cambridge: Cambridge University Press, 1913).

Cook, J., 'אשה זרה (Proverbs 1–9 Septuagint): A Metaphor for Foreign Wisdom?', *ZAW* 106 (1994), 458–76.

——, *The Septuagint of Proverbs: Jewish and/or Hellenistic Proverbs? Concerning the Hellenistic Colouring of LXX Proverbs* (SVT 49; Leiden, New York, and Cologne: Brill, 1997).

Couroyer, B., 'Le Chemin de vie en Egypte et en Israël', *RB* 56 (1949), 412–32.

Cowley, A., *Aramaic Papyri of the Fifth Century BC* (Oxford: Clarendon Press, 1923).

Crawford, S. W., 'Lady Wisdom and Dame Folly at Qumran', *DSD* 5 (1998), 355–66; reprinted in A. Brenner and C. Fontaine (eds), *Wisdom and Psalms* (A Feminist Companion to the Bible, Second Series 2; Sheffield: Sheffield Academic Press, 1998), 205–17.

Crenshaw, J., 'Method in Determining Wisdom Influence upon "Historical" Literature', *JBL* 88 (1969), 129–42.

——, *Education in Ancient Israel: Across the Deadening Silence* (ABRL; New York: Doubleday, 1998).

Day, J., 'Foreign Semitic Influence on the Wisdom of Israel and its Appropriation in the Book of Proverbs', in J. Day, R. P. Gordon, H. G. M. Williamson (eds), *Wisdom in Ancient Israel: Essays in Honour of J. A. Emerton* (Cambridge: Cambridge University Press, 1995), 55–70.

——, *Yahweh and the Gods and Goddesses of Canaan* (JSOTS 265; London and New York: Sheffield Academic Press, 2000).

Delitzsch, Franz, *Biblischer Commentar über die poetischen Bücher des Alten Testaments*, vol. 3: *Das Salamonische Spruchbuch* (Leipzig: Dörffling &

Franke, 1873), ET, *Biblical Commentary on the Proverbs of Solomon*, translated by M. G. Easton (Edinburgh: T&T Clark, 1874–5).

Denning-Bolle, S., *Wisdom in Akkadian Literature: Expression, Instruction, Dialogue* (Mededelingen en Verhandelingen van het Vooraziatisch-Egyptisch Genootschap 'Ex Oriente Lux' 28; Leiden: Ex Oriente Lux, 1992).

Depla, A., 'Women in Ancient Egyptian Wisdom Literature', in L. J. Archer, S. Fischler, M. Wyke (eds), *Women in Ancient Societies: An Illusion of the Night* (London: Macmillan, 1994), 24–52.

Derousseaux, L., *La Crainte de Dieu dans l'Ancien Testament: royauté, alliance, sagesses dans les royaumes d'Israël et de Juda. Recherches d'exégèse et d'histoire sur la racine 'yârê'* (Lectio Divina 63; Paris: Cerf, 1970).

Devauchelle, D., 'Le Chemin de vie dans l'Egypte ancienne', in R. Lebrun (ed.), *Sagesses de l'Orient ancien et chrétien: la voie de vie et la conduite spirituelle chez les peuples et dans les littératures de l'Orient chrétien. Conférences IROC 1991–1992* (Uer de Théologie et de Sciences Religieuses Institut Catholique de Paris. Sciences Théologiques & Religieuses 2; Paris: Beauchesne, 1993), 91–122.

Devaud, E., *Les Maximes de Ptahhotep d'après le Papyrus Prisse, les Papyrus 10371/10435 et 10509 du British museum, et la Tablette Carnarvon* (Freibourg: s.n., 1916).

Di Lella, A. A., 'The Meaning of Wisdom in Ben Sira', in L. Perdue, B. Scott, W. Wiseman (eds), *In Search of Wisdom: Essays in Memory of John G. Gammie* (Louisville, KY: Westminster / John Knox Press, 1993), 133–48.

Dietrich, M., 'Der Dialog zwischen Šupe-ameli und seinem "Vater": Die Tradition babylonischer Weisheitssprüche im Westen. Anhang von G. Keydana: Die hethitische Version', *UF* 23 (1991), 33–74.

Dor, Y., 'The Composition of the Episode of the Foreign Women in Ezra IX–X', *VT* 53 (2003), 26–47.

Driver, G. R., 'Problems in the Hebrew Text of Proverbs', *Biblica* 32 (1951), 173–97.

Ebner, M., 'Wo findet die Weisheit ihren Ort. Weisheitskonzepte in Konkurrenz', in M. Fassnacht, A. Leinhäupl-Wilke, S. Lücking (eds), *Die Weisheit—Ursprünge und Rezeption: Festscrift für Karl Löning zum 65. Geburtstag* (Neutestamentliche Abhandlungen n.s. 44; Münster: Aschendorff, 2003), 79–103.

Emerton, J. A., 'The Teaching of Amenemope and Proverbs XXII 17–XXIV 22: Further Reflections on a Long-Standing Problem', *VT* 51 (2001), 431–64.

Erman, A., 'Eine ägyptische Quelle der "Sprüche Salomos"', *SPAW* 15 (1924), 86–93, tab. VI–VII.

Eskenazi, T. C. and Judd, E. P., 'Marriage to a Stranger in Ezra 9–10', in T. C. Eskenazi and K. H. Richards (eds), *Second Temple Studies*, vol. 2: *Temple and Community in the Persian Period* (JSOTS 175; Sheffield: JSOT Press, 1994), 266–85.

Farmer, K. A., *Who Knows What is Good? A Commentary on the Books of Proverbs and Ecclesiastes* (ITC; Grand Rapids, MI: Eerdmans, and Edinburgh: Handsel Press, 1991).

Fischer, H. G., 'A Didactic Text of the Late Middle Kingdom', *JEA* 68 (1982), 45–50.

Fischer-Elfert, H.-W., *Lesefunde im literarischen Steinbruch von Deir el-Medineh* (Kleine ägyptische Texte 12; Wiesbaden: Harrassowitz, 1997).

——, *Die Lehre eines Mannes für seinen Sohn: eine Etappe auf dem 'Gottesweg' des loyalen und solidarischen Beamten des Mittleren Reiches* (Ägyptologische Abhandlungen 60; Wiesbaden: Harrassowitz, 1999).

Fitzpatrick-McKinley, A., *The Transformation of Torah from Scribal Advice to Law* (JSOTS 287; Sheffield: Sheffield Academic Press, 1999).

Fontaine, C. R., *Traditional Sayings in the Old Testament* (Bible and Literature Series; Sheffield: Almond Press, 1982).

——, 'Wisdom in Proverbs', in L. Perdue, B. Scott, W. Wiseman (eds), *In Search of Wisdom: Essays in Memory of John G. Gammie* (Louisville, KY: Westminster / John Knox Press, 1993), 99–114.

——, 'The Social Roles of Women in the World of Wisdom', in A. Brenner (ed.), *A Feminist Companion to Wisdom Literature* (The Feminist Companion to the Bible 9; Sheffield: Sheffield Academic Press, 1995), 24–49.

——, *Smooth Words: Women, Proverbs and Performance in Biblical Wisdom* (JSOTS 356; London and New York: Sheffield Academic Press, 2002).

Fox, M. V., 'The Pedagogy of Proverbs 2', *JBL* 113 (1994), 233–43.

——, 'World Order and Maʿt: A Crooked Parallel', *Journal of the Ancient Near Eastern Society of Columbia University* 23 (1995), 37–48.

——, 'Ideas of Wisdom in Proverbs 1–9', *JBL* 116 (1997), 613–33.

——, 'Who Can Learn? A Dispute in Ancient Pedagogy', in M. L. Barré (ed.), *Wisdom, You Are My Sister: Studies in Honor of Roland E. Murphy, O. Carm., on the Occasion of his Eightieth Birthday* (CBQMS 29; Washington, DC: Catholic Biblical Association of America, 1997), 62–77.

——, 'Wisdom and the Self-Presentation of Wisdom Literature', in J. C. Exum and H. G. M. Williamson (eds), *Reading from Right to Left: Essays on the Hebrew Bible in Honour of David J. A. Clines* (JSOTS 373; London: Sheffield Academic Press, 2003), 153–72.

——, *Proverbs 1–9: A New Translation with Introduction and Commentary* (AB 18A; New York: Doubleday, 2000).

Gardiner, A. H., 'The Tomb of Amenemhet, High-Priest of Amon', *ZÄS* 47 (1910), 87–99.

——, *Hieratic Papyri in the British Museum. Third series: Chester Beatty Gift* (London: British Museum, 1935).

——, *Late-Egyptian Miscellanies* (Bibliotheca Aegyptiaca VII; Brussels: Édition de la Fondation égyptologique reine Elizabeth, 1937).

Gemser, B., 'The Instructions of ꜥOnchsheshonqy and Biblical Wisdom Literature', *SVT* 7 (1960), 102–28.

Goedicke, H., 'A Neglected Wisdom Text', *JEA* 48 (1962), 25–35.

Grabbe, L., 'Reconstructing History from the Book of Ezra', in P. R. Davies (ed.), *Second Temple Studies*, vol. 1: *Persian Period* (JSOTS 117; Sheffield: Sheffield Academic Press, 1991), 98–106.

——, *Ezra-Nehemiah* (London and New York: Routledge, 1998).

Greenfield, J. C., 'The Background and Parallel to a Proverb of Ahiqar', in A. Caquot and M. Philonenko (eds), *Hommages à André Dupont-Sommer* (Paris: Librairie d'Amérique et d'Orient Adrien-Maisonneuve, 1971), 49–59.

——, 'The Wisdom of Ahiqar', in J. Day, R. P. Gordon, H. G. M. Williamson (eds), *Wisdom in Ancient Israel: Essays in Honour of J. A. Emerton* (Cambridge: Cambridge University Press, 1995), 43–52.

Gruber, M. I., 'Fear, Anxiety and Reverence in Akkadian, Biblical Hebrew and Other North-West Semitic Languages', *VT* 40 (1990), 411–22.

Grumach, I., *Untersuchungen zur Lebenslehre des Amenope* (Münchner Ägyptologische Studien 23; Munich and Berlin: Deutscher Kunstverlag, 1972).

Habel, N., 'The Symbolism of Wisdom in Proverbs 1–9', *Interpretation* 26 (1972), 131–56.

Hadley, J., 'Wisdom and the Goddess', in J. Day, R. P. Gordon, H. G. M. Williamson (eds), *Wisdom in Ancient Israel: Essays in Honour of J. A. Emerton* (Cambridge: Cambridge University Press, 1995), 234–43.

Harrington, D. J., *Wisdom Texts from Qumran* (The Literature of the Dead Sea Scrolls; London and New York: Routledge, 1996).

——, 'Ten Reasons Why the Qumran Wisdom Texts are Important', *DSD* 4 (1997), 245–54.

Harris, S. L., *Proverbs 1–9: A Study of Inner-Biblical Interpretation* (SBL Dissertation Series 150; Atlanta: Scholars Press, 1995).

Helck, W., 'Zur Frage der Enstehung der ägyptischen Literatur', *WZKM* 63/64 (1972), 62–6.

Hieke, T., 'Endogamy in the Book of Tobit, Genesis, and Ezra-Nehemiah', in G. Xeravits and J. Zsengellér (eds), *The Book of Tobit: Text, Tradition, Theology. Papers of the First International Conference on the Deuterocanon-*

ical Books, Pápa, Hungary, 20–21 May, 2004 (SJSJ 98; Leiden: Brill, 2005), 103–20.

Hornung, E., *Der Eine und die Vielen: Ägyptische Gottesvorstellung* (Darmstadt: Wissenschaftliche Buchgesellschaft, 1971); ET, *Conceptions of God in Ancient Egypt: The One and the Many,* translated by John Baines (Ithaca: Cornell University Press, and London: Routledge & Kegan Paul, 1982).

Humbert, P., 'La Femme étrangère du livre des Proverbes', *RES* 4 (1937), 49–64.

——, 'Les Adjectifs "zâr" et "nokrî" et la "femme étrangère" des Proverbes Bibliques', in *Mélanges syriens offerts à monsieur René Dussaud, secrétaire perpétuel de l'Académie des Inscriptions et Belles-Lettres par ses amis et ses élèves* (Paris: Librairie Orientaliste Paul Geuthner, 1939), vol. 1, 259–66.

Jasnow, R., *A Late Period Hieratic Wisdom Text (P. Brooklyn 47.218.135)* (Studies in Ancient Oriental Civilization 52; Chicago: Oriental Institute, University of Chicago, 1992).

Kaplony, P., 'Die definition der schönen Literatur im alten Ägypten', in J. Assmann *et al.* (eds), *Fragen an die altägyptische Literatur: Studien zum Gedenken an Eberhard Otto* (Wiesbaden: Reichert, 1977), 289–314.

Kayatz, C., *Studien zu Proverbien 1–9: Eine form- und motivgeschichtliche Untersuchung unter Einbeziehung ägyptischen Vergleichsmaterials* (WMANT 22; Neukirchen-Vluyn: Neukirchener Verlag, 1966).

Keel, O., *Die Weisheit spielt vor Gott: Ein ikonographischer Beitrag zur Deutung des mesahäqät in Sprüche 8, 30f* (Freibourg: Universitätsverlag Freiburg Schweiz, and Göttingen: Vandenhoeck & Ruprecht, 1974).

Kitchen, K. A., 'Studies in Egyptian Wisdom Literature: I. The Instruction by a Man for his Son', *OA* 8 (1969), 189–208.

Klostermann, A., 'Schulwesen im alten Israel', in N. Bonwetsch *et al.* (eds), *Theologische Studien: Theodor Zahn zum 10. Oktober 1908* (Leipzig: A. Deichert'sche, 1908), 193–232.

Kottsieper, I., *Die Sprache der Ahiqarsprüche* (BZAW 194; Berlin: de Gruyter, 1990).

Kramer, S. N., 'Sumerian Literature: A General Survey', in G. E. Wright (ed.), *The Bible and the Ancient Near East: Essays in Honour of William Foxwell Albright* (London: Routledge, 1961), 249–66.

Krispenz, J., *Spruchkompositionen im Buch Proverbia* (Europäische Hochschulschriften Ser. 23, 349; Frankfurt: Peter Lang, 1989).

Küchler, M., *Frühjüdische Weisheitstraditionen: Zum Fortgang weisheitlichen Denkens im Bereich des frühjüdischen Jahweglaubens* (OBO 26; Freibourg: Universitätsverlag Freiburg Schweiz, 1979).

Lambert, W. G., *Babylonian Wisdom Literature* (Oxford: Clarendon Press, 1960).

Lang, B., *Die Weisheitliche Lehrrede: Eine Untersuchung von Sprüche 1–7* (Stuttgarter Bibelstudien 54; Stuttgart: KBW, 1972).

——, *Wisdom and the Book of Proverbs: An Israelite Goddess Redefined* (New York: Pilgrim Press, 1986).

Laporte, J., 'Philo in the Tradition of Biblical Wisdom Literature', in R. L. Wilken (ed.), *Aspects of Wisdom in Judaism and Early Christianity* (University of Notre Dame Center for the Study of Judaism and Christianity in Antiquity 1; Notre Dame, IN: University of Notre Dame Press, 1975).

Levenson, J. D., 'The Sources of Torah: Psalm 119 and the Modes of Revelation in Second Temple Judaism', in P. D. Miller, P. D. Hanson, S. D. McBride (eds), *Ancient Israelite Religion: Essays in Honor of Frank Moore Cross* (Philadelphia: Fortress Press, 1987), 559–74.

Lichtheim, M., *Ancient Egyptian Literature* (Berkeley: University of California Press, 1973, 1976, 1980).

——, *Late Egyptian Wisdom Literature in the International Context: A Study of Demotic Instructions* (OBO 52; Freibourg: Universitätsverlag Freiburg Schweiz, and Göttingen: Vandenhoeck & Ruprecht, 1983).

——, *Ancient Egyptian Autobiographies Chiefly of the Middle Kingdom* (OBO 84; Freibourg: Universitätsverlag Freiburg Schweiz, and Göttingen: Vandenhoeck & Ruprecht, 1988).

Lindenberger, J. M., 'The Gods of Ahiqar', *UF* 14 (1982), 105–17.

——, *The Aramaic Proverbs of Ahiqar* (Johns Hopkins Near Eastern Studies; Baltimore: Johns Hopkins University Press, 1983).

Loprieno, A., 'Loyalistic Instructions', in A. Loprieno (ed.), *Ancient Egyptian Literature: History and Forms* (Probleme der Ägyptologie 10; Leiden, New York, and Cologne: Brill, 1996), 403–14.

Mack, B. L., 'Wisdom Myth and Mytho-logy: An Essay in Understanding a Theological Tradition', *Interpretation* 24 (1970), 46–60.

——, *Wisdom and the Hebrew Epic: Ben Sira's Hymn in Praise of the Fathers* (Chicago Studies in the History of Judaism; Chicago: University of Chicago Press, 1985).

McKane, W., *Proverbs: A New Approach.* (OTL; London: SCM, 1970).

McKinlay, J. E., *Gendering Wisdom the Host: Biblical Invitations to Eat and Drink* (JSOTS 216; Gender, Culture, Theory 4; Sheffield: Sheffield Academic Press, 1996).

Maier, C., *Die 'fremde Frau' in Proverbien 1–9: Eine exegetische und sozialgeschichtliche Studie* (OBO 144; Freibourg: Universitätsverlag Freiburg Schweiz, and Göttingen: Vandenhoeck & Ruprecht, 1995).

Maier, C., 'Conflicting Attractions: Parental Wisdom and the "Strange Woman" in Proverbs 1–9', in A. Brenner (ed.), *A Feminist Companion to Wisdom Literature* (The Feminist Companion to the Bible 9; Sheffield: Sheffield Academic Press, 1995), 92–108.

Marböck, J., *Weisheit im Wandel: Untersuchungen zur Weisheitstheologie bei Ben Sira*, 2nd edn (BZAW 272; Berlin and New York: de Gruyter, 1999).

Marcus, R., 'The Tree of Life in Proverbs', *JBL* 62 (1943), 117–20.

——, 'On Biblical Hypostases of Wisdom', *HUCA* 23 I (1950–1), 157–71.

Martínez, F. G., and Tigchelaar, E. J. C. (eds), *The Dead Sea Scrolls Study Edition*, paperback edition (Leiden: Brill and Grand Rapids, MI: Eerdmans, 2000).

Meinhold, A., *Die Sprüche*, vol.1: *Sprüche Kapitel 1–15* (Zürcher Bibelkommentare 16.1; Zürich: Theologischer Verlag, 1991).

Michel, D., 'Proverbia 2: ein Dokument der Geschichte der Weisheit', in J. Hausmann and H.-J. Zobel (eds), *Alttestamentlicher Glaube und Biblische Theologie: Festschrift für Horst Dietrich Preuss zum 65. Geburtstag* (Stuttgart: Kohlhammer, 1992), 233–43.

Mies, F., ' "Dame Sagesse" en Proverbes 9: une personnification féminine?', *RB* 108 (2001), 161–83.

Miles, J. E., *Wise King—Royal Fool: Semiotics, Satire and Proverbs 1–9* (JSOTS 399; London and New York: T&T Clark International, 2004).

Miosi, F. T., 'God, Fate and Free Will', in G. E. Kadish and G. E. Freeman (eds), *Studies in Philology in Honour of Ronald James Williams: A Festschrift* (SSEA publications 3; Toronto: SSEA, 1982), 69–111.

Moers, G., 'Travel as Narrative in Egyptian Literature', in G. Moers (ed.), *Definitely: Egyptian Literature*. Proceedings of the symposium *Ancient Egyptian Literature: History and Forms*, Los Angeles, 24–26 March 1995 (Lingua Aegyptiaca Studia Monographica 2; Göttingen: Seminar für Ägyptologie und Koptologie, 1999), 43–61.

Moore, R. D., 'Personification of the Seduction of Evil: "The Wiles of the Wicked Woman" ', *RevQ* 10 (1981), 505–19.

Morentz, L. D., 'Literature as a Construction of the Past in the Middle Kingdom', in J. Tait (ed.), *'Never Had the Like Occurred': Egypt's View of its Past* (Encounters with Ancient Egypt; London: UCL Press, and Portland, OR: Cavendish, 2003), 101–17.

Müller, A., *Proverbien 1–9: Der Weisheit neue Kleider* (BZAW 291; Berlin and New York: de Gruyter, 2000).

Muraoka, T., 'Sir. 51, 13–30: An Erotic Hymn to Wisdom?', *JSJ* 10 (1979), 166–78.

Murphy, R. E., 'Religious Dimensions of Israelite Wisdom', in P. D. Miller, P. D. Hanson, S. D. McBride (eds), *Ancient Israelite Religion: Essays in Honor of Frank Moore Cross* (Philadelphia: Fortress Press, 1987), 449–58.

——, 'Wisdom and Eros in Proverbs 1–9', *CBQ* 50 (1988), 600–3.

——, 'The Personification of Wisdom', in J. Day, R. P. Gordon, H. G. M. Williamson (eds), *Wisdom in Ancient Israel: Essays in Honour of J. A. Emerton* (Cambridge: Cambridge University Press, 1995), 222–33.

——, *The Tree of Life: An Exploration of Biblical Wisdom Literature*, 2nd edn (Grand Rapids, MI: Eerdmans, 1996).

——, *Proverbs* (Word Biblical Commentary 22; Nashville, TN: T. Nelson, 1998).

Nel, P. J., *The Structure and Ethos of the Wisdom Admonitions in Proverbs* (BZAW 158; Berlin and New York: de Gruyter, 1982).

Newsom, C. A., 'Woman and the Discourse of Patriarchal Wisdom: A Study of Proverbs 1–9', in P. L. Day (ed.), *Gender and Difference in Ancient Israel* (Minneapolis: Fortress, 1989), 142–60.

Niccacci, A., 'Proverbi 22.17–23.11', *LA* 29 (1979), 42–72.

Nougayrol, J., *et al.* (eds), *Ugaritica, 5: Nouveaux textes accadiens, hourrites et ugaritiques* (Mission de Ras Shamra 16; Bibliothèque archéologique et historique/Institut français d'archéologie de Beyrouth 80; Paris: P. Geuthner, 1968).

O'Connell, R., 'Proverbs VII 16–17: A Case of Fatal Deception in a "Woman and the Window" Type-Scene', *VT* 41 (1991), 235–41.

O'Connor, D., 'Egypt's Views of Others', in J. Tait (ed.), *'Never Had the Like Occurred': Egypt's View of its Past* (Encounters with Ancient Egypt; London: UCL Press, and Portland, OR: Cavendish, 2003), 155–85.

Östborn, G., *TŌRĀ in the Old Testament: A Semantic Study* (Lund: Ohlssons, 1945).

Parkinson, R. B., *The Tale of Sinuhe and other Ancient Egyptian Poems 1940–1640 BC* (Oxford: Clarendon Press, 1997).

——, 'The Dream and the Knot: Contextualising Middle Kingdom Literature', in G. Moers (ed.), *Definitely: Egyptian Literature*. Proceedings of the Symposium *Ancient Egyptian Literature: History and Forms*, Los Angeles, 24–26 March 1995 (Lingua Aegyptiaca Studia Monographica 2; Göttingen: Seminar für Ägyptologie und Koptologie, 1999), 63–82.

——, *Poetry and Culture in Middle Kingdom Egypt: A Dark Side to Perfection* (London and New York: Continuum, 2002).

Pemberton, G. D., 'The Rhetoric of the Father in Proverbs 1–9', *JSOT* 30 (2005), 63–82.

Perdue, L. G., 'Wisdom Theology and Social History in Proverbs 1–9', in M. L. Barré (ed.), *Wisdom, You Are My Sister: Studies in Honor of Roland*

E. Murphy, O. Carm., *on the Occasion of his Eightieth Birthday* (CBQMS 29; Washington, DC: Catholic Biblical Association of America, 1997), 78–101.

——, *Proverbs* (Interpretation; Louisville, KY: John Knox Press, 2000).

Plath, S., *Furcht Gottes: Der Begriff* ירא *im Alten Testament* (Arbeiten zur Theologie 2.2; Stuttgart: Calwer, 1963).

Plöger, O., *Sprüche Salomos (Proverbia)* (BKAT 17; Neukirchen: Neukirchener Verlag, 1984).

Porten, B. and Yardeni, A. (eds), *Textbook of Aramaic Documents from Ancient Egypt*, vol. 3: *Literature, Accounts, Lists* (Hebrew University, Dept. of the History of the Jewish People, Texts and Studies for Students; Jerusalem: Hebrew University, 1993).

Posener, G., 'L'Exorde de l'instruction éducative d'Amennakhte (Recherches littéraires, v)', *RdE* 10 (1955), 61–72.

——, 'Quatre tablettes scolaires de Basse Epoque (Aménémopé et Hardjedef)', *RdE* 18 (1966), 45–65.

Puech, E., *Qumrân Grotte 4. XVIII: Textes Hébreux (4Q521–4Q528, 4Q576–4Q579)* (DJD 25; Oxford: Clarendon Press, 1998).

Quack, J. F., *Studien zur Lehre für Merikare* (Göttinger Orientforschungen IV Reihe, Ägypten 23; Wiesbaden: Harrassowitz, 1992).

——, *Die Lehren des Ani: Ein neuägyptischer Weisheitstext in seinem kulturellen Umfeld* (OBO 141; Freibourg: Universitätsverlag Freiburg Schweiz, and Göttingen: Vandenhoeck & Ruprecht, 1994).

Quesada, J. J., 'Body Piercing: The Issue of Priestly Control over Acceptable Family Structure in the Book of Numbers', *Biblical Interpretation* 10 (2002), 24–35.

Quirke, S., *Egyptian Literature 1800 BC: Questions and Readings* (London: Golden House, 2004).

Ray, J. D., 'Egyptian Wisdom Literature', in J. Day, R. P. Gordon, H. G. M. Williamson (eds), *Wisdom in Ancient Israel: Essays in Honour of J. A. Emerton* (Cambridge: Cambridge University Press, 1995), 17–29.

Richardson, H. N., 'Some Notes on *lyṣ* and its Derivatives', *VT* 5 (1955), 163–79.

Robert, A., 'Les Attaches Littéraires Bibliques de Prov. I–IX', *RB* 43 (1934), 42–68; 172–204; 374–84; *RB* 44 (1935), 344–65; 502–25.

Römheld, D., *Wege der Weisheit* (BZAW 184; Berlin and New York: de Gruyter, 1989).

Ruffle, J., 'The Teaching of Amenemope and its Connection with the Book of Proverbs', *Tyndale Bulletin* 28 (1977), 29–68.

Sacchi, P., *The History of the Second Temple Period* (JSOTS 285; Sheffield: Sheffield Academic Press, 2000).

Sachau, E., *Aramaische Papyrus und Ostraca aus einer jüdischen Militärkolonie zu Elephantine* (Hilfsbuecher zur Kunde des Alten Orients 4; Leipzig: J. C. Hinrichs, 1911).

Sanders, J. A., *The Psalms Scrolls of Qumrân Cave 11 (11QPs)* (DJD 4; Oxford: Clarendon Press, 1965).

Schäfer, R., *Die Poesie der Weisen: Dichotomie als Grundstruktur der Lehr- und Weisheitsgedichte in Proverbien 1–9* (WMANT 77; Neukirchen: Neukirchener Verlag, 1999).

Schenkel, W., 'Eine neue Weisheitslehre?', *JEA* 50 (1964), 6–12.

Schipper, B., 'Die Lehre des Amenemope und Prov 22, 17–24, 22: eine Neubestimmung des literarischen Verhältnisses', *ZAW* 117 (2005), 53–72, 232–48.

Schmid, H. H., *Wesen und Geschichte der Weisheit* (BZAW 101; Berlin: Töpelmann, 1966).

Schnabel, E. J., *Law and Wisdom from Ben Sira to Paul: A Tradition Historical Enquiry into the Relation of Law, Wisdom and Ethics* (WUNT 2nd series 16; Tübingen: Mohr-Siebeck, 1985)

Schott, S., *Bücher und Bibliotheken im alten Ägypten: Verzeichnis der Buch- und Spruchtitel und der Termini technici* (Wiesbaden: Harrassowitz, 1990).

Schroer, S., 'Wise and Counselling Women in Ancient Israel: Literary and Historical Ideals of the Personified HOKMÂ', in A. Brenner (ed.), *A Feminist Companion to Wisdom Literature* (The Feminist Companion to the Bible 9; Sheffield: Sheffield Academic Press, 1995), 67–84.

——, *Die Weisheit hat ihr Haus gebaut: Studien zur Gestalt der Sophia in den biblischen Schriften* (Mainz: M. Grünewald, 1996); ET, *Wisdom Has Built Her House: Studies on the Figure of Sophia in the Bible*, translated by Linda M. Maloney and William McDonough (Collegeville, MN: Liturgical Press, 2000).

Scott, R. B. Y., 'Priesthood, Prophecy, Wisdom, and the Knowledge of God', *JBL* 80 (1961), 1–15.

——, *Proverbs, Ecclesiastes* (AB; Garden City, NY: Doubleday, 1965).

——, 'Wise and Foolish, Righteous and Wicked', in *Studies in the Religion of Ancient Israel* (SVT 23; Leiden: Brill, 1972), 146–65.

Sevenich-Bax, E., 'Schule in Israel als Sitz der Weisheit', in M. Fassnacht, A. Leinhäupl-Wilke, S. Lücking (eds), *Die Weisheit—Ursprünge und Rezeption: Festscrift für Karl Löning zum 65. Geburtstag* (Neutestamentliche Abhandlungen n.s. 44; Münster: Aschendorff, 2003), 59–77.

Shupak, N., 'The "Sitz im Leben" of the Book of Proverbs in the Light of a Comparison of Biblical and Egyptian Wisdom Literature', *RB* 94 (1987), 98–119.

Shupak, N., *Where Can Wisdom be Found? The Sage's Language in the Bible and in Ancient Egyptian Literature* (OBO 130; Freibourg: Universitätsverlag Freiburg Schweiz, and Göttingen: Vandenhoeck & Ruprecht, 1993).

Simpson, W. K., '*Belles Lettres* and Propaganda', in A. Loprieno (ed.), *Ancient Egyptian Literature: History and Forms* (Probleme der Ägyptologie 10; Leiden, New York, and Cologne: Brill, 1996), 435–43.

Skehan, P. W., 'The Seven Columns of Wisdom's House in Proverbs 1–9', *CBQ* 9 (1947), 190–8.

——, *Studies in Israelite Poetry and Wisdom* (CBQMS 1; Washington, DC: Catholic Biblical Association of America, 1971).

——, 'Structures in Poems on Wisdom: Proverbs 8 and Sirach 24', *CBQ* 41 (1979), 365–79.

Skehan, P. W. and Di Lella, A. A., *The Wisdom of Ben Sira* (AB 39; New York: Doubleday, 1987).

Smend, R., 'The Interpretation of Wisdom in Nineteenth-Century Scholarship', in J. Day, R. P. Gordon, H. G. M. Williamson (eds), *Wisdom in Ancient Israel: Essays in Honour of J. A. Emerton* (Cambridge: Cambridge University Press, 1995), 257–68.

Snijders, L. A., 'The Meaning of זר in the Old Testament', *OTS* 10 (1954), 1–154.

Soll, W. M., 'Babylonian and Biblical Acrostics', *Biblica* 69 (1988), 305–23.

Steiert, F.-J., *Die Weisheit Israels—ein Fremd Körper im Alten Testament? Eine Untersuchung zum Buch der Sprüche auf dem Hintergrund der ägyptischen Weisheitslehren* (Freiburger theologische Studien; Freiburg im Breisgau: Herder, 1990).

Strugnell, J., 'Notes en marge du volume V des "Discoveries in the Judaean Desert of Jordan"', *RevQ* 7 (1970), 163–276.

Tait, W. J., 'Demotic Literature: Forms and Genres', in A. Loprieno (ed.), *Ancient Egyptian Literature: History and Forms* (Probleme der Ägyptologie 10; Leiden, New York, and Cologne: Brill, 1996), 175–87.

Tambling, J., *What is Literary Language?* (Open Guides to Literature; Buckingham and Bristol, PA: Open University Press, 1988).

Tan, N. N. H., 'The "Foreignness" of the Foreign Woman in Proverbs 1–9: A Study of the Origin and Development of a Biblical Motif', Ph.D. thesis (University of Durham, 2004).

Thissen, H. J., *Die Lehre des Anchscheshonqi (p. BM 10508)* (Papyrologische Texte und Abhandlungen 32; Bonn: Habelt, 1984).

Thomas, D. W., 'Textual and Philological Notes on some Passages in the Book of Proverbs', SVT 3 (1955), 280–92.

Toy, C. H., *A Critical and Exegetical Commentary on the Book of Proverbs* (ICC; Edinburgh: T&T Clark, 1899).

Ullendorf, E., 'The Bawdy Bible', *BSOAS* 42 (1979), 425–56

van der Toorn, K., 'Female Prostitution in Payment of Vows in Ancient Israel', *JBL* 108 (1989), 193–205.

van der Woude, A. S., 'Wisdom at Qumran', in J. Day, R. P. Gordon, H. G. M. Williamson (eds), *Wisdom in Ancient Israel: Essays in Honour of J. A. Emerton* (Cambridge: Cambridge University Press, 1995), 244–56.

Van Leeuwen, R. C., 'Scribal Wisdom and a Biblical Proverb at Qumran', *DSD* 4 (1997), 255–64.

Veldhuis, N., 'Sumerian Proverbs in their Curricular Context', *JAOS* 120 (2000), 383–99.

Waltke, B. K., *The Book of Proverbs: Chapters 1–15* (NICOT; Grand Rapids: Eerdmans, 2004).

Washington, H. C., 'The Strange Woman (אשה זרה/נכריה) of Proverbs 1–9 and Post-Exilic Judaean Society', in T. C. Eskenazi and K. H. Richards (eds), *Second Temple Studies*, vol. 2: *Temple Community in the Persian Period* (JSOTS 175; Sheffield: JSOT Press, 1994), 217–42. Reprinted in A. Brenner (ed.), *A Feminist Companion to Wisdom Literature* (The Feminist Companion to the Bible 9; Sheffield: Sheffield Academic Press, 1995), 157–84.

Weeks, S., *Early Israelite Wisdom* (Oxford Theological Monographs; Oxford: Clarendon Press, 1994).

——, 'Wisdom in the Old Testament', in S. C. Barton (ed.), *Where Shall Wisdom be Found? Wisdom in the Bible, the Church and the Contemporary World* (Edinburgh: T&T Clark, 1999), 19–30.

——, 'Biblical Literature and the Emergence of Ancient Jewish Nationalism', *Biblical Interpretation* 10 (2002), 144–57.

——, 'The Context and Meaning of Proverbs 8. 30a', *JBL* 125 (2006), 433–42.

Weinfeld, M., *Deuteronomy and the Deuteronomic School* (Oxford: Clarendon Press, 1972).

Westermann, C., *Roots of Wisdom: The Oldest Proverbs of Israel and Other Peoples* (Louisville, KY: Westminster / John Knox Press, 1995).

Whybray, R. N., *Wisdom in Proverbs: The Concept of Wisdom in Proverbs 1–9* (SBT 45; London: SCM Press, 1965).

——, *Proverbs* (NCBC; Grand Rapids, MI: Eerdmans, and London: Marshall Pickering, 1994).

——, *The Composition of the Book of Proverbs* (JSOTS 168; Sheffield: Sheffield Academic Press, 1994).

Williams, R. J., 'The Alleged Semitic Original of the Wisdom of Amenemope', *JEA* 47 (1961), 100–6.

Winston, D., 'Wisdom in the Wisdom of Solomon', in L. Perdue, B. Scott, W. Wiseman (eds), *In Search of Wisdom: Essays in Memory of John G. Gammie* (Louisville, KY: Westminster / John Knox Press, 1993), 149–64.

Wright III, B. G., 'Wisdom and Women at Qumran', *DSD* 11 (2004), 240–61.

Yee, G., "'I Have Perfumed my Bed with Myrrh": The Foreign Woman (*'iššâ zārâ*) in Proverbs 1–9', *JSOT* 43 (1989), 53–68.

Yoder, C. R., *Wisdom as a Woman of Substance: A Socioeconomic Reading of Proverbs 1–9 and 31: 10–31* (BZAW 304; Berlin and New York: de Gruyter, 2001).

Zauzich, K. T., 'Neue literarische Texte in demotischer Schrift', *Enchoria* 8/2 (1978), 33–8.

Zehnder, M. P., *Wegmetaphorik im Alten Testament: eine semantische Untersuchung der alttestamentlichen und altorientalischen Weg-Lexeme mit besonderer Berücksichtigung ihrer metaphorischen Verwendung* (BZAW 268; Berlin, New York: de Gruyter, 1999).

Index of Authors

Index of References

Discussion of verses in Proverbs 1–9 will also be found ad loc. in the notes to the annotated translation.

General Index